raDIO
caroLINe

radio
caroline

THE TRUE STORY OF THE BOAT THAT ROCKED

ray clark

The History Press

First published 2013, this updated edition 2019

The History Press
97 St George's Place, Cheltenham,
Gloucestershire, GL50 3QB
www.thehistorypress.co.uk

British Library Cataloguing in Publication Data.
A catalogue record for this book is available from the British Library.

ISBN 978 0 7509 9253 4

Typesetting and origination by Geethik Technologies and The History Press
Printed and bound in Great Britain by TJ Books Limited

To my wife, Shelley, for having to share her life,
for too much of the time, with this other woman – Caroline.

CONTENTS

Forewords

Emperor Rosko

I was utterly shocked and pleased that I was selected to say a few choice words to open this collection of pirate radio information, lovingly put together by my man Ray. We go back quite a long way and he had dozens who he could have asked.

All DJ foolishness aside, Ray knows more than enough to handle and coordinate the info on Radio Caroline (although he doesn't know about my night with a French journalist on board, but that is probably for the better, as she had wanted a real taste of pirate life …)

Enjoy the read and keep the Jolly Roger flying!

Emperor Rosko, EMP, 2013

Keith Skues

My ambition as a schoolboy was to work for the BBC. However, having worked for eighteen months on Radio Caroline I wanted to see the introduction of commercial radio into Britain – and I wanted to be a part of it. Fortunately I was lucky on both counts.

Radio Caroline was the centre of attraction in the Swinging Sixties and the first station that pop stars of the day would turn to in having their records played. Listeners loved the music and the DJs.

In turn Caroline helped to bring about the deregulation of British radio with BBC Radio 1 and BBC local radio in the 1960s. A number of offshore DJs joined Radio 1 in 1967.

We had to wait until the 1970s for the introduction of independent (commercial) radio. Now listeners have a huge choice of stations to which they can listen.

Never in my wildest dreams would I have envisaged we would still be talking about 'pirate' radio fifty years later.

Thank you Radio Caroline for helping me to achieve my ambition.

Keith Skues, 2013

Paul McKenna

I can't overstate how amazing it feels to open the mic and know that you are broadcasting on Radio Caroline. The magic is still there. It feels like coming home.

Over the years, many pirate radio stations have come and gone. I believe one of the factors in them going, as good as they were, was because they were essentially just businesses whereas Radio Caroline is a movement based on freedom.

This wonderful book by Ray Clark captures the drama, excitement and magic of the amazing real life adventures of one of most loved parts of modern pop history. I really hope you enjoy reading about this most wonderful radio station and the extraordinary people who make it what it is.

Paul McKenna, 2019

acKNOWLEDGEMENTS

My grateful thanks go to everyone who has contributed to this book with interviews, photographs and information. Very special thanks are due to Colin Nicol who had the foresight to interview a number of the key players from the early days of this amazing story, recording interviews before it was too late, and for allowing me access to his extensive collection of interviews and memorabilia. Chris Edwards and Francois L'hote of Offshore Echos have provided invaluable help, as have Hans Knot and Jon Myer.

The following websites are essential browsing for anyone wanting even more information on the fascinating topic of offshore radio:

www.offshoreechos.com
www.offshoreradio.co.uk
www.hansknot.com
www.radiolondon.co.uk
www.radiocaroline.co.uk
www.rayradio.co.uk

Special thanks to Nigel Harris and Andy Archer for the use of extracts from their fine books.

Many of the photographs used within this book have kindly been provided by friends and used with their permission; others are from my own collection. I have tried to trace the original owners of the few remaining photographs – they are used for all the right reasons and for the story that they tell. However, if you have an interest in those, please contact the publisher.

Special thanks to my friends, Bill Rollins, Hans van Dijk and Pete MacFarlane for encouraging my unhealthy interest in this topic and forcing me into a reasonably successful radio career.

Thanks also to the team at The History Press, especially Alex for her patience ... and for always finding that extra little bit of space for a few more words.

about the author

Ray Clark has enjoyed a successful radio career for more than thirty years, after fulfilling his dream of working aboard Radio Caroline in the Eighties. Since then he has regularly broadcast on a variety of commercial and BBC radio stations, together with frequent appearances on Pittsburgh's KDKA, the world's oldest radio station. He has won numerous prestigious national and international radio awards.

Ray continues to present programmes on Radio Caroline and BBC and has also written *The Great British Woodstock: The Incredible Story of the Weeley Festival 1971* (The History Press).

INTRODUCTION

Those of a similar age to me will have grown up with memories of listening to Radio Caroline, either through the swinging Sixties, the psychedelic Seventies or the 'loadsa money' Eighties. The music and those playing it – and the conditions that they worked under – certainly made an impression at the time.

My life has been influenced by much of what I've heard on the radio: the music, the fun and what Caroline stood for.

Radio Caroline lit that spark in my imagination from the first time I heard it, Easter 1964. I have followed her ups and downs and stayed loyal – for most of the time. There have been times when Caroline sounded so amazingly good that I found it difficult to turn the radio off; occasionally it was so bad that I only listened because it WAS Caroline.

Radio Caroline was the world's most famous pirate radio station, but did the millions of us tuning in realise just what battles went on behind the scenes? Financed by respected city money men, this is a story of human endeavour and risk, international politics, business success and financial failures. A story of innovation, technical challenges, changing attitudes, unimaginable battles with nature, disasters, frustrations, challenging authority and the promotion of love and peace while, at times, harmony was far from evident behind the scenes.

For one person to tell the full Radio Caroline story would be impossible but in the pages that follow you will read the inside story of much that happened during Caroline's days at sea and since she came ashore, including previously unpublished interviews with the 'pirates' who were there and featuring many rare photographs. Of course there is plenty that will never be written ... there were just so many adventurous, funny, frightening, happy, sad, dangerous, ridiculous, stupid, frustrating and unbelievable events that will be remembered only by those who were involved at the time. I've been lucky enough to have heard many of these stories from those who were there.

The aim of this book is to put on record a very special time that was enjoyed by so many people. I see this as a story of a battle between young people wanting to challenge and provide an alternative to a heavily regulated system of radio, those just wanting to be involved in something different, determined businessmen and equally determined politicians. I leave you to decide who the good guys and the bad guys were.

This is the captivating story of the boat that rocked ... and a story that I am proud to have played a tiny part in.

***

This is Radio Caroline on 199, your all-day music station. We are on the air every day, from six in the morning till six at night. The time right now is one minute past twelve and that means it's time for Christopher Moore.

Hello and happy Easter to all of you. This is Christopher Moore with the first record programme on Radio Caroline. The first record is by the Rolling Stones and I'd like to play it for all of the people who helped to put the station on the air, and particularly for Ronan.

Noon on Easter Saturday, 28 March 1964 and Radio Caroline was on the air. Broadcasting from a ship named *Caroline* which was registered in Panama, owned by a Liechtenstein company called Alruane and hired by Planet Productions – an organisation that was registered in Ireland and benefitted from the business of Planet Sales, which would sell advertising on Britain's first commercial radio station. A complex, and purposely confusing pathway of internationally based operating companies was behind her, but this first broadcast started a radio legacy that continues to this day.

The ship anchored just beyond British territorial waters, north-east of Felixstowe at around 6.30 p.m. on Good Friday 1964. With a towering 168ft high steel transmitting mast, generators powering away to supply the studio equipment and the two American built 10 kilowatt transmitters, test broadcasts started just a few hours later.

On board were the Dutch skipper, Captain Baeker, and his marine crew, Swedish radio engineer Ove Sjöström and two broadcasters, 23-year-old Christopher Moore and Simon Dee, then aged 29. Neither had presented a radio programme before, but it would be their job to make continuity announcements and present occasional live record sessions between pre-recorded programme tapes of popular music.

1

Before Caroline

Before Radio Caroline's first broadcast, radio in Britain was provided by the BBC, and though not controlled by the Government, they did regulate it. Its purpose, as set out by the first Director General, Lord Reith, was to educate, inform and entertain; however, it seemed to concentrate more on the first two objectives and less on the latter. Although British pop music was taking the world by storm in the early Sixties, you could hear very little of it on the BBC.

Radio Luxembourg was the only place for pop music fans to hear the hits of the day. Broadcasting from mainland Europe, English-speaking announcers played pop music and commercials every evening. But the signal was poor; it faded in and out continually, it couldn't be heard in the UK during daylight hours and the programme content was dictated by the major record companies, who bought airtime to promote their own recordings.

Unlike the USA and Australia, Europe had very few commercial radio stations, other than those based in Luxembourg, Monte Carlo and Andorra. In most countries, the state-regulated national broadcasting and European governments saw no need for change. The only way to provide an independent radio station was to operate outside state boundaries and outside the law, selling commercials to finance the broadcasts.

The first commercial radio station playing popular music to a mass market and operating from a ship in international waters started in August 1958, when Radio Mercur (Mercury) came on the air. Listeners in Denmark were able to tune in to broadcasts from homemade equipment aboard a tiny ship, the *Cheeta*, moored off the Danish coast. The idea came after Peer Jansen, the founder of Radio Mercur, heard about the US Government-backed Voice of America radio station which was broadcasting from a ship anchored off the coast. The MV *Courier* was moored in the Mediterranean while transmitting programmes that promoted an American view of the world to listeners in Communist countries in the area, such as Albania.

Jansen and his team studied the broadcasting laws and found a way to broadcast legally … or at least, not illegally. The Danish press called them radio pirates, but Radio Mercur, in various forms, remained on air until 1962, when broadcasts to Denmark were outlawed by the introduction of new laws.

The success of the station had not gone unnoticed; other groups became involved with Radio Mercur and, at various times, three different ships associated with the station were broadcasting off the country's coast.

The next offshore radio venture was a far more professional set up from the start. Jack Kotshack lived in Sweden and, through his contacts, met a Texan, Gordon McLendon, who was visiting the country on business. He owned several radio stations in America including KLIF in Dallas and KILT Houston, both market leaders. McLendon understood commercial radio and was one of America's major players in the business.

Within hours of meeting, McLendon and Kotshack agreed that they should start a radio station similar to Radio Mercur, but aimed at a Swedish audience. It was to be known as Radio Nord and it would be financed by Texan money men. A maximum budget of $400,000 was agreed and, at the start of 1960, the team went looking for a suitable ship. They found a small coaster called the *Olga* moored in Kiel, Germany.

> I think she was one of the ugliest boats I have ever seen. Small and worn, she lay on the dock, surrounded by an overpowering stench of rotting herring, noticeable 20 metres away.
>
> Jack Kotshack[1]

The *Olga*, originally called the *Margarethe*, had been built in 1921 as a steel schooner weighing just 250 tons. Over the years she'd been lengthened and fitted with a low-powered diesel engine and had already had a hard life, surviving five years of coastal work during the war.

On 31 May 1960, she was towed to Hamburg, where she underwent a major refit. The cargo hold was converted into cabins for the crew, with space allocated for transmitters and the generators needed to power a radio station. A new superstructure was built, containing the galley, the messroom and broadcast studios. However, final preparations for her conversion came to a halt when the shipyard was notified that it was illegal under a pre-war German law to install or repair a radio station without government permission. The ship was taken to Denmark for further work, then Finland and, finally, made broadcast-ready once anchored off the Swedish coast.

The *Olga* was renamed *Bon Jour* and became the home of Radio Nord. Many issues delayed the start of the radio station, but once these problems, political and technical, were overcome, the station broadcast successfully off the coast of Sweden for fifteen months, from March 1961 until the close down on 30 June 1962, one month ahead of new laws introduced to outlaw offshore broadcasts to Sweden.

The days of Radio Nord were over, but the American investors still owned the small radio ship housing a complete radio station, able to go anywhere in the world. The immediate future of the ship became uncertain, but she would play a huge part in the story of Radio Caroline in the years that followed.

In April 1960, Radio Veronica had started broadcasts off the Dutch coast. Despite a precarious start, Veronica went on to broadcast successfully from sea until 1974 and later to have a role in the Dutch national broadcast system.

The Dutch VRON (Free Radio Broadcasting Netherlands) was set up by a consortium of Amsterdam businessmen. Dubious financial dealings preceded the first broadcasts of Radio Veronica, but eventually a former German lightship, the *Borkham Riff*, registered in Guatemala was equipped and moored off the Dutch coast. Programmes were recorded on land and played from the ship and, although the audience grew quickly, little money was made in return. Six months after coming on air three brothers, the Verweijs took complete control of the venture – one of the brothers, Bull, was part of the original group of investors.

Veronica's new owners were keen to increase their income and decided to target a British audience, so CNBC (the Commercial Neutral Broadcasting Corporation) was set up. Three English-speaking broadcasters were hired, including Paul Hollingdale, an Englishman who had experience with the British Forces Broadcasting Network, who was given the role of Programme Director.

There were only three people involved with CNBC: Doug Stanley, a Canadian Broadcaster, John Michael, a Canadian and me. The people behind the station were three Dutch brothers, they worked in the textile business in Hilversum, making a fortune manufacturing and selling nylon stockings.

Paul Hollingdale, DJ

You're listening to the radio sound of tomorrow today, the CNBC way. If you dial 192 metres medium wave, you get us. We hope you do, as of this morning this is CNBC broadcasting to the south-east coast of England and other parts, no doubt, of England picking us up. We'd like to hear from you by way of reception reports to find out what it's coming in like.

The show consisted of popular music, a mix between 208 [Luxembourg] and the Light Programme [BBC]. We broadcast until lunchtime with the programmes of Radio Veronica starting after that. All of our shows were recorded in studios that we constructed within the textile factory located in Hilversum. The tapes were then taken aboard the ship for transmission.

CNBC had a London office, located in a newly built block called Royalty House in Dean Street.

Paul Hollingdale, DJ

The CNBC programmes quickly gained listeners in the south-east of England and East Anglia and questions about the broadcasts were asked in Parliament. But politics played no part in the demise of CNBC; the signal just wasn't strong enough, leading to poor reception and interference.

CNBC closed down because the medium-wave signal on 192 metres was too weak to penetrate into London. The project failed when an engineer hired by the Verweij brothers received money from them to buy a more powerful transmitter, but he spent the lot in London on the fast life with women, one of whom became pregnant. We were denied the opportunity of this transmitter and the station closed down.

Paul Hollingdale, DJ

Next came the unlikely named 'Voice of Slough', with plans for Radio LN (London) or GBLN. The intended vessel for this project was a 70-ton fishing boat called the *Ellen*. She was moored in Leith harbour in Scotland and had been detained in port, because she was considered unseaworthy.

The boat set sail on 3 October 1961, under cover of darkness, but didn't get far; the next day she was towed into North Berwick with engine trouble. After repairs she made off again, only to put into Dunbar with further problems. The man behind the plan was John Thompson, a journalist working in Slough who intended broadcasting from a position off Southend-on-Sea in Essex. As with CNBC, the radio station was to pre-record programmes on land, some reports suggested Ireland, and then broadcast them from the ship. Thompson told reporters that the plan was to collect a transmitter that was hidden near an East Coast creek, 'a secret rendezvous has been arranged', although he later said he was still looking for a transmitter; he told the *Southend Standard* that Marconi had refused to sell him one, so his company may well buy American.

Thompson's technical advisor and major financier was a Canadian millionaire, Arnold Swanson, who soon decided to break away from Thompson and launch his own radio station, to be called GBOK (Great Britain, OK!). It seems there was little goodwill between the two after the split, according to a newspaper article from the time.

> This man Swanson has pinched our idea, his station GBOK is a complete copy of our Voice of Slough idea. You can take it from me that our station, GBLN, will be beaming before his.[2]

Thompson was true to his word; a broadcast was heard on 306 metres between 4.15 p.m. and 5.30 p.m. on 5 April 1962. The authorities believed it may have come from Mr Thompson's studio, based in a caravan parked in a builder's yard in Slough; it certainly wasn't from his boat which was still in Scotland, beached in Musselborough.

> *You are listening to Radio Ellen, the Voice of Slough, coming to you from a ship anchored off the Nore.*[3]

It's not known if the boat ever managed to get to the Thames, but Radio LN, Radio Ellen or GBLN was never heard of again. Thompson later told reporters that he had relinquished control of his company and all 'intangible' assets, including advertising contracts, had been handed over to his rival, Arnold Swanson, who had a ship that he planned to use for his station GBOK. The *Lady Dixon* was an 84-year-old former lightship, weighing 570 tons and lying in a mud berth in a creek off the Thames at Pitsea.

The plans for GBOK were impressive; a colour brochure gave detailed programme information and advertising rates. Programmes for future broadcast were recorded in a specially constructed studio at Swanson's home in Oxfordshire. He claimed to have invested £80,000 in the project and had already sold £100,000 worth of advertising through his company, the Adanac Broadcasting Agency.

Post Office officials, who were responsible for regulating broadcasts in Britain, had little detail of the proposed radio station in the early months of 1962, but they did suspect that a lightship would be used and set about looking for it. They initially failed to track down the *Lady Dixon*, but inadvertently they stumbled across what may have been a future offshore radio project without realising what they'd found.

An official report gave details of a boat called *Satellite*,[4] a lightship tender, that had been sold by Trinity House during 1961 and was registered to Mr Allan James Crawford, the owner of a group of music publishing companies. The *Satellite* was moored in East Cowes though no link was found to the GBOK project and no more was heard of the *Satellite*. Mr Crawford would certainly come to the authorities' attention during the months that followed.

As 1962 progressed, plans for GBOK continued, but there were problems when tugs tried to pull the *Lady Dixon* free from its muddy berth in Pitsea Creek. Several attempts were made and eventually three tugs managed to free the hulk and tow her across the Thames to Sheerness, where she was to be fitted out. Press reports suggested that the ship, registered in Liberia, would be on the air within about a fortnight.

As work took place on the ship, Post Office officials observed progress and planned to board her to inspect any radio equipment once it was installed.[5] But by July 1962 Mr Swanson had given up with the *Lady Dixon*, saying she would never be sufficiently sound for the project and he was now looking at using another ship, a 'tank landing ship', that he would name the *Notley Galleon* (his home was Notley Abbey in Thame, Oxfordshire). Whether through lack of finance or official pressure, GBOK, just like GBLN, failed to materialise. By August, the *Lady Dixon* was still moored at Sheerness and the *Ellen* was somewhere between Scotland and

Southend-on-Sea, but a third ship *was* in the Thames Estuary and, unlike the other vessels, she was certainly capable of fulfilling her role as a broadcasting base.

2

ProJect atLanta

Australian Allan Crawford was a music publisher living in London. He'd been employed by Southern Music, one of the biggest publishing houses in the world at a time when sheet music sales were all important, but times were changing and the music business had become more dependent on sales of the new 45rpm records. In 1959, Crawford decided to 'go it alone', setting up his own Merit Music Publishing Company and, later, a variety of record labels, including Rocket, Cannon and Crossbow which featured cover versions of top pop hits of the day, performed by session musicians and singers and available by mail order. He also released original recordings on his Sabre and Carnival labels.

> I was managing director of Southern Music both in Australia and in London; I resigned from the London Company after fourteen years to become independent. Then it hit me that having 300 publishers in London striving to get into any half-hour recorded programme on the BBC or Luxembourg was idiocy; there was no way to win as an independent. The publishers that were getting success were the well-established, wealthy publishers, who could wine and dine people and influence them.
>
> I read an announcement that Radio Luxembourg had made an arrangement with one of the big publishers to form a publishing company between them. Well, I was angry at that, because I could see that favouritism was going on. The main advertisers on Luxembourg for the principal hours in the

evening were EMI and Decca, so naturally it was their numbers that were being played, and, of course, the disc jockeys employed by Radio Luxembourg, by great coincidence, turned out to be the same ones the BBC were using and were they going to cut off their own bread and butter by not playing the records that EMI and Decca wanted? Of course they weren't, they'd have been crazy if they had. It was a very restrictive set-up.

I was annoyed so I wrote a sarcastic letter to the BBC and said, 'Following the announcement in the paper,' and I didn't name the article or what it said, 'I now make the following suggestion: that the BBC and my company, Merit Music, form a sub-publishing company, so that by careful programming, we can do away with such worthy institutions as the Performing Rights Society, the Publishers Association and Phonographic Performance Limited, so that all the numbers being broadcast would belong to Merit Music and the BBC.'

I meant it to be sarcastic, such a thing could never happen. But, you know, they had a fellow ring up, 'Mr Crawford, we have your letter – what does it mean?' I've forgotten the name of the man but I was invited to lunch with the BBC, in the boardroom, there was a butler serving on silver platters a beau-tiful luncheon and we were sitting at a boardroom table a mile long and there were only three of us.

One of the men, I think he was in charge of BBC pro-grammes, was reluctant and a little bit huffy at having been made to come, until he listened to what I was saying and he warmed up as I was explaining how Luxembourg worked.

He wrote out the address of a committee[1] that was meeting to take evidence about the future of radio and he described how they were going to have housewives on this committee and I thought 'my God, we're going to get some sense out of this, aren't we?' [sarcastically]. He said, 'would you please repeat what you said to them,' and I said, 'I'll think about it'.

As I left, I stood outside in Portland Place looking up at the BBC building, I said to myself, 'I'll be dammed if I'll do this. I'm not going to play your game to make [the name of] Radio

Luxembourg black so that there'll never be commercial radio in England. I will do it myself.'

And that was that day that pirate radio was born.

Allan Crawford[2]

Before his meeting at the BBC, Crawford was already aware of radio broadcasts from ships off the coast, in particular the Dutch Radio Veronica and the English CNBC service.

Both Doug Stanley and I came to know Allan Crawford while we were with CNBC. We met on several occasions and he could see the value of pirate radio to break the BBC monopoly. He became aware of the debacle concerning the Verweijs problem, the absconding of thousands of guilders by the rogue engineer they had contracted to buy a powerful AM transmitter from RCA in the US. Allan's thoughts towards Radio Atlanta occurred shortly after CNBC closed down in 1961.

Paul Hollingdale, DJ

Another of Crawford's acquaintances was a theatre literary agent called Dorothy 'Kitty' Black, she sold plays, he sold music, their business interests were similar and they obviously moved in the same circles.

Kitty Black had been aware of Radio Mercur when she'd been on holiday in Sweden in the late 1950s, so she already knew about offshore radio. She was to play a major role in Crawford's future plans for commercial radio in the UK.

I was introduced to an Australian called Allan Crawford. I asked him to come and see this musical and because we were both 'beastly colonials' – I come from South Africa, he from Australia – we clicked and became great friends and seemed to have the same sort of ideas about most things. One day, Allan told me that he had been approached by the stocking manufacturers who owned the pirate ship called Radio Veronica and they were prepared to sell a half share for something like

£60,000. Allan had been over to see the ship and came to the conclusion that for £100,000 it would be possible to buy a ship, install the radio equipment and start our own operation in this country.

Kitty Black[3]

There was certainly contact between Crawford and Veronica, though any proposed deal was probably more complex than Kitty Black remembered, or was aware of.

I had gone to meet the people in the Dutch ship, the Verweij brothers, and I took a great liking to them. They needed money very heavily in 1961 because they'd struck opposition from the authorities, people were afraid to advertise. I found a small English bank willing to listen and I took them [the bank] over there. The day was such a nice day and the English were so bloody light-hearted, they started to get flippant. The Dutchmen didn't like it, I mean they were in trouble, they wanted money and they weren't interested in anyone getting flippant on a nice summer's day. We came back to England with them not having reached a decision, and it's always bad not to clinch a thing on the spot. But within days, one of the biggest advertisers had some kind of adverse thing against one of their products and they needed a quick way to offset this unfavourable publicity. They choose to advertise on Veronica and, overnight, they were making 2,000 a week instead of a loss. Now they didn't need us.

Allan Crawford[4]

With Allan Crawford aware of Veronica's situation and the costs involved, he searched for investors prepared to put money into his own radio station. His plan was 'Project Atlanta', a radio station to broadcast off the English coast. It was, potentially, a very risky business, but also one that could become extremely profitable.

There was no way that I would embark on something unless
we had sufficient capital to operate for a minimum of three
months. So the sums were gone into over and over again; the
cost of the ship, the cost of the equipment, the weekly running costs, the transport between shore and ship, the cost of
recording the tapes, the cost of an onshore office – everything
that you can think of had been calculated. The problem was
always to persuade the backers to put up the money that we
needed. Somebody would put up ten thousand, somebody else
would then say they would put up another five thousand and
then we go to somebody else who said they would put up
another ten thousand, so we had twenty five thousand. But by
this time, the person who had said that he was going to put
up the initial ten thousand had changed his mind, so we were
back to fifteen thousand. This was the appalling situation that
we were in, neither of us had the kind of financial connections that were needed for this sort of operation, but at this
point Allan met up with a very interesting man called Oliver
Smedley. He'd stood for Parliament as a Liberal candidate and
had great financial ideas as to how things should be operated,
he was very go-ahead, very open to new ideas and he became
fired with enthusiasm for the pirate radio ship operation.

Kitty Black[5]

When Project Atlanta Ltd was registered on 30 July 1963, the
company attracted more than 150 investors, some owning just
twenty shares, but others owning considerably more. The largest
shareholder was CBC (Plays) Ltd, a company registered in April
1960 to act as agents and managers, Crawford and Black were
both directors of this company.

Allan Crawford studied the legalities very carefully, guided
by the experiences and research of previous ventures and further legal advice. It's likely that he had access to papers from the
CNBC venture operated from Royalty House, just a few yards
away from his own Merit Music office in London's Dean Street.

The ship would be owned by a Panamanian company. It would
be run by a company in Lichtenstein which would enter
into agreements with us to sell advertising time in England,
which legally we could do. In other words, we had a company that didn't own the ship but did have a contract with
the owner to sell advertising time. The crew would be paid
from Lichtenstein, the company that employed the disc jockeys would get so much every month from Lichtenstein and
the company selling the advertising would be Project Atlanta
Ltd. My lawyers went to the Treasury for permission for the
money to go overseas, and the Treasury people said, 'Yes, this is
absolutely above board. It conforms to all English law. You can
do it'. From that moment, we knew that we could go and get
money legitimately from people to invest.

                                                Allan Crawford[6]

Every time you went round to see somebody to ask if they
would put up money for our project you had to explain
what you were doing. You were going to buy a ship, anchor
it outside the 3-mile limit and you needed two flags of convenience. If the first one was challenged you always had the
second in the locker which was your secret flag, all of which
cost money. When we met anybody who showed any signs
of putting up any money they obviously needed to be given
chapter and verse as to how the operation was completely
legal, but we were laying ourselves wide open to having all
our ideas pirated.

                                                Kitty Black[7]

Crawford needed a ship and his search for a suitable vessel took
him to Sweden, where, after a faltering start, the American-
financed Radio Nord was proving to be very successful.
It was one of three offshore radio stations operating off the
coast of Sweden and Denmark: Radio Syd (south) and DCR
(Danmarks Commercielle Radio) were the two more recent
additions to the offshore fleet. The Swedish Government

was in the process of introducing new laws that would make operating the stations illegal and the Americans behind Radio Nord wanted to withdraw from their nautical radio business with as little financial loss as possible. The sale of a complete radio broadcasting station on a ship, together with the equipment from the onshore studios would certainly look good on their balance sheets, and Allan Crawford and his Atlanta project looked a likely buyer.

> My attention was drawn to the fact that Radio Nord was operating in the Baltic off Stockholm. I ended up meeting the owners, who were Americans, Texans, and very nice people. Then the ship came up for sale, they were closing down business because of suppressive Government acts and I could see that there was an opportunity.
>
> Allan Crawford[8]

The law to close Radio Nord was passed in May 1962 and came into effect on 1 August 1962, but the company chose to close down a month earlier, at midnight, 30 June 1962. The man running Radio Nord, Jack Kotshack, was hopeful of a deal with Atlanta:

> At the time, it seemed as if we were in the final stages of negotiations with an Australian businessman, Allan Crawford and his consortium Project Atlanta Ltd. He planned to start a radio station in international waters outside the Thames Estuary, the station was expected to reach an audience of millions of radio listeners in the London area. Allan's intention was to use his radio station to promote his record label operations, and Radio Nord's vacant broadcasting ship was offered to him on 4 July 1962, four days after Radio Nord's closing. She left her anchorage with a newly recruited Polish crew on board, to take her out of the Baltic Sea. In recent months the MV *Bon Jour* had been re-registered as MV *Magda Maria*. On board was all the studio equipment, the equipment used in the studios in

Stockholm and the entire gramophone library. All the commercial value of the company was in the ship and its cargo and
the owners were concerned about any intervention from the
authorities on her passage through the narrow strait between
Denmark and Sweden, but the ship had an easy trip to the
North Sea.

                                                    Jack Kotshack[9]

In various interviews Jack Kotshack suggests the name 'Atlanta'
was chosen by US radio man, Gordon McLendon, advisor to
Radio Nord, as a tribute to the Texan city that was his home,
but Allan Crawford always denied this. Kotshack, in his story of
Radio Nord, written after the station's closure, also referred to
Project Atlanta's original idea of equipping their ship called SS
Atlanta. Could this have been the former lightship tender *Satellite*,
that the British authorities discovered while searching for the
GBOK ship some months earlier, registered to Crawford and
moored at East Cowes on the Isle of Wight?

While negotiations continued between Project Atlanta and
Radio Nord's owners, British government departments had taken
the unusual step of talking to each other and sharing information,
a trend that, had it continued, may have seriously threatened the
future of offshore radio. The Postmaster General was informed by
an internal memo of 'a disquieting development'. The same document shows that plans for Radio Atlanta were at an advanced
stage as early as summer of 1962.

In August we received from the treasury a copy of a proposed
agreement between a British company CBC (Plays) Ltd and
a Liechtenstein registered company, Atlantic Broadcasting
Services Establishment. The latter proposes to lease the ship
Magda Maria, anchor it outside UK waters and broadcast commercial programmes to the UK. CBC (Plays) Ltd will acquire
under the agreement the rights to sell advertising time in the
programmes.[10]

The exact movements of the *Magda Maria* over the next eight-een months would tell a fascinating story. She took a month to travel from the coast of Sweden to El Ferrol in north-west Spain, arriving on 2 August 1962, where she underwent res-toration work, presumably as part of the deal for the change of ownership. Two weeks later the former *Bon Jour* and latterly *Magda Maria* had once again been renamed, she was now called *Mi Amigo*.

> The *Magda Maria* anchored outside UK territorial waters some 5 miles south of Clacton pier on 24 September. It has been to the Hook of Holland for a few days but is understood to be returning soon. So far as we are aware no broadcasts have yet been made from the vessel. If it starts, as it is Panamanian regis-tered and there is as yet no UK legislation of the type discussed at the Council of Europe, there is little we can do to stop it.[10]

But the programmes of Radio Atlanta failed to materialise; something had gone wrong with the deal. An incident off the coast of Denmark was blamed for the delay. DCR, a radio station aboard a ship in the Baltic called *Lucky Star* and asso-ciated with Radio Mercur, had returned to the air just days after the introduction of the anti-pirate radio law. Three days of broadcasts followed before Danish police boarded the ship and towed the vessel to the port. Some of Project Atlanta's backers became nervous after this move by the Danish author-ities and, fearing they might lose their investment, withdrew their funds, leaving Crawford with insufficient capital to com-plete the deal. But were Crawford's cautious investors the real reason for the deal failing, or was he perhaps holding out for a better deal, a deal where Project Atlanta was exposed to far less risk?

Nobody was really sure what the reaction of the British authorities would be to a radio ship broadcasting off the coast and, should they have raided the ship once Radio Atlanta went on the air, the group would have lost everything. But, if the ship was still owned by the Americans it might have caused the British Government to delay any action for fear of the situation involving other nationalities and becoming far more complicated, thus acting as insurance for Crawford.

> I tried to persuade them that they could remain owners and I could operate off England, but they didn't like that idea, and while I was busy with the formula under which we could successfully operate in England, they got scared, as money men often do, and they took it all back to Texas.
>
> Allan Crawford[11]

Just how close Radio Atlanta came to becoming Britain's first offshore commercial radio station broadcasting from the UK coast in September 1962 will probably never be known, but the radio ship was in position and she was ready to go. Instead the *Mi Amigo* spent the next four months at various anchorages and ports around the North Sea; for a while she was moored close to the Radio Veronica ship off Holland. She then entered the Belgian port of Ostend and later reports placed her in the port of Flushing.

Various rumours about the ship being used for television broadcasts and even being sold to the Cuban authorities circulated. Belgian newspapers reported the 'mysterious radio ship' was to anchor off the French coast with daily commercial radio broadcasts starting on 18 December 1962. According to 'a reliable source', a British millionaire had paid 5 million Belgian Francs for her. But all of these plans and rumours came to nothing, the owners decided that a deal was unlikely and ordered the *Mi Amigo* to sail to Galveston.

> My Texan friend, who had seven radio stations, was considered one of the bright executives of America, rang me and said, 'we've got it from the horse's mouth that you'll never be able to get away with opening a ship there' and he withdrew

his ship to Texas. I was broken-hearted; I depended on getting that damned ship, the *Mi Amigo*, for us, because it was already equipped for radio.

Allan Crawford[12]

The transmitting mast was partly removed and, on 26 January 1963, the *Mi Amigo* sailed from Belgium, with reports of a stop on the way at Brest in western France to repair the steering gear, before crossing the Atlantic and eventually mooring at Pier 37 in Galveston, Texas on 14 March 1963.

The plan now was to remove the radio equipment and convert the *Mi Amigo* into a luxury yacht or recreational fishing vessel. Her crew were all paid off on arrival and she spent the long summer months in Galveston. She became a feature of the harbour with little activity around her; newspaper reports called her 'The Lady of Intrigue' and speculated that she had broadcast as the Voice of America, fighting for the freedom of the west against the communists.

Later reports revealed that radio equipment on board had been bought by local radio station KILT, another of Gordon McLendon's stations; although it was likely that the radio equipment onboard *Mi Amigo* was dismantled sometime after arrival in the Texas port.

We replaced the older cartridge machines and all studio mics with the relatively new Collins machines and Telefunken microphones that were removed from the MV *Mi Amigo*, which was home to McLendon's pirate radio ship operation off the coast of Norway. When Radio Nord was disassembled at Pier 37 in Galveston, KILT was the recipient of a good bit of studio gear.[13]

Bill Weaver, KILT's programme controller and local representative of the Rosebud Shipping Company of Panama, the registered owners of the ship, told local journalists that the ship was for sale. Newspaper reports described her Panamanian flag as tattered and her green-painted hull in need of care. The *Mi Amigo* was to stay alongside the pier in Galveston for eight months.

3

THE 'WHY NOT' BUSINESS

Radio Caroline was the first of the British offshore radio stations. It was started by Irishman Ronan O'Rahilly and without him there would have been no Radio Caroline, but what led O'Rahilly to start this radio revolution in the UK?

Ronan O'Rahilly had legitimate Irish Republican credentials; his family were part of the recent history of the island of Ireland. His grandfather was Michael Joseph O'Rahilly, shot by British soldiers while taking part in the 1916 Easter Rising in Dublin. Known in legend as The O'Rahilly, his life was celebrated in a poem by Yeats and a street in Dublin close to where he fell bears the family name.

Married to an American, Ronan's father, Aodhogen, also had an interest in the politics of Ireland; he stood for election to the Dail, the Irish parliament, in 1932, but failed to win a seat. As an educated engineer, he became a successful businessman with involvement in the peat and building industry and forestry. In the mid-1950s he bought the port of Greenore in County Louth from British Railways for £15,000. Earlier in the century it had been an important rail and ferry port for onward travel to England, but with closure of the railway in 1951 the ferry service to England came to an end and the whole site had lain redundant. Ronan O'Rahilly came from this wealthy background.

Born in 1940, O'Rahilly took pride in being a rebel; he claimed that he was expelled seven times from school. He moved to London at the start of the 1960s and quickly got to know the people who frequented the coffee bars of Chelsea. It was a place to be hip and cool and with his charm and good looks, he soon became one of the coolest in the Chelsea set. Whether he benefitted from family wealth, or not, money didn't seem to be a problem.

He became involved in a drama school, Studio 61, in the Fulham Road, practising method acting, a technique created by Russian Constantine Stanislavski. The actor 'becomes the part' and takes on the persona of the person being portrayed. Also attending these classes was Giorgio Gomelski, who would become involved with the Rolling Stones in the band's early days and go on to become an influential music producer. Another student at Studio 61 was former RAF man Cyril Nicholas Henty-Dodd, soon to be known by millions as Simon Dee. Whether Ronan was qualified to teach isn't clear, but he then moved to London's club land in Soho, running the Scene Club in Ham Yard off Great Windmill Street. This was one of a number of hip clubs in London, a place where rhythm and blues ruled. Artists playing here included Geno Washington, Chris Farlowe and Zoot Money; most of them were on the books of impresario, promoter and club owner Rik Gunnell, but their management was the responsibility of others. The Rolling Stones also appeared at the Scene, appearing on stage on four occasions in June and July 1963.

I believe Ronan was the owner of the Scene, at least that's what we all believed. The Scene club was dark, cramped and narrow, with a small bar, what passed as a dance floor and a stage too small for anything other than a DJ who had to make room for live bands and their equipment; consequently, it was very loud. There were some tables at the back, but I'm not sure anyone sat at them. It always seemed crowded, even when, quite often, it seemed there were only twenty people in there. The walls were invariably running with condensation, I don't remember seeing an emergency exit anywhere, I didn't go near the toilets due to pushers plying their trade, so maybe there was one there. One of the reasons that the Scene was not one of my favourite venues was because you almost always got hassled by someone wanting to sell you drugs, usually pep pills like purple hearts or bomber or dubes and I was not into that even though it was as common then as smoking is now amongst my contemporaries. The place rocked though, they got records straight from the States so you heard stuff that never would have got played on the radio.

Steve Cook, roadie with Zoot Money

The musicians performed the songs they'd heard on the imported American records that were played during the band breaks at the Scene: blues, jazz, soul and ska; black music, so different to the hits performed by established British artists, accompanied by strings and orchestras and played on the radio at the time.

Ronan O'Rahilly was responsible for the day-to-day management of a number of artists at this time; he was certainly working with harmonica player Cyril Davis and legendary blues musician Alexis Korner. Another of Ronan's protégés was blues singer Ronnie Jones, an American serviceman based in Britain.

Well, he started out trying to tame Alexis Korner. He invested in suits and stuff which the guys took and laughed about. I was still in the American Air Force being discharged and it was then that Ronan asked me to return. Alexis had asked me too, and I was undecided. I chose Ronan; I figured it'd be the shortest step to success. How wrong was I? Apart from my first two recordings he wasn't around that much. I do know he never gave me a dime for the singles that were produced on the various Decca and CBS labels, just a weekly salary and he paid for my flat in the first three months.

Ronnie Jones, musician

Ronan was instrumental in bringing the Alan Price Combo to London from Newcastle. Keyboard player Price, lead singer Eric Burdon, John Steele, Hilton Valentine and Chas Chandler became The Animals during this time.

We were resident at The Club A'GoGo in Newcastle and Ronan came up to see us, and he was moving with the smart set in London. We were taken down there and had a meeting at the Carlton Towers, a swish hotel. Ronan knew how things were done, he was very hip, he really fancied himself, but he had a lot of 'get up and go' and verve. He helped to launch The Animals, but he and the manager had a split up and he always felt slightly resentful that he didn't get a slice of The Animals – but he was there at the birth.

Alan Price, musician

Keyboard player and vocalist Georgie Fame had a residency at the Flamingo Club and he also performed at the Scene and it was Ronan's attempts to promote a recording of Georgie Fame that, he claims, led him to start a radio station.

I can remember well going round with an acetate of Georgie after I'd discovered that the BBC wouldn't play it at all because it wasn't on EMI or Decca, and I suddenly realised that the whole thing was locked up. I remember sitting with the head of Luxembourg and he had two of his colleagues in the office with him and I said, 'here's the acetate. How many plays can I get, will you play this?'

I knew I needed airplay in order to get the thing to function and when I'd finished rabbiting about how many plays I'd get, there was spontaneous laughter. The idea that somebody could walk in and believe they could get a recording played … and then he pointed out all these boards on the wall and there was EMI Show, Decca Show, EMI Show, Decca Show all listed and I said, 'do you mean to say that every record I'd ever heard on Luxembourg was paid for?', and he said,' you're absolutely right. We're booked up for five years'. I said, 'well, it looks like I'll have to start a radio station of my own', and with that they became very unhappy and they said, 'you can't do that' … I said, 'well why not? You've done it.'

Ronan O'Rahilly[1]

Ronan has said that he was aware of other radio stations broadcasting from ships, in particular the Voice of America and the Dutch Radio Veronica, but now there were two would-be radio operators chasing the same dream. The question that many have puzzled over is who came up with the idea first? Interestingly, although Project Atlanta was formed in 1962, it wasn't until February 1964 that Planet Productions, the company behind Caroline, was registered. Allan Crawford has always maintained that he had the idea first.

> One of the people I met, who came into my office was Ronan O'Rahilly, it must have been late 1962, and he's a very personable bloke, a very likeable bloke, charming manners and so on, and naturally one likes him and, like an idiot, I trusted him, especially when he said, 'my father's a rich man, living in a beautiful house in Dublin and I'll take you to meet him. If you give me a set of the papers I'll take them to him and interest him in being one of your investors'.
>
> So I went over to Ireland, he was absolutely right, beautiful house on the outskirts of Dublin. The father himself drove us to the border abutting Northern Ireland and there was this port. It hadn't been used for a long time and it had fallen into neglect, but there was a jetty for ships to tie up alongside and he said 'you can come here, it'll be kept quiet. You can equip your ship, and I'll see to it that you won't have any trouble.'
>
> Allan Crawford[2]

Ronan might have had the idea of operating a radio station before meeting Allan Crawford, but Crawford's associate, Kitty Black, was convinced that O'Rahilly used the Atlanta business plan:

> Ronan O'Rahilly met up with Allan and said he owned a harbour in Ireland and he could do the whole thing without any problems at all, this seemed like the answer to our prayer. Although he wasn't prepared to put up any money, the

fact that he could offer this harbour with the facilities that we
needed seemed to be sufficient reason for including him in the
deal. Therefore, in order to convince Ronan of the viability
of our totally legal operation, Allan had to give him the full
details of the entire set-up with details of the banking facilities,
the flags of convenience and the amount of money that had
already been promised. Ronan was therefore fully conversant
of the *modus operandi* of the entire set-up. He said that he was
totally in sympathy with the project, and that he couldn't agree
more with the way it had been set up. He was absolutely, one
hundred per cent committed and the port facilities would be
made available in Eire.

Kitty Black[3]

But although Project Atlanta had come close to securing the purchase of the *Mi Amigo* in 1962, the man operating Radio Nord
remembered others showing an interest in the ship.

In the last days of Radio Nord I was visited by a shipown-
er's son who was named Ronan O'Rahilly, together with a
Swede. They wanted to buy the boat, but their appearance and
impression on me was that it was empty talk, so I didn't bother
to take their offer seriously.

Jack Kotshack[4]

Armed with all the facts and figures needed, however they were
obtained, O'Rahilly set out to start a radio station of his own.
One of the few who Ronan had shared his idea with was another
Chelsea character, Christopher Moore. Ian Ross shared a flat
with him.

I'd only recently known Chris. I was 19 and had come to
London from the family home in Haslemere, but we became
great friends and shared a flat together in Milner Street,
Chelsea. Chris was a hustler, a sort of Kings Road cowboy that
seemed to exist in those days. They'd sit in the Kenya coffee

bar in Kings Road and pull birds and drink cappuccino, that was Chelsea in 1963.

Ian Ross

Ian Ross had a very wealthy father, New Zealand-born Charles Ross, a financier in the City, who had interests in numerous businesses; including a London bank, the Jenson car company and the Buxted chicken brand, although he had no connection with the Ross fisheries company, which would have great relevance later in the Radio Caroline story.

In 1963 Dad was 63 years old and still operating in the City with his chums, who used to have lunch and do deals. These were people who had umbrellas and wore bowler hats, though my dad didn't. They had lunch at the Savoy, shook hands on some sort of insider dealing and all made a s★★t of a load of money and up yours to the rest of you – we're alright.

Ian Ross

Ronan O'Rahilly needed to finance his radio station and the money he needed was heading straight in his direction.

This was spring 1963, Chris knew Ronan and he said, 'there's someone I'd like you to meet, you'll really like him, and he's got this idea.' We went to the Kenya, waited for ages for this guy to show and then this little leprechaun arrives, 'How's it goin'? How are ya?', that sort of thing. In those days you just didn't speak to people like that; everyone was cool and didn't speak to one another. He had a big impact on me. I'd never met anyone like him; he was most entertaining, and everything he told me was pretty much the opposite of how I'd been brought up. If you asked Ronan what he did, he'd say he was in the 'why not' business. This impressed me a great deal. Then I was told that he'd only met me to see if I was cool, if I was 'up to it', if I could 'dig it'. It wasn't so much of 'can he get the money?' because both Chris and Ronan knew perfectly

well that I was the complete lamb to the slaughter, a rich dad,
and what they didn't know, a rich dad who was prepared to do
almost anything to find me an occupation in life, other than
crashing cars and getting drunk.

We met again later the same day at the Carlton Tower, there
was a bit of corridor and he'd set up a sort of headquarters
there, so you'd appear and he'd be there with his documents
and his whole bullshit and you'd think … yeah …, so we met
again and I had my car downstairs, it was an MGB and he said,
'don't worry, I'll drive'. He drove my car at about 180mph
all the way to Haslemere, with me in the back and Chris in
the front and my dad's there looking annoyed and fiddling
around with his tractor. He was a New Zealander and he had
an ambivalent attitude towards the English upper classes. He
used to have to deal with them every day, yet he wasn't one
of them; he was an outsider, a complete outsider. There was
something about Ronan that he immediately really liked, he
just loved the guy, and I think they had some common bond
in being anti-establishment. My dad just sat there nodding and
drinking his gin and tonic, he didn't say anything. Then we had
dinner … and he still didn't say anything. He was a bit like that.
Then he just got up, went into the sitting room and rang his
mates, Jocelyn Stevens, John Sheffield and these stockbroker
guys who were in his kind of gang. They were very much the
establishment, the absolute figures of the establishment. Dad
was involved with a little bank called Close Brothers that was
his base, I think they came in. If he recommended something,
people bought it; he had a reputation, they thought it was a
flutter. Anyway they put the money in that night.

So this unlikely group of people came together on my dad's
say-so and everyone put in a bit of money, a punt it would be
for them – they were all rich – but they were entrepreneurs.
They all thought it would be great; Ronan said it would make
millions a month, it sounded great. He sat there and gave the
spiel to 'old Jimmy'. I can't believe that he would call my dad
Jimmy; the whole idea of it was unbelievable … 'Jasus Jimmy,

you won't believe it when you see this …' as he stabs this pile of papers, so my father goes overboard for Ronan and all of this was done in a day.

The money was delivered; we got the cash. I think we got it from the bank and we ended up with a suitcase with £150,000, which in those days was a fortune, a huge amount of money and I know it affected us all in the same way, me, Chris and Ronan. We went to mine and Chris' flat and we 'just destroyed the place, we threw the money in the air, we danced around the place', we went crazy. We were going to start a radio station.

Ian Ross

Not only had Ronan got his hands on enough money to bring his dream to fruition, he'd also done it in style, with finance from the top echelons of British society. The three of them made an unlikely alliance: the grandson of an Irish Republican fighter; John Sheffield, a descendant of the Duke of Buckingham, John Sheffield; and his son-in-law, Jocelyn Edward Greville Stevens. Stevens was a flamboyant Old Etonian, who was married to Jane Sheffield, a lady-in-waiting to Princess Margaret. Jane's father, John Sheffield, owned a highly successful company called Norcros, which, in turn, financed many well-known companies at the time. Stevens had inherited around £1 million from a trust set up after his mother died, shortly after his birth. On his 25th birthday he'd bought the staid society magazine *Queen* for £10,000. He re-launched it as a satirical magazine which included glossy photographs taken by a new wave of society photographers, including Antony Armstrong-Jones, 1st Earl of Snowdon, who was married to Princess Margaret. Stevens, the magazine's contributors and many of its readers were considered to be part of the early 1960s London jet set.

With the finance in place, work started on setting up the radio station. The task of finding a suitable ship was obviously top priority; assistance was sought from the Dutch Wijsmuller company. They supplied crews for vessels around the world and were

renowned as a ship delivery and salvage company; their business
was ships. Chris Moore was despatched to Holland to buy a ship
for the radio adventure.

> Chris went to Rotterdam, I think he'd worked as a gigolo on a
> cruise ship, he was a very good-looking guy, supposedly a stew-
> ard or in the purser's office, but I'm sure a seducer of women
> and he was deemed to be our man who knew about ships. So
> he went off with 20,000 quid in cash to Rotterdam and buys
> this really great ship. She was a beauty and I remember when
> Chris got back, we were in Ronan's flat, we'd bought the ship,
> laughing and giggling, the phone rings and it's John Sheffield,
> and he's the most serious, conservative, important guy you
> could meet and he starts by asking Ronan what's going on?
> 'Well, we've bought a ship John. It's a beautiful thing', so John
> asked, 'what kind of ship?' so Ronan puts his hand across the
> mouthpiece and says, 'he wants to know what kind of f★★★★★g
> ship it is', 'err John, Chris tells me it was some kind of ferry
> boat'. 'What … a ferry boat!?'" was the response, so Ronan says,
> 'if you think about it John, there are a lot of inland water-
> ways in Holland!' and he put the phone down. We were crying
> with laughter.
>
>   Ian Ross

The MV *Fredericia* was a former Danish ferry boat. She was
already more than thirty years old and had been laid up in 1963,
but now this 763-ton ship was destined to become the base for
Britain's first commercial radio station. Next, the radio equipment was needed before the ship could be turned into a fully
functioning broadcasting unit. Ronan flew to Dallas to buy the
equipment from Continental Electronics, the company who
built the two 10 kilowatt transmitters that would eventually
find their way onto the *Fredericia*. Also with business interests in
Dallas, were Gordon McLendon and his associates, who owned
the *Mi Amigo*, which was tied up in Galveston and was still for
sale in late November 1963. The studio equipment later fitted on

the Caroline ship was very similar to that already in place on the *Mi Amigo*, made by American company Gates. So, did O'Rahilly fly to Texas to simply do the deal for the equipment, or was he trying to acquire the *Mi Amigo* before the deal was done with Crawford, who was still trying to raise the funds?

The story goes that it was while Ronan was flying to Texas that he came up with the name for his radio station. He was reading a magazine which featured photographs of American President, John F. Kennedy, working in the Oval Office of the White House, as his children John Jnr and Caroline played around him. Interestingly, it was some months after Caroline came on air that this version, of how the name came about, first materialised. It is possible as O'Rahilly has always been a huge fan of the Kennedy family, but there are other credible versions: Reginald Maudling was Chancellor of the Exchequer at the time; his daughter was a model and actress and Ronan knew her.

> Reginald Maudling had a daughter called Caroline and Ronan met her at a party and thought that he would be able to influence Mr Maudling in his favour by naming it after her. He couldn't do a thing and he never did, quite rightly. So, we gained nothing from this bloody silly name, Radio Caroline.
>
> Allan Crawford[5]

> It would have been great but I doubt it, but it might have been a nice juxtaposition, a pirate radio station named after the daughter of a Tory!
>
> Caroline Maudling[6]

There was also a third, more likely, reason as to why the name Caroline was chosen. *Queen* magazine was owned by Jocelyn Stevens who, besides part financing the radio station, also seemed to take charge of business matters, especially in the early days of the venture. The magazine had a style guide for all writers who offered material for publication: this was the market they were aiming at.

This is Caroline. Look at her carefully and don't ever write anything Caroline wouldn't understand. Caroline was the sort of person one ended up in bed with. Caroline had fair long hair, and went to school and thought, '16 and out!'[7]

CHUG-a-LUG, CHUG-a-LUG, CHUG-a-LUG

While Ronan and his team were planning their radio station, Allan Crawford had finally found the finance that he needed; it was 'game on' for both Caroline and Project Atlanta. The race to be first on air was underway. During November 1963, the *Mi Amigo* left her mooring in Galveston for repairs at a local shipyard.

> The hull is deteriorating rapidly, it will be scraped of barnacles and receive a new paint job. The propellers are rusted and the ships motors are unable to operate, this will be corrected.[1]

A deal on the ship had finally been agreed with Project Atlanta and after eight months in harbour, the *Mi Amigo* slipped her moorings and left Galveston. Whilst it was unclear if all the onboard broadcast equipment had been removed in Galveston, much of it was certainly back onboard before her return to European waters, arriving in the Spanish port of El Ferrol on 30 January 1964. Here, work to improve her stability was carried out, in preparation for a new radio transmitting mast to be fitted. Had that mast been fitted in the Spanish port, Atlanta might have been on the air first, but Crawford had made the decision to go to Ireland for the work to be carried out.

The Irish port of Greenore was isolated and little-used; it was the ideal place to fit out a floating radio station. The Caroline ship was already there, but the *Mi Amigo* also needed a secluded port for her new transmitting mast to be erected. Both ships would use Greenore.

I was down in the south looking for a ship mast maker in aluminium and I met this marvellous ship rigger. In the summer
he would be with crews, running up the mast and down again,
huge, powerful hands, a lovely man with a marvellous accent
you could cut with a knife, and he was the rigger that rigged
our ship. But, Ronan got on to him through me too, so he was
rigging both ships.

Allan Crawford[2]

It was Harry Spencer,[3] based in Cowes, on the Isle of Wight, who
did the job. He and his team were experienced at fitting masts to
racing yachts and the principal of building a transmitting mast
was the same, just on a larger scale. His company was hired to
design, source and build, not just the masts for both ships, but the
stays and support wires to keep these huge structures upright in
the most testing of conditions.

Nearly all programmes on previous offshore stations had been
pre-recorded and that was the plan for these two new operations.
Atlanta had studios which were made available to Caroline in
exchange for the use of the facilities in Greenore. Both organisations needed staff: Ronan already had Chris Moore, Ian Ross
and another friend from his acting studio days, Michael Joseph,
working with him and the search for DJs led him to recruit two
experienced actors and an estate agent. Cyril Nicholas Henty-
Dodd, as Simon Dee, was signed up with actors John Junkin and
Carl Conway.

I was first approached through my agent. I was doing voice-overs
for television commercials and acting jobs, and she said, 'There's
some mysterious radio station. I don't know anything about it,
they won't tell us anything, but you can go along for an interview
or an audition if you like.' I went along to this studio and Michael
Joseph, who was Ronan's right-hand man, he was holding the
auditions and he said, 'Just sit on the stool and talk in a nice
relaxed way and chat along to the people, that's the sort of thing
we want, and introduce a few records' which I did, and he had a

chat with somebody back in the office and right away he came
back and said, 'Well, we'd very much like to have you with us'.

Carl Conway, DJ

At the same time Allan Crawford was signing up suitable radio
talent to work for him. As an Australian he favoured those from
his own country who already had radio experience, something
that was lacking on the Caroline team, but the man appointed
as general manager for Radio Atlanta was Richard Harris, an
Englishman who had broadcast whilst in the forces.

I was playing a double bass and during a break in the recording,
I was talking to one of the technicians and he was on about
this guy who was going to operate a radio station off the East
Coast, so I asked who he was. 'Oh,' he said, 'I don't know, he's
some music publisher'. So I then set about trying to find this
mythical character and eventually it led me to the offices of
Southern Music in Soho and Allan Crawford. At that time he
didn't have any regular staff as such; he introduced me to Kitty
Black. We'd discuss the setting up of the studio, programme
format, and how it was going to be and eventually I sort of
became general manager of Project Atlanta Ltd. The ship was
the *Mi Amigo* and Project Atlanta Limited was PAL (my friend,
pal) and he liked this, he used to keep saying, 'I love it'. He used
to keep on about the fact that the *Mi Amigo* and the PAL was a
thing and he liked the name Atlanta and, indeed, so did I.

Richard Harris, DJ[4]

The number of Australian broadcasters in London at the time
was fortuitous for Allan Crawford; he knew many of them from
his music publishing days in Australia. Ken Evans was another
experienced radio man.

I met Allan Crawford in late May of 1963; we had known
each other in Sydney when I was programme director of radio
station 2CH and Allan was plugging records for Southern

Music. We had dinner at a nearby Chinese restaurant and Allan told me about his radio plans. He asked me to look out for radio people from Commonwealth countries: Australia, Canada and so on.

Ken Evans, programme controller[5]

Allan said to me, 'Who are we going to have to broadcast?' and I said, 'We should have Australians'. We didn't want Americans and there were no Brits who were capable of doing this, or at least I didn't think so because it was so new, and let's face it commercial radio in Australia had been around for a long, long time. Allan replied, 'I'm glad you said that because I've got a whole bunch of Australians', and he mentioned Tony Withers, Colin Nicol, Ken Evans and Dermot Hoy, who was in those days an engineer, but would eventually became Bryan Vaughan on air, and that was virtually the nucleus at that time.

Richard Harris, DJ[6]

Studios had been built in the Dean Street offices of Radio Atlanta, and the DJs began rehearsing and recording programmes. Allan Crawford's recordings, on his various labels, were featured heavily. He was covering the hits of the day with session singers; the most famous at the time was Ross McManus, who featured in many of the shows on the BBC Light Programme. Because of Musicians' Union rules in force at the time, the BBC was only allowed to broadcast a limited number of hours from gramophone records (needle time). For example, the latest Beatles record would receive very few plays on the BBC, but the likes of Ross McManus and the Northern Dance Orchestra would be playing away, seemingly all day.

With the preparations for Radio Atlanta finally underway, Allan Crawford told members of his team about the rival group behind Caroline. Manager Richard Harris was incredulous when he heard:

Allan told me that the *Mi Amigo* had crossed the Atlantic from
Galveston and it was having its mast put on in Ireland. When
I asked him how did you organise that?, he said, 'well this guy
Ronan O'Rahilly', who I never heard of before, 'has got a
father who had a bit of Ireland which included a port and he
said that we could put the *Mi Amigo* there and get the mast put
on it'. I said, 'well, why can't we put it in an English port? He
replied, 'as soon as we went in there, they'd slap a writ on the
mast and that would be it; we couldn't move it'. We asked him
why it couldn't be done in Spain and he said, 'well, because he'd
been offered this port in Ireland which was so much nearer and
this is where he'd decided to have it done'. Then of course, he
said, 'Oh by the way, Ronan has bought a ship, but ours will
be ready first, of course, he's not going to do the dirty on us or
anything like that' and I couldn't believe this. I said, 'But, Allan,
you're mad – of course he will. He'll get his out first and in the
meantime his people are wandering all over the *Mi Amigo*, they
see exactly what equipment is there, exactly what is required to
put an offshore radio station out to sea, he's obviously going to
do it'. 'Oh, no, no, no', he said, 'He won't do that'.

Richard Harris, DJ[7]

Programme controller Ken Evans was one of the first to meet the
Caroline team as they started recording their programmes in the
Dean Street headquarters of Atlanta.

In late 1963 Allan told me, 'We could have competition; there
could be another ship involved'. Then a group of men arrived
in our studios and I was instructed to prepare a series of musical programmes to be recorded in our studios by these people.
I did some of the panel operating; they were Carl Conway,
Simon Dee and John Junkin.

Ken Evans, programme controller[8]

We were training these guys. l remember a young guy who
came in, just out of the RAF as a corporal, who called himself

Simon Dee, and it was us who actually taught him how to broadcast. We sat him in that cubicle and we used to twiddle the knobs for him outside while he was in there and we'd teach him exactly how to do it.

Richard Harris, DJ[9]

Another experienced Australian recruit was Colin Nicol, who was to present the pre-recorded breakfast show on Radio Atlanta.

We rehearsed at the Soho studios and trained others, including those who were later to prove our rivals, and recorded hour-long tapes of programmes in preparation for broadcast when the ship came on air. The point being, we were not to be on the ship ourselves; all programmes were to be recorded with carefully synchronised time-checks and then played out from the ship by technicians. We were recording rival Radio Caroline disc-jockeys in our studios because Allan had, or so he thought, reached an agreement that Ronan's ship, the *Caroline* [*sic – Fredericia*], would take up a position on the north-west of England, off the Isle of Man, while ours would go to its original intended location off Essex in the South East.

Colin Nicol, DJ[10]

By accepting the offer of the port facilities at Greenore, Crawford and his team played into the hands of O'Rahilly, who had realised the huge benefits of being the first to go on air. But the Caroline crew had other concerns, they feared that the Radio Atlanta format and it's music, made up largely of Crawford's cover versions, would frighten off potential listeners should Atlanta be first on air. The cool Chelsea cats behind Caroline wanted to promote the music that was so popular with those who frequented the London clubs. They planned to play established R&B acts like Ray Charles, Jimmy McGriff and the new wave of British performers like Georgie Fame, The Animals and The Rolling Stones. Crawford was intent on playing cover versions from his own record labels.

Allan Crawford unfortunately had the same idea as us and he'd bought a ready-made radio ship and it was sailing towards our designated pitch off Harwich, and this was a crisis. Allan had really bad taste in music; he'd do cover versions. His great launch programme was going to be called 'Mid-morning Musicale'. We thought if that happens then we're out of business right away.

Ian Ross

A complex web of companies was behind both radio stations, with different enterprises registered in different countries taking charge of the various aspects of the business, from ship owning, to sales and employing staff. Crawford claimed that the only difference between his plans and Caroline's were the lawyers that O'Rahilly had used. Ronan has always maintained that Caroline had been set up completely independently of Atlanta, with his own business model, and his team believed that too.

Our corporate structure was modelled on the Dutch, Radio Veronica. Our ship had a Panamanian flag and also a Bolivian flag. Planet Productions was an Irish company based in Dublin and leased airtime from a Lichtenstein company who had the ship, and a London Company leased airtime from the Irish company.

Ian Ross

Radio Atlanta, like Caroline, had a complicated business set up. CBC Plays was the major shareholder of Project Atlanta, an organisation which sold advertising in the UK. Atlanta's airtime was leased from Atlantic Broadcasting Services in Lichtenstein, and this company rented the ship from Rosebud shipping, but also supplied payments to the disc jockeys and engineers through a British company called Hengown Ltd.

As preparations for Radio Atlanta got underway on land, the *Mi Amigo* made her way to Greenore, but the Caroline ship, *Fredericia*, was ahead of her, having sailed from Rotterdam on

13 February 1964. The *Mi Amigo* left Spain on 15 February, a longer, slower voyage lay ahead of her, and already Caroline had taken the lead.

> Signals were sent to the skipper to bring the *Mi Amigo* round from Spain to this port called Greenore in Southern Ireland, which was going to take her some time because she was not very a big ship; she had to hug the coastline and so she was coming chug-a-lug, chug-a-lug, chug-a-lug, very slowly. Nobody thought that time was the essence for the operation. But we didn't know Ronan O'Rahilly.
>
>   Kitty Black[11]

The port of Greenore on Carlingford Lough, including the substantial railway buildings and grand hotel, had remained unused for many years and much of the site had fallen into disrepair. It was secluded and provided deep-water berths, the only way to view work on the dockside was from the water and visitors were discouraged.

Both groups sought technical advice from former BBC and Marconi men. Overseeing Caroline's set-up was Arthur Carrington, he'd been involved in the development of television cameras capable of working underwater. Another former BBC man, A.N. Thomas, worked with Atlanta. He was an aerial expert. John Gilman and George Saunders worked on the *Mi Amigo* for Atlanta and one of the original Swedish Radio Nord engineers from the *Mi Amigo*, Ove Sjöström, was now signed up for Caroline. There was much more to be done on the *Fredericia*, now renamed *Caroline*. She had to be converted into a radio ship; transmitters and generators to power them, a broadcast studio, the aerial mast and a heavy-duty anchoring system to allow a permanent mooring, had to be fitted. The *Mi Amigo*, despite arriving days later had little work to be done; she'd been designed and fitted out very well, but she had no radio mast.

Although both the Caroline and Atlanta teams were ultimately aiming for the same end result, there was little co-operation between them and any advice given was often misleading. Atlanta engineer George Saunders remembers plenty about this remote Irish port.

> Greenore was the creepiest place I've ever been to; the large hotel lay empty, the last passenger ship had docked years ago, but there were still posters displayed from years earlier. I always felt that I was being watched. The original plan was for the stronger ship, *Fredericia*, now *Caroline*, to go to a position off the Isle of Man; she was fitted with a steel mast weighing 13 tons. The *Mi Amigo*'s mast was made of aluminium and weighed just 3 tons. Caroline's people were certainly hostile to Atlanta; they wouldn't tell Atlanta what they were doing, but the Caroline engineering was in a state; at least on Atlanta we had the expertise.
>
> George Saunders, broadcast engineer

While the engineers worked at preparing the ships, Ronan, Chris Moore and Ian Ross would check on progress.

> Without Greenore this whole thing just wouldn't have happened. Ronan had been to Galveston, bought the equipment and it was all shipped over. We went to see the ship, there were guards on the gates, we'd fly over there. It was a laugh from start to finish.
>
> Ian Ross

With both ships in the same harbour and the harbour owned by the father of one of the ship's owners, there was only going to be one winner, and that would be Caroline. Delays were slowing Radio Atlanta's progress at every stage, adding to Crawford's frustration.

> Oh, there were hundreds of incidents. I had people reporting to me by phone every day. There'd be things mysteriously – wires cut – all kinds of things. You couldn't get on our ship without climbing over the other one first and it was much

bigger. I had a hell of a lot of headaches there because when
the two ships were tied up and getting ready, the sabotage that
was going on in my ship to stop it getting ready was colossal.
In fact, the influence that Ronan brought to bear was such that
our ship was ordered out of harbour several times by the harbour master. The captain was forced to go out during a storm
and it was so bad that the ship touched bottom in the harbour
and he turned round and came straight back in and said, 'Up
yours, I'm going to stay here', and knowing what they were
doing, they didn't dare do too much about it.

                                                    Allan Crawford[12]

Radio Atlanta now had a number of people on the payroll, and
were advertising for more to join the team, but the radio station
still showed no signs of getting on air and earning any money.
Colin Nicol suggested Radio Atlanta could still be first on the air,
beating Caroline, by abandoning the ship and taking over one of
the disused military forts in the Thames. Within months the forts
would be used, but not by Atlanta, and they'd play a huge part in
the British offshore radio story.

I told him, it was early 1964, over a Chinese meal – if Ronan
is getting the jump on us, move onto a fort and beat him to it.
Allan would not take the risk, he had investors to consider and
felt that was too risky a tactic, legally. I think that was one of
the things I said that got Allan a bit off-side with me. He didn't
accept advice.

                                                    Colin Nicol, DJ[13]

5

GENIUS

Caroline was ready to sail, programme controller Chris Moore, announcer Simon Dee, engineers and the marine crew led by Dutch Captain Baeker, were on board, as the ship prepared to slip her moorings and leave Greenore, but not before the whole area had been made aware of the real purpose of this strange-looking ship. As the transmitters were turned on and tested for the first time, the signal could be heard on every television, radio and even telephone in the immediate area, as the huge radiated power from the ship blasted out music by Ray Charles, causing interference to just about everything electrical.

> I had to start from the beginning; we started to put in the transmitters and all the necessary things. The pieces came in and we put it together. We had to be sure everything was working, it blocked out television reception and you could see on the harbour lights that the lamps were blinking to the music. You could see the music in the lamps.
>
> Ove Sjöström, Engineer

On 23 March 1964, the MV *Caroline*, flying a Panamanian flag and looking like no other ship on the high seas with her 168ft-high mast, left Greenore destined, as Allan Crawford and his Project Atlanta team thought, to a position little more than 50 miles away, off the Isle of Man. According to Simon Dee, the Caroline ship did head for the island, but only to shelter while the weather calmed down. The voyage continued, but until she dropped anchor on Good Friday evening at a position 3½ miles north-east of Felixstowe, no one knew of her final destination.

> The weather of that week was appalling. I was ready to be sick, but I was not ready to leave my body in the way I did in the first few days. It was so bad that we had to anchor off the Isle of Man in one of the bays. We stayed there for a bit whilst we hoped the storm abated, it didn't, and we had to go on. We pulled out the following morning and we turned south from the Isle of Man and started sailing to our anchorage.
>
> Simon Dee, DJ[1]

Coastal stations were tracking the movements of this strange looking ship on her voyage south through the Irish Sea, turning east up the Channel and then heading north into the Thames Estuary.

> North Foreland telephoned and reported that a series of link calls had been passed on 27th March from a Panamanian vessel named CAROLINE in 'very guarded and incomprehensible language' from which it had been deduced that a broadcasting service might be started from the vessel whilst at sea between 9am and 10am and noon and 1pm on 28th March. Also that on Easter Sunday special broadcasts directed at the UK would begin. On first contact the position of the vessel was given as 'off Dungeness' but later, on being requested an evasive reply 'east for orders' had been given. It was thought that the vessel was anchored in the vicinity of the Cork light vessel off Harwich.[2]

The Government weren't alone in having an interest in *Caroline*'s movements. Allan Crawford and his Project Atlanta colleagues were following the course that the Caroline ship was taking.

> Ronan O'Rahilly kept saying in no way did he wish to compete with Project Atlanta's plans. So the *Fredericia* set sail from Greenore bound, as everybody thought, or as they had declared, for a course that would take her to a station off the Isle of Man.

As she departed from Greenore, it became obvious that there was no intention of turning smartly left or port; she was continuing on a southerly course which was going to take her round the Lizard and ending up, eventually, somewhere in the North Sea.

Kitty Black[3]

Although Caroline had stolen a march on Atlanta, there were two pieces of information that Allan Crawford had hung onto: the best position off the coast to anchor the ship and the best frequency to broadcast on:

I tracked down a set of pilots operating the ships in and out of London. They were great blokes and of course, they knew the waters like the palm of their hands. They brought in shareholders that they knew, people with money, so there was a little clique of investment from that direction that was always friendly with me. They found a perfect spot for our ship, and that was one of things I always withheld from Ronan, all he knew was that it was off Frinton, but he didn't know where.

Allan Crawford[4]

Keith Martin, who'd been involved with the GBLN and GBOK projects in 1962, but never got to broadcast, was now a member of the Atlanta team:

The *Fredericia* went chugging around the coast and set out to find an anchorage somewhere off Harwich, but a Trinity House pilot advised us as to where we should anchor Radio Atlanta to the best advantage, bearing in mind that she would have to be serviced both from Harwich and from Holland in the event of any problems with English Maritime laws. The spot was outside territorial waters and in an area where the slack water was likely to make life comparatively comfortable for the DJs who were going to have to live and work aboard her.

Keith Martin, DJ[5]

Project Atlanta had also researched the best frequency to broadcast on and obtained the crystals for the transmitter, but here
there were problems:

> A man called Thomas Chatsfield was high up in BBC engi-
> neering and he was asked to identify good frequencies to
> broadcast on. Four crystals, two for each ship, were ordered
> from the States, but Caroline kept all of them.
>
> George Saunders, broadcast engineer

The Government had got wind of a likely assault on the British
airwaves a few weeks earlier. The Postmaster General, Reginald
Bevins, who was responsible for the control of radio broadcast,
was asked in the House of Commons, on 5 February 1964, if he
was aware of plans to broadcast commercial radio programmes
to Britain from a ship moored off Harwich and what action he
proposed to take:

> Yes, I am aware of these plans. Such broadcasting would con-
> travene International Regulations and endanger international
> agreements on the sharing of radio frequencies. It would
> almost certainly cause serious interference to radio-communi-
> cations in this, and other countries. The Council of Europe has
> under consideration, a Convention aimed at preventing broad-
> casting from ships on the high seas. This may point to the need
> for new legislation in due course. Meanwhile, I am glad to say,
> that I have had very encouraging indications that responsible
> interests in this country have no intention of supporting any
> such venture. I am keeping a close watch on the position.[6]

But although the Government were aware of Project Atlanta,
they knew nothing of Caroline until the transmitters were fired
up for her first broadcasts:

> A project of 'Radio Atlanta' came to notice in mid-1962 …
> by the beginning of 1964 the indications were that Radio

Atlanta would start broadcasting within a month or two …
On 28th March 1964 a ship 'Radio Caroline' started broadcasting … the Post Office had not, until 28th March, had any
knowledge of the existence of this project.[7]

Test broadcasts started soon after the MV *Caroline* dropped
anchor on that Friday night. Swedish engineer Ove Sjöström,
formerly with Radio Nord, was responsible for the transmitters onboard.

When the moment came to turn on the Radio Caroline transmitter there were many people around. There was a big switch
to operate the transmitters. I was down in the transmitter room
the whole time. After the switch-on, I walked around looking
for sparks or signs of any problems.

Ove Sjöström, Engineer

Soon-to-be disc jockeys, Chris Moore and Simon Dee, were
on board. They were to be the 'live' voices. John Junkin and Carl
Conway would also be heard on this new radio station, but their
programmes had been recorded on ten-inch reels of tape. Now these
programmes were stashed aboard the ship and ready to be played on
the professional Ampex tape machines in the control room.

Those involved with the organisation on land waited eagerly
to learn if, and how well, the signal could be heard. It had been
planned to use a code word, 'genius' to avoid any confusion with
any other broadcast that might have been received. Ray Charles
was the 'genius' and it would be Ray Charles' music that was
played for the tests.

As the seas made the ship pitch and roll on this blustery Friday
evening, Carl Conway and Ian Ross were on dry land, tasked
with listening for the test transmissions from the radio ship. How
far would the signal reach and how clear would it be?

I was driving around Canterbury, Herne Bay, Margate,
Ramsgate because Ronan said we wanted to know how

it's being covered on my part of the coast, so 'would I drive around as much as you can, as far as you can and as quickly as you can and make a note of where it's fading and where it's coming in strong?' It was a great thrill to hear it, it was lovely. I thought, crikey, I'm part of this exciting new venture – yes that was exciting.

Carl Conway, DJ

Simon Dee was on board with Chris Moore and the plan was to play Ray Charles, either 'The night time is the right time' or 'I got news for you' and use the code word 'genius'. I was driving around Kent and Surrey listening out for 'genius'. Simon Dee had refused to go on air, locking himself in his cabin, so Chris had to do everything for those tests, including pulling the switch to go on air for the first time – that was a revolutionary act.

Ian Ross

Radio knob-twiddlers in East Anglia on Saturday morning must have been surprised to hear a Ray Charles record played over and over again on 199 metres and weird voices repeating 'The genius' now and then, Caroline, anonymously, was testing for the big moment.

Simon Dee, DJ[8]

This audacious scheme, destined to challenge the monopoly of the BBC and effectively declare broadcasting war on the Government, was about to kick off. In London, a group of journalists had been invited to listen to the birth of this radio adventure. Ronan was there, together with Jocelyn Stevens, representing the financiers, although, at this stage he wasn't keen to be seen publicly as part of the project.

The ship gets on station, *Mi Amigo* is still effectively impounded, and we had this press conference. Jocelyn had this highly ambivalent attitude towards the whole project and the public in general; he was the chairman – then he wasn't, then he was and he wanted to be there, but incognito. So, we had this press conference where he appeared in his overcoat and he wore this sort of trilby pulled over his face, as if the whole press core didn't know who he was, he was a blue-blooded Fleet Street press baron. Then Ronan appears with this enormous radio and all these Fleet Street hacks are sitting there drinking and he switches it on and nothing ... nothing happens, it's a complete fiasco. Because of the steel structures, the signal wasn't getting through.

Ian Ross

But outside, in the street, the signal was loud and clear; the newspapers had their headline story for the next day editions and radio, and perhaps the complete culture of Britain, was about to be challenged in a way that could not have been foreseen by anyone, least of all those involved in Radio Caroline.

6

Your all-Day Music Station

This is Radio Caroline on 199, your all-day music station. We are on the air every day from six in the morning till six at night. The time right now is one minute past twelve, and that means it's time for Christopher Moore.

We were both scared, because suddenly this is the big moment and all the lads, all our friends, were waiting in London and with a meeting of the press. Up until now it'd been quite a lot of fun and a bit of heartache, but suddenly it was there, the pile of records, the microphone, the big switch, everything was there.

Christopher Moore, DJ[1]

Britain now had a choice of BBC radio and a commercial radio station, though it would be some time before any advertisements would be heard. The newspapers were full of the story and the Government, and in particular the Post Office, which was in charge of radio broadcasts, went into apparent meltdown. Ship-to-shore telephone facilities were suspended immediately.

A programme of pop records had been heard with no identification or conversation between records. North Foreland was informed that if it was established without doubt that the vessel was conducting a broadcast service, all link calls and radio telegrams, except those concerning the safety of life or navigation should be refused.[2]

There were claims of interference from Caroline's transmitters; Coastguards in particular complained of their messages having to compete with pop music, but if there was a problem with Caroline's signal, it was quickly fixed or the effects had been exaggerated.

> Interference experienced the previous day has now ceased and adjustments have now been carried out on the transmitter on the *Caroline* to remove spurious emissions.

> The pirate's emissions were not as 'tidy' as that of the BBC station, but were not very much worse. As we suspected, the interference to coastguard services from pirate stations was due, primarily, to the inadequacy of the coastguard's receiver.[3]

A telegram was sent within hours of Caroline's first broadcast to Panama, requesting that Caroline was stopped from broadcasting. According to the reply, the ship's registration was withdrawn, though whether this actually happened is debatable. The establishment, so used to having things their own way, appeared unable to comprehend such an assault on the world that they governed. The flurry of activity behind the scenes appeared to be manic, with official memos and correspondence fired off in all directions, they just didn't know what had hit them and there appeared to be very little that they could do about it, apart from bluster.

Sir Joseph Lockwood, Chairman of EMI, all but demanded the Government blow the ship out of the water, requesting that the Government Act immediately and suggested the record industry, of which his company had the lion's share of the market, consider financing a ship of their own to jam Caroline's signal. He claimed that Caroline's programmes would result in a reduction of record sales. The Government did look into the possibility of jamming the Caroline broadcasts, with enquiries about cost and availability of transmitters capable of preventing people in Britain from tuning in. Caroline was certainly seen as a serious threat by many government officials and politicians.

It is estimated that the cost of providing and installing the equipment would range from about £4,000 for a 1 kilowatt transmitter to £13,000 for a 10 kilowatt transmitter. The cost of operating the service is estimated to be in the order of £60 a week ... The delivery of one could well take anything from three to eighteen months.[4]

The British Copyright Council and the Musicians Union and PPL wasted no time at all in attacking Caroline, calling for immediate action from the Government. Writs were threatened by Phonographic Performance Ltd, the group that controlled the broadcasting of gramophone records. There were even threats made to the listeners by the Post Office:

Radio listeners are entitled only to listen to authorised stations. Listeners to Radio Caroline are liable to a £10 fine on a first conviction and to a £50 fine for any subsequent offence.[5]

Until now the BBC had a complete monopoly of radio broadcasting in Britain, and they weren't going to accept this newcomer gladly, the British Broadcasting Corporation was outraged. Memos flew around Broadcasting House, with staff assigned to recording and transcribing every word spoken and details of every song played from this 'pirate'. The Director General's office was quick to feed the Radio Services Department at the GPO, with every titbit of information they gleaned from 'private sources'. Suggested names of investors included the Chairman of the British Printing Corporation, one of whose member companies printed the BBC's own Radio Times. Also links to Swiss bankers, the London based Close Brothers merchant bank and the Irish PYE radio company were reported.[6]

The British PYE company already provided equipment to commercial television operators and in 1960 published 'A plan for local radio broadcasting in Britain', a report that, had the Government's Pilkington Committee found in favour of introducing commercial radio to Britain in 1962, might have been used as a basis for the project.

Pye would obviously have been keen to provide the equipment, in fact, Manx Radio – based on the Isle of Man and the first authorised commercial radio station within the British Isles – was supplied with a Pye transmitter and studio equipment when it came on air in 1964, just weeks after the arrival of Radio Caroline. There were claims that Pye had even supplied Caroline with equipment, manufactured by the company, but branded with a fictious company name to avoid being openly linked to 'pirate' radio, but no evidence can be found of this.[7]

But the listeners just loved what they were hearing; no number of government threats would make them switch off. Within days of the first broadcast a huge proportion of the population were aware of this new pirate radio station, with thousands tuning in and writing to Caroline. By Wednesday morning, just two postal days after Caroline came on air, Don Murrison of Anglia Marine, said he had 300 letters waiting to go out to the ship. Listeners of all ages immediately took to the relaxed style of presentation and the music that was played. Listen back now to those early programmes and you begin to understand just how boring and staid the BBC programmes must have been and how there was a hunger for something more entertaining, yet those programmes from the early days of Caroline, many of them pre-recorded, were hardly imaginative, and the music choice was very uninspiring.

> Presentation: very brief (average 4 seconds) identification of title and artist. Back announcements are rare. Two discs segue about every ten minutes. I have so far heard four different DJs – two of them are live, and I think the other two may have taped 20-minute phases (on terra firma?). Voices are young, pleasant, without strong characteristics.[8]

A few programmes were presented live from the ship by Simon Dee, albeit with an engineer playing in his records. Live announcements could be identified by the sound of generators pulsating throughout the ship whenever the microphone was opened. The pre-recorded programmes made in the London studios of Atlanta filled the rest of the broadcast day.

On 7 April 1964 Caroline was discussed in Parliament, with the Postmaster General telling the house that, 'concerted action from the countries of the Council of Europe' could be expected before long and he was 'relying on British advertisers not to use this or any other similar unauthorised service'.[9]

More crew members were enlisted; one of the first to join was a former British Forces broadcaster Alan Turner, initially employed as a studio engineer, his job was to play the records for the on-air announcer, but he was soon on air himself.

My wife Elaine worked in central London and I'd often drive through London to pick her up in the car and on this particular day I bought the *Evening Standard* newspaper to read while I was waiting and, as I was thumbing through the pages, my eyes caught an advert which said, 'staff wanted for broadcasting venture, apply to the following address ...' the address was in Fetter Lane, and I was parked in Fetter Lane. I looked out of the car window and there, about two doors up the road, was the number where I should respond to this advert. I wandered in there; it was the publishing offices of *Queen* magazine. I walked in and the girl on reception had no idea what I was talking about, so I showed her the advert and she went off then came back saying, 'well, apparently there are a couple of men in a room on the top floor, I think you should go up and talk to them about it'. I went up and found Ronan O'Rahilly and a guy called Chris Moore, I told them my background and they said, 'Can you go out on the ship tomorrow?' I couldn't go out prior to the ship starting broadcasts, so I went out immediately after Easter on the tender that took Chris Moore back to land. A couple of days later Doug Kerr, a Canadian DJ, turned up. Simon Dee was on board still, so it was Doug Kerr, myself and Simon.

Alan Turner, DJ and technician

The studio operation on Caroline had been designed to broadcast tapes; initially there were no plans to have DJs on-board – all the programmes were to be recorded in London and taken out to the ship – so there was the operating unit and a very small continuity studio, but this soon changed.

Sometimes the tender would come out from Harwich with the tapes and wasn't able to get alongside. We couldn't broadcast programmes as envisaged, so we started having DJs on board. I had no audition, I was just going to handle the management of the studio on board and do the continuity announcements, but as we found out very quickly, that wasn't going to work. Doug Kerr and Simon couldn't operate the panel, so I then produced the shows for them. It was just myself and Swedish engineer Ove Sjöström that did most of the shows in the early days because there was nobody else to do it.

Alan Turner, DJ and technician

The ship was necessarily anchored outside territorial waters, so all fuel, food, water, supplies and personnel had to be ferried from land. Anyone travelling to and from the ship, had to pass through numerous checks such as customs and immigration and, with the Government obviously smarting from Caroline's challenge to their authority, they were hardly going to make life easy for the pirates.

In the early days we had quite a lot of different tenders, mostly tugs. One of these was called *Hooligan*, it wasn't really suitable for us and after a while we stopped using him. The skipper was a really gruff-speaking cockney and I remember this really deep East End voice calling us on the ship's radio saying, 'Caroline, Caroline, Caroline, 'ooligan, 'ooligan, 'ooligan. The tenders were organised by Anglia Marine, the agents in Church Street, Harwich, run by Don Murrison. He was an unsung hero of the early days of Caroline, for the first months he was basically underwriting all the costs himself. It was because of his word that a lot of the fuel was delivered to the ship, and food. He was saying to the suppliers, 'well don't worry, I'll cover the costs', until money started coming in from advertisers.

Alan Turner, DJ and technician

The Government might have been under the impression that Panama had relinquished the ship's registration; perhaps they had. Confusion was certainly an ally to Caroline – the whole business plan was built on loopholes and confusion – and whether or not the ship was on Panama's books, the Government would take care not to act against the *Caroline* if there was any doubt about her registration.

She flew the Panamanian flag occasionally. I remember them painting the word 'Panama' on a board and hanging it over the stern after it was reregistered. It was painted on a plank. When she was in Greenore they tried to chisel off the name *Fredericia* and they only got part of it off because it was welded into the ship's hull. If you look at photographs of the ship you can see where they started and tried to remove it, it never was removed.

Alan Turner, DJ and technician

While Atlanta had yet to get on air, Caroline's audience was massive, and continued to grow daily. The race to be first on air had been won and the prize was a wealth of publicity worldwide.

We had no communication with the shore, one of the first things the Government did was stop our ship to shore communication, we had no idea what was going on ashore. We just sat there and played records, we knew the signal was going out because we could see it on the oscilloscope. It was about three or four weeks after we started broadcasting that someone came out from head office in London and said, 'I think you'd better sit down, we have some important news for you'. We sort of looked at each other and sat down, and they said, 'you've got almost six million listeners.

Alan Turner, DJ and technician

There was another prize that Caroline and Atlanta both needed if they were to survive – advertisers; without them there would be no finance to enable the broadcasts to continue. The Postmaster General had appealed to advertisers to have no dealings with the offshore stations, but on 1 May 1964 the commercials started. Initially the majority of those advertising were smaller, local businesses: a holiday camp at Hopton-on-Sea, a radio and television dealer from Westcliff-on-Sea and a furniture store in Gidea Park, all featured on the first day of advertising. The very first commercial broadcast was for the Duke of Bedford's Woburn Abbey:

The only time I appeared on air was doing the radio commercials for the Duke of Bedford's Woburn Abbey, because he liked my posh voice and I knew how to say Wooburn, not Woburn. The Duke was very keen on me and Chris. He liked to come to the *Queen* office and he'd invite us to dinner, and we'd sit there and chat and he'd dream up these commercials. One day Jocelyn was in his office and the Duke of Bedford had come and gone without him knowing, 'WHAT, WHAT? … I've had enough of you bloody people', he was really angry about that. 'You don't have dukes coming to call at *Queen* magazine without me knowing about it.

Ian Ross

Alan Turner was responsible for playing the commercials out on the ship between segments of the pre-recorded programme tapes.

The first main ad was for Bulova watches, because they provided a quartz clock for the studio and we used the Bulova time check for a long time.

> *This is Radio Caroline, your all-day music station, the time is exactly*
> *10 o'clock, that's Bulova watch time, B U L O V A, Bulova, when*
> *you know what makes a watch tick you'll buy a Bulova.*

Some of the ads were on tape, some on 'Spotmaster' [a tape
cartridge machine], some were live reads. On the hour and half
hour you were busy, you had to interrupt the tapes, have reel
to reel tapes cued up, Spotmaster ready and scripts if they were
live reads, and of course we had to log all the times that the ads
went out.

> Alan Turner, DJ and technician

From 25 May, regular mentions for well-known brand names
started to appear on air, including William Hill Bookmakers,
Harp Lager, *News of the World*, Reveille and Kraft Dairylea. Small,
local retailers were also keen to have their name on air and heard
by tens of thousands, the vast majority never likely to use their
services. The Government's plea to advertisers to avoid using the
radio ships had gone unheeded.

We are not out to annoy the Government and our impression
is that the climate has changed. It is up to us to go for the best
value for money in our advertising and you can't find out if
you have value unless you experiment.[10]

Caroline was also keen on dealing with smaller, unknown companies, appealing for agents to sell their products such as perfumes
and nylons. There was controversy when the Government's Egg
Marketing Board booked time. A really clever campaign using
casual mentions of eggs during the breakfast programme, and
even the use of 'chicken' jokes, which were very popular at the
time was a big success. Simon Dee seemingly adlibbing around
the subject of eggs, although the adlibs had been written by an
advertising agency!

Once advertising really started to take off the amount of commercials was phenomenal: I remember we had ads for the egg marketing board – go to work on an egg.

Alan Turner, DJ and technician

The fact that a government quango, the Egg Marketing Board, had booked commercials on Radio Caroline didn't go down well with the politicians; the deal was discussed in the House of Lords.

I wish to ask Her Majesty's Government whether reports are true that the Egg Marketing Board are contributing to the revenue from advertising of pirate radio stations operating in breach of international agreements; and, if so, whether they propose to take any action.[11]

My Lords, I am informed that the Egg Marketing Board has entered into a contract for advertisements to be broadcast by one or more of the unauthorised broadcasting stations which are at present operating off our shores. The Government strongly deprecate this action, and in response to their representations the Board have agreed not to renew the contract without prior discussion with my right honourable friend the Minister of Agriculture, Fisheries and Food.[12]

Radio Caroline broadcast twelve hours a day from 6 a.m., when transmissions opened with a Jimmy McGriff instrumental 'Round midnight', much in keeping with the laid-back, blues style of music favoured in the early days of the station. The same recording was also used each evening as the day's transmissions ended. The *Caroline* bell appeared on the hour for the station identification spot and preceded every commercial. The bell also featured on stationary and tee-shirts.

The *Caroline* bell was hung around Simon Dee's neck and Chris Moore hit it with a spoon.

Ian Ross

I think it had been an impromptu thing. The first recording of the bell was terrible, a really poor recording, all 'wowing', and I said to engineer Ove one day, 'Shall we get this bell rerecorded so it sounds like a proper ships bell?' and the *Caroline* bell that you hear to this day came from that recording. We took a microphone cable right out across the deck and recorded the audio.

Alan Turner, DJ and technician

Another new voice to join the broadcast team in the very early days of Caroline's broadcasts was Jerry Leighton. He would eventually become one of the longest serving staff members in the sixties.

I had no broadcast experience, but a friend of mine, an actor named Carl Conway, had been doing some shows on Radio Caroline. He said. 'You'd be good at that; you can talk, and you have the gift of the gab. Let me take you round to the office.' They gave me an album and told me to talk about track seven. I said, 'What do you mean?', they said, 'Well, just read from the sleeve.' Then they said, 'Can you be at Harwich Quay on Monday?' I turned up at Harwich Quay and I was on the boat.

Jerry Leighton, DJ[13]

The new radio station was seldom out of the news – every time a politician asked a question about 'these pirates of the airwaves,' the newspapers reported the story; it was great publicity that just could not be bought. Weeks after coming on air a government department inadvertently gave Caroline another front-page story when a customs vessel drew alongside the MV *Caroline*. The incident was reported in detail on air by Simon Dee.

You're tuned to Radio Caroline on 199, the time is twenty-nine minutes past one and here is a Radio Caroline news report. At 12.20pm today, May 6th 1964, Her Majesty's vessel Venturous, *flying the blue ensign drew close on* Caroline's *port side. Permission was asked for them to board and see our bonded stores. The captain of the* Caroline *said this was against the law as we sit in international waters, but would allow one man to come across in a lifeboat, this offer was not accepted. At 12.33 the* Venturous *drew off and after drifting close for some moments turned and steamed away. We shall of course interrupt any scheduled programmes at any time to bring you news as, and when it happens, but now, everything's alright.*

On the same day the matter was raised in Parliament by Labour MP Roy Mason, already showing himself to be an opponent of the new radio station, he asked the Chancellor of the Exchequer why one of Her Majesty's ships had approached the pirate radio ship *Caroline* and why a boarding did not take place?

> The revenue cruiser *Venturous*, which is in the service of Her Majesty's Customs and Excise approached the motor vessel *Caroline* in the normal course of operations relating to the safety of the revenue and the observance of Customs requirements. The commander of the *Venturous* asked for, and was given, certain information about stores carried by the *Caroline*; there was never any question of boarding the vessel.[14]

Mr Mason was certainly not a fan of the offshore stations, asking numerous questions in Parliament about flags, frequencies, interference and requesting assurances that British companies would avoid using Caroline to advertise their goods and services. But the listeners just couldn't get enough of this new radio service. Announcements for the Caroline Club started on 26 May 1964; the club was quickly established to provide listeners with information about the radio station. In return for five shillings (25p) listeners received a selection of DJ photographs, a membership card, a car sticker proclaiming 'I love Caroline on 199' and a booklet containing technical information. It looked very professional, but behind the scenes there were frantic efforts to keep up with the huge demand. Nobody had foreseen just how big this thing was going to be.

7

THE SHIP THAT ROCKS THE OCEAN

In Greenore, work continued to equip the *Mi Amigo*. Radio Atlanta had been beaten in the race to be first on air and Allan Crawford's team needed to start broadcasting as soon as possible; Project Atlanta needed to make some money.

> The *Mi Amigo* was still alongside the port of Greenore, with work on the mast and everything else technical that they needed, then chief technician John Gilman had an absolutely hideous experience when he fell off the gangplank between the ship and the jetty and very narrowly avoided being crushed to death by the ship, he was hauled aboard again, practically at death's door. But eventually the *Mi Amigo* was made operational, upped anchor and set out in hot pursuit of the first ship.
> Kitty Black[1]

Granada television was planning a *World in Action* programme on the pop pirates and a film crew were on board in Greenore, filming final preparations as the *Mi Amigo* left. The programme would be broadcast on Atlanta's first day on air. She sailed south, leaving Greenore overnight on 19 April 1964, but problems with loose aerial stays during the voyage brought worries that the huge mast would topple overboard. The ship needed assistance but there was concern on board that she might be impounded if she entered territorial waters, the same concerns that had led to Greenore being used to fit the mast in the first place. The crew dropped anchor off the coast of Cornwall, but as the weather blew up, the *Mi Amigo* had to run for the shelter of Falmouth harbour and

Harry Spencer, the mast rigger, was summoned from the Isle of
Wight. The mast was repaired and the *Mi Amigo* was allowed to
leave without interference from the authorities.

> I got a telephone call at about four o'clock in the morning,
> the ship had been in heavy seas off Falmouth and it had to go
> in because the mast was coming adrift. So I had to send £100
> in cash to get my rigger to get in his car to get straight to
> Falmouth and repair this.
>
> Allan Crawford[2]

The *Mi Amigo* sailed to a position a few miles south of the
Caroline anchorage, arriving on 27 April. She anchored in the
position suggested by the Trinity House investors, in the Wallet
channel off the Essex seaside town of Frinton-on-Sea. The
nearby Gunfleet sands offered protection against the rough seas
stirred up by winds from most directions. Because the waters of
the Thames Estuary are so shallow, the 'short' waves can make
life on an anchored ship extremely uncomfortable. Caroline's
position to the north was further out to sea and more exposed
than Atlanta's.

The frequency for the transmissions was controlled by a crystal and, as Caroline had the originals, Atlanta's test transmissions
had to rely on temporary replacements supplied by Continental
Electronics, the transmitter company, but they weren't suitable for
European frequencies, so the early test broadcasts were 'off channel' and accompanied by a heterodyne whistle.

> Our very first test broadcast was done by trickery because we
> broadcast in French so that people couldn't tell that we were
> testing. My secretary, Margaret, did this and we sent the tape
> out, so we had our test done.
>
> Allan Crawford[3]

The *Mi Amigo* was at anchor for almost two weeks, before going
on air officially; test transmissions had started three days earlier.

The long delay was partly due to the wait for the correct crystals to arrive.

> I had the job of taking the new crystals down to Brightlingsea to go out to the *Mi Amigo*, which was going to make our signal more powerful and clearer and easier to pick up, and I remember I was down at the jetty with a whole lot of Caroline people and we thought at one time that they were going to try and nick our crystals, but they didn't, they were sort of lurking about, watching us.
>
> Richard Harris, DJ[4]

Texan father and son Bob Scott and Johnny Jackson both had radio experience and were in the country visiting relatives, when they heard about Radio Atlanta. They made contact with Allan Crawford, who offered them both jobs on board as continuity announcers.

> We met Allan Crawford at a little English village on the coast, where the liaison ship would leave from to service the *Mi Amigo*. He was worried about getting the frequency crystal through customs. He handed it to me and asked if I had any ideas. Jokingly I said I could just pop it down my pants; as it turned out that's the way we got the crystal on board. No one bothered to check as we told the Customs officials we were going on board as advisors. We did the test transmissions with only a handful of records, most were cover versions of current hits that Allan had from his record company.
>
> Johnny Jackson, DJ[5]

> Bob Scott and Johnny Jackson were father and son. To our horror they started broadcasting while we were testing. This was not at all the idea because we'd prepared a first day's programme schedule in which we were all introduced and that was supposed to be the first programme to go over the airwaves from Atlanta.
>
> Richard Harris, DJ[6]

Radio Atlanta was subject to one final delaying tactic by the Swedish engineers from Caroline. Ove Sjöström and Jan Gunnarsson were now working for Caroline, but both had previously worked on the *Mi Amigo* for the Swedish station, Radio Nord.

> We went in one of our lifeboats and told them that we were two technicians that were once working on that boat and we were interested to come on board to see how it looked like now. Jan and I had decided what to do, but Jan was not too keen on the idea. So he took the people aside and I went down in the transmitter room and did a couple of things so they were delayed, I think for ten days until they received spare parts from the USA. That was enough so they got behind and Caroline managed to establish themselves and took all of the market. I know that they had some suspicions as they realised the day after when they tried to start the transmitter and then they got the information that two Swedes had been on board and that we had been working on the ship before. But I did it in a way so that there was no evidence, I knew how to do it, it was not too complicated. That was not a pretty thing to do but I was young and wanted to help my company.
>
> Ove Sjöström, broadcast engineer[7]

At an official launch attended by many of the shareholders, a presentation was made to the press and the advertising industry at the Waldorf Hotel. Crawford claimed that his station 'would be a worthy alternative for the BBC. The programmes will be of the light entertainment type and specially designed for family listening.'[8] Allan Crawford's dream of Radio Atlanta had finally come to fruition. The radio station went on air on 12 May 1964, with programmes starting at 6 p.m., just as Caroline closed down for the night. Atlanta used the same frequency as Caroline, in an attempt to pick up some of their listeners. There were now two offshore commercial radio stations off the English coast; the battle for listeners, and advertisers was on. Both ships operated under very similar conditions, but using different ports for their supplies, with boats going out to the ships almost on a daily basis. Caroline was tendered from Harwich, Atlanta from the smaller port of Brightlingsea. Atlanta used a local sand barge, the *Cecil Guilders*, which delivered supplies and the taped programmes to the ship, the tapes having been recorded in the London studio and then driven the 50 miles or so to the coast.

> We used to get the tapes down to Brightlingsea and the only way we could get out to the ship was in a dreadful old shingle barge, a terrible thing. I've known it to take five hours to get out there, with two old East Anglian crew members who used to sit there in the freezing cold always drinking gallons of tea, with all the tapes mixed up in the shingle. It was incredible; we were working about eighteen hours a day. I remember I was taking a whole load of tapes down from the studio. Allan had these huge great coffin-like boxes with the tapes sort of slotted in, in order, so that all they had to do on board the *Mi Amigo* was to take them out and feed them into the transmitter and everything should work according to plan, and it did. It was remarkable how the programmes went out on time and in the correct sequence. I was going down once in the car with a load of these coffins to go out to the ship and had the radio tuned into Radio Atlanta and it was near Chelmsford and a guy was hitch-hiking. I stopped and he got into the car and as it happened it was me who was broadcasting at the time. As I was talking to him he kept looking at the wireless and looking at me and in the end he couldn't stand it any longer, he said, 'That sounds like you, your voice is so like that bloke's on the wireless' So I said, 'It is', and he said, 'It can't be, you're here'.
>
> Richard Harris, DJ[9]

> *You're in tune with the right side of radio, the good ship Radio Atlanta, operating to you and everyone else at 201 metres.*
>
> *This is Radio Atlanta on 201 metres, medium wave – the ship that rocks the ocean.*

On 201 metres, our business is show business and you're in tune with the show boat, the good ship Atlanta.

You're listening to the dolphin of the sea, the good ship Radio Atlanta.

While the Caroline DJs sounded relaxed and informal, their counterparts on Atlanta were noticeably upbeat and excitable. With their experience of working in competitive commercial radio markets in Australia and America, their presentation style certainly stood out, perhaps too much for a British audience, but the Atlanta signal was stronger and clearer than Caroline's.

Atlanta had advertisers from the start, including the *News of the World*, Contact watches and of course there were plenty of mentions for Crawford's cover version record labels. In an effort to catch up with Caroline's lead in the market, Radio Atlanta stayed on air each evening after Caroline had closed down. Unlike Caroline, where most programmes were now presented by a live DJ and lasted two or three hours, Atlanta's daily broadcast schedule was made up of shorter segments and, in many ways, was programmed in the style of the BBC.

I never understood why Radio Atlanta wasn't a straight Top 40 station; instead it was a mini clone of the BBC. One day, Allan Crawford walked by and I was listening to a transistor radio with one of the little earpieces, he asked, 'what are you listening to?' I said, 'Radio Caroline' and he asked 'why?' I said 'because we are playing show tunes from *My Fair Lady* in the middle of the afternoon'. He looked at me, turned and walked away. I don't know if he was more upset that I was listening to Caroline, or that Atlanta was playing show tunes. On another occasion he discussed jingles, I think he had a demo tape from PAMS[10] in Dallas. He was concerned about sounding too American and thought he could produce his own jingles. I mentioned that Caroline had the ship's bell, the minute you heard it you knew it was Caroline. That comment got a reply

of, 'Oh yes, the ship's bell … amazing isn't it?' That was the end
of the conversation.

Johnny Jackson, DJ[11]

As spring 1964 turned to summer, the reliability of the broadcasts
from both ships improved and it was obvious that they were here
to stay, at least for the foreseeable future. Politically, they'd chosen
just the right time to go on air and establish themselves, an election was due later in the year and closing down popular radio
stations was hardly likely to enamour voters to the incumbent
government, so immediate political action was avoided. The radio
stations were, for the time being, safe. This prompted others to
set up their own radio stations; Screaming Lord Sutch was first
in line, but with a very amateurish set-up when compared to
Caroline and Atlanta, broadcasting from the disused wartime forts
in the Thames Estuary, with former war-department equipment.

8

THE CAROLINE NETWORK

Although Caroline and Atlanta were each out to gain the biggest possible audience, they both managed to attract advertising, but they were both competing for the same audience. It was only a matter of time before the two groups looked at sharing resources and just three months after Caroline's first broadcast, an amalgamation was announced.

A press release issued on 2 July 1964 announced that Atlanta would now be known as Radio Caroline South and the original Caroline, based on the bigger ship, would sail to a position off the Isle of Man to become Radio Caroline North. No announcement was made on air about the closure of Radio Atlanta, probably because the crew knew nothing of the plan when they closed down on the previous evening; Radio Atlanta was never heard again. The *Caroline* upped anchor from her position off the Suffolk coast and hove-to a few hundred yards from the *Mi Amigo*. The captain of the *Caroline* went to the *Mi Amigo* for discussions and on his return a transfer of DJs took place, with Tom Lodge, Jerry Leighton and Alan Turner choosing to stay on their ship and go north. The remaining broadcasters, including Simon Dee and Doug Kerr, would stay in the south, where they would join those already on board the *Mi Amigo*, including Colin Nicol, the Atlanta breakfast presenter.

There was that definitive moment, at the merger of Caroline and Atlanta when, without warning, their ship hove alongside and Simon Dee stepped aboard to tell me we were about to become Radio Caroline South. I had hastily taken security precautions as MV *Caroline* closed in on us but we maintained a courteous exchange and sent messages ashore to sort it all out.

Colin Nicol, DJ[1]

The transmitter crystals were exchanged, together with a selection of records and the MV *Caroline* sailed off. At 6 a.m. on the Saturday morning, when Caroline started broadcasts for the day, the listeners were completely unaware of the ship, frequency and crew changes that had taken place overnight. But the merger wasn't quite what it seemed, the two organisations would operate separately; Caroline South would be run by Crawford's Project Atlanta and Planet Productions would run Caroline North, with airtime sold on behalf of both organisations.

We were forced into each other's arms in July of '64; it would have been within a matter of days of the agreement being made in Lichtenstein. I went over with my Chairman, and certainly Ronan met us there, I don't know who else was with Ronan, I forget, it might have been Jocelyn and our mutual lawyer. They [Caroline] were unwilling to go for a straight fifty-fifty split, and, as always, we were at the disadvantage, having the smaller ship. The income wouldn't have mattered – I mean it was barely paying its way at that point. Someone had to be cooperative, and I swallowed my pride, having been the creator and I was losing my own created name. So we became Radio Caroline North and South with the agreement that his ship would go round to the Irish Sea off the Isle of Man and we would operate as a network and share the income. It was agreed that it would be fifty-five to his lot because they said they'd put in more money for the bigger ship, and forty-five to us, and at a certain stage of income it would merge at fifty-fifty. I made another mistake there, which was not to set a time limit on that; in other words, if the income didn't come to a certain point within a certain time, it would go to fifty-fifty anyway. So, we were always at a handicap from an income point of view as compared to Ronan's side.

Allan Crawford[2]

The MV *Caroline* left the East Coast, broadcasting as she sailed west; listeners were able to follow the ship's progress as she passed along the English coast. Alan Turner was one of the voices heard throughout the voyage:

I was offered a choice of staying south or going north. It was midnight on that Friday that we set off on that epic voyage. At about 8 o'clock the next morning Tom burst into my cabin and said take a look through the porthole, and the whole of Beachy Head was just packed with people, Saturday morning, a nice summer's day. I went up to the bridge and thought I could signal them. I went down into my cabin and over each hand basin was a large mirror, I unscrewed that and took it up on deck and started flashing the shore. Some people cottoned on to this very quickly and we were getting isolated flashes from the shore all the way along, miles apart some of them, but then we started saying on air that I was going to flash from the ship and we could see maybe 20 or 30 miles to the west and it was just magical. It was as if someone had flicked a switch on because there were hundreds of these lights flashing back at us from mirrors on the shore, it was incredible to see.

Alan Turner, DJ and technician

Thank you all for flashing your lights in Rottingdean and Peacehaven, it's a wonderful sight believe me, and also stand by in Brighton because we'll be passing you at 12.15, or thereabouts. So keep a lookout for the ship with the big, big mast, that's Radio Caroline, broadcasting on 199 metres, your very first commercial radio station.[3]

The route was outside the Isle of Wight and along the South Coast, we broadcast quite late into the evening, but there were only three of us on board, so we couldn't manage more. The captain joined us and gave an update of our position on air.

Alan Turner, DJ and technician

We are on our way along the South Coast of England … we will be at Portland Bill at nine o'clock tonight … Start Point will be the next point at two o'clock tomorrow morning, Sunday morning, to Lizard Point, eight o'clock tomorrow morning and then we go rounding Land's End and heading north … and at noon on Monday will be journey's end on the Isle of Man. [4]

We were off the north Cornish coast, I think it was a garage owner who came out in a speed boat, and he caught up with us and threw a selection of papers aboard. We eventually arrived in Ramsey Bay, sailing up the East Coast of the Isle of Man and picked up the anchorage, we looked at the shore and … nothing. Not one single boat or yacht came out to meet us, but we'd arrived on Tynwald Day, a public holiday. We'd been at anchor for a couple of hours or so and then someone shouted 'there's a boat coming'. We looked through the binoculars and it was a tiny two-seat canoe, and these two lads said they'd heard about us and wanted to see what we were all about. They gave us a sprig of lucky white heather.

Alan Turner, DJ and technician

The north ship, now anchored off the Isle of Man, soon became an additional attraction for holidaymakers, many of them tempted to visit the island by Caroline's frequent mentions of its beauty on both the north and south services.

Isle of contrasts, Isle of beauty, the Isle of Man. Nowhere in the British Isles is there so much choice and variety for a holiday as on the Isle of Man, the happy holiday island. [5]

The relationship between Caroline and the people of the Isle of Man would prove to be beneficial for both, with Caroline promoting tourism, and the island's Government, Tynwald, fighting for Caroline's survival against Westminster just three years later.

> We started mentioning the Isle of Man hundreds of times each day. The benefit to the tourist trade on the island was immense, and when we went ashore the crowds of people were amazing. We always flew back to London via Cambrian airways who we also mentioned.
>
> Alan Turner, DJ and technician

Following the merger, a number of the original Atlanta DJs resigned and new recruits were taken on. One of the first to join the new radio station was a singer with a band from Bournemouth. Within days of contacting Radio Caroline, Tony Blackburn was on air and soon became a favourite with the listeners.

> I read an advertisement in the NME wanting disc jockeys on Radio Caroline. I did an audition and that was it really, I was out on the boat. When I first saw it, I was struck by how small it was; it seemed a very small boat for being out on the North Sea. I was amazed that this little boat, bobbing about on the North Sea was making so many political storms. It was a very cosy little ship, but I always felt it wasn't quite big enough for what it was doing. I joined Caroline only three months after it started and I was aware that it was going to alter the whole of radio because of the response we were getting to it. At the time we had the Home Service and the Light Programme, it was really quite frightful for young people, so I really did know that what we were doing was quite important.
>
> Tony Blackburn, DJ

Former British Forces broadcaster Keith Skues was another early recruit to Radio Caroline.

My very first visit to the office was on the day of the merger in July 1964. I was signed for the south ship and my first trip to the *Mi Amigo* was on Monday 31 August. I travelled to Harwich with Doug Kerr, Tony Blackburn and Keith Martin. We caught the 8.30 a.m. train from Liverpool Street and arrived at Parkestone, Harwich around 10 a.m. I was met by the liaison officer for Caroline, Bill Scadden who asked if I had my passport.

Keith Skues, DJ

Bill Scadden dealt with the complexities of supplies and the transfer of personnel to and from the ship and oversaw all contact between land and the ship. He also operated a clandestine radio link from his home overlooking the sea in Frinton, with sight of the *Mi Amigo* at anchor. He was a former CID inspector at Scotland Yard and had been a chief security officer in Nigeria.

I had a phone call from Ronan O'Rahilly and he said, 'our chief engineer's name is Gilman and he wants to have a chat with you'. I was in the amateur radio book you see. So I met John Gilman in Thorpe-le-Soken and he said he wanted some-body to act as agent down here and that he understood that I was a bit of a wizard with two-way communications. He asked me to go up to Caroline House, so I went and met O'Rahilly and Crawford and before I knew where I was they'd offered me a job. Ronan said 'well now look, we haven't got a lot of money, we can't pay you a lot of money, but we'll give you £30 a week plus expenses.' I wasn't worried about the money really.

Bill Scadden, liaison, Caroline South[6]

Every departure and arrival to and from the ship was treated as leaving and entering the UK. Wherever the ships were regis-tered, in Panama or elsewhere, it was a foreign land and passports were needed.

Leaving the country to go to the ship involved dealings with HM Customs and Excise, HM Waterguard, Special branch of CID, HM Immigration, British Railways, Trinity House, Board of Trade, Ministry of Transport, Harwich Harbour Board and the Port health authority, and this every time we left the country for the ship. We sailed aboard the *Offshore 1*, weighing 60 tons she was registered in Baarn in the Netherlands and wasn't comfortable. She had a crew of three and the journey to the *Mi Amigo* took about two hours. It was Tony Blackburn's second time and my first trip out and it was the first time that I'd seen the *Mi Amigo*. She was very rusty and had a silver-coloured hull.

Keith Skues, DJ

Following the merger, the servicing of both ships had been taken over by the Offshore Tender and Supply Company, which was part of the Dutch Wijsmuller salvage company. *Offshore 1* was the regular supply boat for Caroline South and later other radio ships that would anchor off the Essex coast. The larger *Offshore 2* would make trips from Holland to supply fuel, water and bulk supplies. *Offshore 2* would also make the longer journey to the north ship, although Caroline North was supplied by a local boat, the *Essex Girl*, based in Ramsey IOM where George Hare had a role that was similar to Bill Scadden's in the south.

During the summer months, there were daily visits from the tourist boats. The *Lady Kent* and the *Viking Saga* made several trips out to the *Mi Amigo* each day in the holiday season from Clacton and Walton. Although the fans weren't allowed on board, they were able to see the DJs, shout out and handover requests and letters. Some, like listener Vivien Barnard, made regular visits out to the ship.

I went to the pier in order to go out on the pleasure boat the *Lady Kent*, which made trips out to the *Mi Amigo*, the Radio Caroline ship, for five shillings. When we reached the ship, I noticed that the hull was painted dark green and the top part was painted white. There were some men on deck, drinking cans of 7up. I recognised one of them to be Simon Dee from the photo I had and called out to him. He confirmed he was Simon Dee and blew me a kiss.

Vivien Barnard, listener

The DJs and crew had little to do other than present and prepare their programmes. Some used their spare time to write to listeners – the mail arrived by the sack load – others took the chance to study, or just sleep, although in the early days of Caroline there was no late-night broadcasting and a twenty-four-hour service was still some years away.

I used to have lots and lots of time and I used to just sit down and write these jokes in exercise books. I've still got some of the original exercise books that I wrote in those days; I'm still using the same jokes.

Tony Blackburn, DJ

I went out on the *Lady Kent* for my sixth visit to the *Mi Amigo*. I took some *Weekend* magazines, a thriller story, and a joke book to give to the disc jockeys. Seven men came out on deck with one woman; one of the men who came out was Tony Blackburn who started working on Caroline in the last week of July. He had a Beatle haircut.

Vivien Barnard, listener

By now most of the programmes were presented live by the on-board DJs playing the chart hits, but only within certain programmes. The music was prepared by Programme Manager Ken Evans and his team of two Australian women, Marion Cochrane and Dorothy Wight, both with experience of programming top radio stations in Sydney. Maureen Blackburn was the third woman who occasionally worked on the ship. Although publicly the record companies complained that Caroline was playing their records without permission, the radio station and the DJs were bombarded with free copies of the new releases every week. Big star interviews were also broadcast, these were recorded by the DJs when they were ashore or by Carl Conway who, after a very short spell at sea, was now permanently based in London.

> I was very lucky I had a film spot, I used to go out to the film studios and interview the big stars like Alfred Hitchcock, when they came over from America, Roger Moore when he was doing the Saint … and any big star that was around; because Radio Caroline was very important in those days everybody wanted to be part of the scene. So we got all the big stars, the American stars had heard all about it.
>
> Carl Conway, DJ

Simon Dee presented *Soundtrack*, a daily programme featuring music from the shows and film scores. This continued under the new regime on Caroline South. Allan Crawford's cover version records were still being sent out to the *Mi Amigo* to be played, as they had been when it was Radio Atlanta. They were also sent to the north ship, but it was unlikely that many were played, and not all of them made it on air in the south either.

> I always remember Simon Dee standing at the bow of the ship, throwing Allan Crawford's records into the sea. Simon refused to play anything he didn't like and especially Allan's cover versions of hits. He also felt advertisements interfered with the flow of his show and began refusing to allow commercials, adding to the financial stresses of the operation.
>
> Ken Evans, programme controller[7]

The north ship broadcast more of a hit-music format to their audience in the northern cities and Scotland, Ireland and Wales, not least because it was difficult for the stations' management in London to hear the output. But it seemed wherever you went, everyone was tuned to Caroline, the all-day music station.

If you listen back to tapes of Radio Caroline now, they sound very old fashioned. In the early days it was very slow and Radio Caroline was really playing all sorts of music. In the morning we used to play pop music and then Simon Dee would come on with show music, then it went back to pop music and then it went to big band music.

Tony Blackburn, DJ

We had a playlist and we were asked to include some records but it was never demanded. There was no Payola as far as I knew; whether any of the record companies paid anything directly to Caroline I do not know. The incentives we were offered were simple; behave and do your job well and you get to keep it.

Norman St John, DJ

In the early days the two ships were completely different in musical output. The north was heavily pop oriented whereas the south was more akin to the BBC Light Programme with the choice of music. We were expected to play records selected by Allan Crawford that had been released through his own record labels Rocket, Sabre and Canon. We were given freedom to select and play our own choice of music and follow the format of the radio station. Caroline North was a very successful station and had a huge audience, the DJs on the north ship had complete freedom from Ronan to choose and play the music they knew their listeners wanted to hear. Crawford was very keen to ensure, as a music publisher, that his Merit Music records were regularly played on Caroline South. The station played more middle-of-the-road music with songs from shows and film sound tracks.

Keith Skues, DJ

Some records were promoted heavily on Radio Caroline and deals were obviously done between the radio station and some record producers and promoters. It was Ken Evan's job to ensure that these records were played.

It might be a case of a record being bought for twelve or fifteen plays a day, two weeks was the general thing, I would work out so that there wasn't going to be a repeat under about two hours. They were records that might have a chance of becoming hits and they were from promoters who knew their chances of getting onto the BBC were next to nothing, they might get one or two plays if they were extremely fortunate, but here was a method by which they could have a record on the air over an eighteen hour time-span. One day Christopher Moore said to me, 'Ken, we want you to make the programming system identical for the north and south ships'. Well, this was absolutely impossible, they had records up there which the southern ship didn't have and the southern ship had records which the northern ship didn't have, we would have to have scrapped umpteen hundreds of records. I remember seeing a lot of the cabaret-type artists, and they were mixed in with the current pops on both ships. It was just impossible, they had too much stuff of their own on each ship and they were two very different stations. There was Caroline North and Caroline South with Atlanta undertones. However, we did have good programming and it covered what was happening and introduced many new artists, publishers and record companies.

Ken Evans, programme controller[8]

Caroline needed more space for their offices on land; the organisation had outstayed its welcome in Jocelyn Stevens' *Queen* magazine office in Fetter Lane. A temporary address in Regent Street was used before a move to a huge property in London's Mayfair. The intention was to show that Radio Caroline was a big operation. However, 6 Chesterfield Gardens, London W1 had plenty of space that was surplus to requirements and it soon became one of the most famous addresses in the country.

We rented a mansion off Curzon Street; the GPO dug up
Chesterfield Gardens and put in a forty-line switchboard, even
though they wanted to get rid of us. Jocelyn wanted us out of his
Queen office. Eventually he threw us out, but we just about had
Caroline House ready. I did the design for the interior. I was supposed to decorate Caroline House but went terribly over budget,
but it was beautifully done with lots of carpet. Ronan alone had
about an acre of this blue carpet in his office with his vast desk.

Ian Ross

Caroline House became home to the various factions that made
up the Caroline organisation, Ronan with his office on one floor,
Allan Crawford on another. It was from here that the commercials were recorded and scheduled for broadcast on both ships
and the Caroline Club was also run from this building, but by late
summer 1964 it was struggling to cope with the huge number of
applications for membership:

I have discovered that there is a list of 15,000 people who have
paid their subscription and have not yet received their membership package. This backlog started to build up immediately
after the merger. The MV *Caroline* sailed north broadcasting
the Caroline Club commercial, and continued to do so for
some days on its arrival off Ramsey until a message reached
the ship to cease.[9]

A number of musicians and their management also had their
offices within 6 Chesterfield Gardens.

All these hustlers just moved in, most of them had nothing
directly to do with Radio Caroline, but they represented the
Chelsea faction. Everyone was there. You'd see people like the
Stones sitting in the foyer. John Fenton, the Moody Blues'
manger was there, Denny Cordell[10] had a job licking stamps
for him and I helped.

Ian Ross

Track Records and Kit Lambert, who looked after The Who, as well as actor, Terence Stamp, had an office in the building and there was also a photographic studio on the top floor.

> I was assistant to Chris Moore in a company called Radio Programme Planners, that was me and Chris sitting in a room smoking various things and we'd built these little studios that had been ripped out from the *Queen* magazine office. We used Ronan's school of acting ideas; it was one of his great beliefs that with this method of acting you can be anything you want to. His theory was you could take almost anyone and turn them into a disc jockey. I'm not sure that Tony Blackburn went through that method, but I know we had a problem with him because of those jokes; Chris was a purist, and he didn't like jokes. Neither did he like disc jockeys doing any personal, pro-motional activities of their own; he thought they should play the record then say 'that was … and here is' and move on.
>
> Ian Ross

Getting a job on Radio Caroline was often dependent on being in the right place at the right time. The idea of playing the latest pop hits to an audience of tens of thousands certainly seemed exciting, but in reality it was far from glamorous. Living in cramped conditions, in a potentially dangerous situation, dis-turbed by the roar of generators operating twenty-four hours a day, sitting at anchor in, sometimes, atrocious sea conditions, with no company other than like-minded DJs, engineers and Dutch marine crew, didn't suit everyone; you needed to be an unusual sort of person to cope. There was even the fear that the radio waves from such high-powered transmitters operating in such a confined space, might lead to impotence. But the rewards, at least for the lucky few, could be big money and stardom.

> A girl that I went to college with was working as PA for Chris Moore and she rang me and asked if I'd ever thought of being a disc jockey? I said 'no never' I wasn't particularly interested in

pop music at that time, and she said, 'Oh that's a pity because you're coming in to make tapes for us tomorrow morning'. I went in and did a dreadful audition and for some reason they asked me to go back in the afternoon and Chris Moore said, 'that was dreadful, what did you earn last year?' So I doubled it and told him and he said 'well we can just about pay you that'. I have to say it wasn't a great deal of money.

So, on August Bank Holiday Monday, with a chap named Jerry Leighton, I found myself on a plane to the Isle of Man and joined Caroline North. I was there for six months, had a slight run in with Chris and he decided that he didn't want me working on the northern ship anymore, so I came home. Within minutes the phone rang and it was Simon Dee and he said, 'I understand you're not working on the northern ship anymore. Will you come and work on the southern ship?' Between me saying yes and arriving on the ship, Simon was fired and we had a new programme director. I was there for six months, but life on the ship was a giggle a minute.

Roger Gale, DJ

Mike Ahern was living in Liverpool and listening to the radio, the programmes of Caroline captured his imagination as he dreamed of being a DJ and it changed his life.

I wrote to Caroline House in London asking for a job and they wrote back and said 'we're getting four thousand letters a week like yours'. So I wrote back again and said, 'well you may be getting four thousand letters a week, but I'm the best disc jockey in the north of England'. So they wrote back and said, 'well if you're so good at it you'd better come down to Chesterfield Gardens for an audition'. I went down to London, did the audition and I didn't hear anything for two or three weeks, so I called them up and they said, 'Oh we're glad you called, can you start next week?' and there I was, Michael A on Radio Caroline North. When I did the audition I just sounded like the people I was listening to on Caroline

North, I just copied it and I was lucky. The magic of Caroline was the music; people weren't hearing the music that they wanted to hear on the BBC and also this very informal style of presentation. The BBC had been terribly well spoken and very upper class, and then suddenly you had people coming on like me, 'ello dare like, dis is Radio Caroline North on erm 199 metres' [exaggerated Liverpool accent]. Listeners could identify with that, because that's how people spoke and I think that, coupled with the magic of the music, where they could hear the Stones and they could hear the Beatles all the time and the romance of being at sea, the idea of these guys on a ship.

When I first started I couldn't eat, I used to be sick – not from sea-sickness but just from sheer excitement. They had me doing Caroline requests at night between six and seven, and then my two weeks were up and Jerry Leighton said to me, 'Look we're short can you stay on an extra week?' I would have happily stayed on for three years. 'I would like you to do the nine to midday shift' and I thought nine to midday wow! It was wonderful to get up in the morning and the steward would have breakfast ready and you would walk in and he would say 'Good Morning what would you like?' and you'd say, 'I'll have some orange juice, cornflakes, oh some bacon and eggs' and this would be about 8 o'clock. You would sit there and you could hear the guy doing the break-fast programme on the internal P.A. system and you'd look out and see the Isle of Man sitting there on a calm morning and think, my god look at this and the ship would have a gentle sway and you sat there and thought, and I'm getting paid for this.

At the end of the three weeks it was time for me to go off but it was very rough and they pulled the tender in alongside, they tried to come in a couple of times and the guy on the tender is saying, 'No we can't get in, we can't get anything off and we can't get anything on' and Jerry said, 'Give it one more try' so he comes in really close and it's pitching up and down and the *Caroline* was high out of the water and Jerry said, 'Jump, now' and I jumped because he had thrown my case down and I flew through the air and I can see as I'm going down, the tender dipping away and starting to pull out. I don't know how I made it, but I landed on the side of the ship and caught the underneath of my chin on the rail outside the cabin on the tender. Apart from bruising my chin, I was ok.

When we got into Ramsey, I went up to this small office which was the shipping company and I was paid three weeks' pay, £60 plus a week off, £80 in total, I thought I was the richest person. I had £80 in my pocket, I'd had a ball and done what I liked, after the first week the mail had started to come in addressed to Mike Ahern, and then it started to come in by the bag full and it was just unbelievable. When I got home my mother said, 'Everybody has heard you they are all talking about you. You are the local hero' and I suddenly found I could get all these girlfriends, all the girls from school who I'd fancied but who wouldn't go out with me because I wasn't good looking enough, suddenly they all wanted to know me.

Mike Ahern, DJ[11]

The Traffic Department is a vital part of any commercial broad-casters business, placing the commercials where the customer or advertising agency wants them and ensuring that they are booked for the correct dates, avoiding clashes, such as two similar products advertised side by side. The commercials, certainly during 1964/5, were recorded in Caroline House on 10-inch reels of tape in order of broadcast and each preceded by the *Caroline* bell. The tapes and a log sheet were then sent out to each ship where it was the job of the DJs to play the commercials at the correct time and in the correct order, and then sign the log to confirm their actions. If the ads weren't played, the customer wouldn't pay, or at best for the station, would demand extra free spots.

I started working for Caroline in the summer of 1964, it was an admin job. I'd been working for ITV, Granada and Westward TV, sorting advertising time. A mate of mine called me and asked, 'how do you fancy working for the pirates?' I thought that didn't sound very safe, but I spoke to my dad and he said, 'well you're young, you can afford to take the chance', so I did. I was again slotting in advertising, but I also had more general jobs, like getting batches of records out to the ship and liaising with general points of contact on the Isle of Man and Harwich and it was just generally running this stuff from Caroline House in Chesterfield Gardens. They certainly didn't need all the floors of Caroline House, there was a basement, which is where I was tucked away, the black hole of Calcutta was what we called it, the ground floor, which had a lot of the sales staff, the first floor was home to the directors and people like Ronan O'Rahilly, the second and third floors had press and publicity. It was incredible; it was a great big mansion in the centre of London. It must have rattled from time to time with the few people who were in there.

Colin Berry, news reader/commercial traffic

Sunsilk Shampoo, Times Furnishing, Weetabix, Horlicks, Harp Lager, Fynon Bath Salts, Kraft, Lucozade, Princes Food, Tesco, Ribena, Mars, Sunblest, Frys Chocolate and Magicote paint were just a few of the nationally known products that chose to advertise on Caroline in the first year and many of them stayed with the station throughout the 1960s. Caroline was very popular with cigarette brands. At this time cigarettes could still be advertised on British television, at least until 1965, but most major brands used Caroline. A number of fifteen-minute pre-recorded programmes for some long-established companies, such as Chappell pianos, Andrews Liver salts and Bulova watches were also broadcast. Although they brought in much-needed income, the radio station had little control over their content and often they were presented by artists who seemed completely out of touch with the image that Caroline was trying to portray. Anne Shelton and Charlie Drake were amongst the recognised names presenting these programmes, but they certainly seemed at odds with the pop stars of the day that listeners tuned in to hear. Most of these programmes were a legacy of Radio Atlanta's advertising deals.

9

YOU're HearING THINGS ...

As Caroline's first winter on air approached, there were rumours of more radio stations on the way. By now, both the Shivering Sands and Red Sands wartime forts in the Thames had been occupied by radio pirates. Radio Sutch had become Radio City and was now being operated by music manager and promoter Reg Calvert – Screaming Lord Sutch was one of his protégés; Radio Invicta was now operating from the Red Sands fort. But the rumour of a major radio project backed by American finance led to an attempt to improve the signal into London from Caroline South. The *Mi Amigo* was moved to a position closer to the city and near to the Shivering Sands forts. The signal was certainly much stronger for listeners in London, but operating conditions on the ship at this anchorage proved to be extremely uncomfortable and she returned back to her original position within days.

> The *Mi Amigo* sailed near the Shivering Sands fort to see what happened to our signal in London. Our trip was dreadful. We were very sick, the ship rolled and pitched dreadfully, and the sea was very rough. We also had a fire in the engine room which put us off the air.
>
> George Saunders, broadcast engineer[1]

The *Mi Amigo* was taken further down to the Thames Estuary and we broadcast from there for three or four days, perhaps almost a week. It was at that time that everyone in London enjoyed the best signal they had ever heard from

Radio Caroline South but the trouble was that the water was very shallow and the boat rocked to and fro violently and it changed course so often because of currents. The original site that was selected for the boat was obviously the right one, so back we went.

Keith Martin, DJ[2]

In calm seas, just the length of chain connecting the anchor to the ship was enough to hold the vessel on station, but in rough seas, when the heavy chain was fully extended and the whole weight and force of the ship, increased by strong winds, huge strain was put on the system. In really heavy seas the ship would pull on the chain and anchor, dragging them along the seabed. There was also the danger that the shackles of the chain, twisting and turning with every tide change, would be weakened; it just takes one link to fail and the anchor can be lost. The seas around the British coast are capable of being some of the roughest in the world and with the two Caroline ships at anchor in the Irish Sea and the North Sea the risk of breaking adrift was always present.

The mooring was on a triple anchor on a swivel spread out on segments of a circle with a ring swivel at the top. The idea was that the ship herself would swing round the swivel and depending on the tide or the wind, would always be pointing with her nose into the weather, whatever the prevailing wind was. Unfortunately, we had one, if not two, major disasters, when the anchor chains starting wrapping themselves round the swivel, which in turn started to drag the ship down. It cost a fortune to send a diver down to investigate what was causing the problems. I think one of the fascinating angles behind pirate radio was the incredible expertise that had to be called in on every single aspect of the operation.

Kitty Black[3]

During the winter of '64/'65 we had hurricane-force gales off the Isle of Man. We had an anchor weighing 5 tons and we dragged that nearly 4 miles. We lost windows out of the bridge and at one time the skipper got us all together, DJs and crew, in the saloon in case we needed to leave the ship. It was really, really rough, frighteningly rough. In the saloon the tables were bolted down, but the chairs were loose and we had long settees from the ferry days, and when the ship rolled you had no option but to run downhill and jump up out of the way or the chairs would crush your legs. We had one period where we had to wait to go out from the Isle of Man for a few days because of the rough weather, we persuaded the skipper to attempt a journey and as we left the harbour this boat, which weighed about 60 tons went up in the air and came down at right angles to the harbour. The skipper shouted, 'We're going back!

Alan Turner, DJ and technician

Each ship normally had at least one transmitter engineer on board, a captain and crew, who were responsible for keeping things shipshape. Professional riggers visited the ships for routine maintenance on the aerial mast, but sometimes emergency situations needed immediate solutions with those on board making the climb high above deck level.

It was an amazing experience when the aerial nearly parted company and in a full gale one of the engineers went up and sat cross legged at the top of the mast and mended the aerial, I was half way up, none of us tied on, carrying the weight of the rope that he had to bring the aerial down with.

Roger Gale, DJ

The mast was nearly 200ft high. It had a ladder that went all the way up the aft side of the mast and at the top was a huge red lamp installation for warning aircraft. I think there were three 150 watt bulbs inside this domed cover. I nominated myself to be the chief bulb changer, going up with no safety harness. I just hooked my leg through the rungs of the ladder

and even on a calm day the ship was swaying by 15 to 30ft out
to the vertical either side.

Alan Turner, DJ and technician

Audience polls had shown that within weeks of Caroline coming
on air, there were more than 4,000,000 listeners and this just
through word of mouth. More detailed reports gave breakdowns
of male/female listeners and age variations. Interestingly, unlike
today's audience figures, the peak audience in Caroline's early
days was between 10 a.m. and 4 p.m., peak audiences now are
invariably at breakfast time. Later in the same year, further surveys
showed that Caroline was reaching more than 7,000,000 listeners
weekly. Finances were looking good too; sales of £47,952 for the
period November/December 1964 were recorded by Caroline
Sales, serving both Planet Productions for Caroline North and
Project Atlanta for Caroline South.

Radio Caroline was keen to shake off the 'pirate' image and
gain respectability. A request was made to the BBC for a copy
of the Queen's Christmas Broadcast to be relayed at 3 p.m. on
Christmas Day. 1964. The reply from the corporation was less
than cooperative.

I asked whether he represented an authorised broadcasting station. He was unable to give me a satisfactory reply but referred
to the authorisation which he considered to be provided by
'12 and a half million listeners'. I said that I could not take him
seriously and added that if and when he could provide evidence of his credentials as the representative of an authorised
broadcasting station we might be able to consider his request.[4]

But the BBC's unwillingness to cooperate was the least
of their worries as a new and serious challenge to Caroline
was soon to arrive. A Texan-backed radio station was set to
target the British radio market and with the experience and
money that was available to them, it was obvious that they
meant business. Ronan O'Rahilly realised this and made an

approach with a view to a merger between the stations, even before they went on air. His proposal would see the Caroline network established to sell airtime on all three radio ships. Caroline North would continue, Caroline South would close and became Radio Continental, serving a foreign audience and the new radio station, Radio London, would take the place of Caroline South.

The proposal was dismissed by the Radio London investors, but O'Rahilly was deeply concerned by this imminent threat of competition and the fear that another powerful radio station would force the Government into immediate action to close all the stations down. He made a further proposal to charter the new radio ship, presumably to broaden the Caroline network, in return, a draft contract was drawn up that was totally unacceptable to Caroline and the two groups went their own way.[5]

Meanwhile the new radio ship had arrived off the coast. The *Galaxy*, a former US minesweeper, dropped anchor close to the Shivering Sand but, realising they were close to the territorial limits, the *Galaxy* moved closer to the *Mi Amigo*.

I was doing the breakfast show on Radio Caroline one day and out of the mist this massive great mine sweeper suddenly appeared. We'd heard that it was coming, it was the MV *Galaxy*, and I remember listening to the test transmissions. It was the very first time that I'd heard these wonderful, terribly professional Radio London jingles, Big L, and I thought, that's the station that I want to work for. It was more professional than Radio Caroline, it was better run, the whole thing was just a different organisation and it was professional radio. It was the very first time that we'd heard proper formatted radio, Top 40 radio. In other words, rather than playing the first thing the DJ thought of, this was well thought out, it was American radio. The Americans were well ahead of what we were doing over here.

Tony Blackburn, DJ

Radio London was a very professional and successful enterprise from the start, with a slick Top 40 format. It had a stronger signal than Caroline, disciplined DJs and a very professional sales team. It quickly attracted a huge radio audience.

> *You're hearing things (you're hearing things) on … Wonderful Radio London.*

All of us on board *Caroline* agreed: What a truly professional station it was and we loved those radio jingles. There was no way we could compete; they had truly slick DJs, great music, strict Top 40 format; clever adverts, a larger and more luxurious ship and a very powerful transmitter.

Keith Skues, DJ

The death occurred in January 1965 of Britain's war time leader, Sir Winston Churchill and a state funeral was held on 30 January. Radio Caroline marked the occasion with a change to normal programmes. The soundtrack from the film *The Finest Hours* was played followed by solemn music for much of the day.

> They then proceeded to play music of such funereal character that it made our solemn music sound like the wedding march.[6]

As quickly as Caroline had gained listeners when she first came on the air, she was now losing them to Wonderful Radio London. More importantly, Caroline was losing out on advertising, with the big London agencies favouring Radio London. The income for the start of 1965 had dropped considerably and there was great concern over this slump in revenue.

Radio London had expensive custom made jingles, produced in Dallas by the world leader in radio production, PAMS. Radio London listeners constantly heard jingles singing the radio station logo:

> *Wonderful Radio London, Big L.*

Nothing like it had been heard in the UK before.

Radio Caroline introduced jingles, but these were poor attempts, many of them appeared to have been made on board, with the DJs singing:

> *This is Radio Caroline, fourteen hours a day: Music all day and every day, this is Radio Caroline, seven days a week.*

Caroline also used generic American jingles produced by the National Association of Broadcasters:

> *Just take a lively companion wherever you go take a portable radio.*

Some jingles had added voice-overs by Caroline House-based Bill Hearne with his deep Canadian voice:

> *Aah come on doll, quit fooling with the antenna, I'm trying to listen to my favourite station, Radio Caroline on 199.*

Some of the DJs had jingles sung for them by a selection of bands, often those eager to have their songs played on Caroline:

> *Have yourself a time, tune into Caroline and Cardboard Shoes ... Keith Skues.*

A group called The New Faces were responsible for a series of personalised idents for Tony Blackburn:

> *Wherever you go, whatever you do, go go with – The Tony Blackburn Show.*

> *It's in the air – The Tony Blackburn Show.*

Tony Blackburn also sang station jingles himself:

> *It's time right now for a good guy sure shot on Radio Caroline 199.*

Let's go over and see what's happening in the USA.

There were also professional 'soundalikes' of recent chart hits:

If you listen it sounds like Caroline. [To the tune of The Searchers hit, 'Take Me for What I'm Worth']

Everything's fine on Caroline. [Based on The Rolling Stones hit, 'Satisfaction']

It would be spring 1966 before the station had a recognisable identity and character to its jingles:

Sounds fine, it's Caroline.

Caroline the sound of the nation, Caroline the sound of the land … Caroline!

In an attempt to make Caroline sound more like a pop music radio station, The Caroline Sounds of '65 pop chart was introduced and a pre-recorded programme from top New York DJ, Jack Spector, of radio station WMCA, was broadcast every evening on both ships:

From New York City it's the Jack Spector show for Radio Caroline.

Compared to the laid-back, very British style of broadcasting from most of the Caroline team, Spector sounded manic, using all the tricks and antics from his afternoon show in the States, such as echo and sound effects. Caroline also adopted another feature from WMCA, the DJs were seen in sharp suits and became the Good Guys – Caroline was now The Good Guy station. The idea worked in New York and on 2SM in Sydney Australia, but the Caroline Good Guys were distinctly uneasy with the new image.

Caroline tried to revamp its image and came up with the Good Guys promotion. We were all kitted out in blue blazer and grey trousers and wore the uniform to all the gigs we attended. We also introduced the Sounds of '65 charts; I believe this was to compete with Radio London's Fab 40 which was a huge success in the audience ratings.

Keith Skues, DJ

10

Bringing News to the Nation, Fast and Factual

Despite claims from the Government that the pirates' days were numbered, Caroline celebrated her first birthday over Easter 1965. Four special 'Caroline Bell Awards' were presented to mark the occasion: 'House of the Rising Sun' by The Animals was song of the year, Petula Clark's 'Downtown' was the best female recording, best male vocal went to Tom Jones for 'It's Not Unusual' and The Beatles received their award for best and most consistent artists from Caroline DJ Simon Dee. Throughout the Easter weekend, messages of support from just about every major recording artist of the time were broadcast. Whatever battles and disputes there might have been going on behind the scenes, Radio Caroline was certainly giving the impression of a successful, professional organisation.

Legendary keyboard player Jimmy Smith, performed live on board the *Mi Amigo* on 5 May 1965, accompanied by a guitarist and drummer. The trio performed live on deck – because the delicate Hammond organ brought out on the tender wouldn't fit through the doors of the ship. The repertoire included 'Hip Ship Blues', 'Moonlight in Vermont' and 'Satin Doll', all tunes showing Caroline's continuing favour towards jazz and the blues, rather than the Top 40.

In August 1965, Radio Caroline South increased its hours of broadcasting and we were given shift changes which meant we had less time off duty; our two weeks on land was cut down to one week. We were not best pleased and made our feelings known to management. Suddenly DJs were axed or they left of their own accord, some had been there since 1964, including Mike Allen, Roger Gale, Doug Kerr, Gary Kemp and Jon Sydney. Management had introduced a new format of radio and believed we weren't being over enthusiastic about our Good Guys image on air and not competing with Radio London.

Keith Skues, DJ

As some staff left, others replaced them. Caroline made use of transient DJs from Australia and Canada, visiting the UK on working holidays. Graham Webb was an Australian radio man with many years' experience:

I wasn't posh enough for the BBC, I needed a job, thought who do I know? Allan Crawford, he's running a thing called Radio Caroline. So I thought, bold as brass, need a quid, need a job, walk in, so I did. Thirty quid a week first up, it turned into forty quid before I left, but thirty was about the best I could get out of them. The ship itself, well there was this little thing bobbing around in the sea, I thought this things gonna sink any minute from now. I decided it was time for Caroline to become a bit more legitimate and I thought we should be doing news as well as just pumping out pop music. I suggested it to Ronan O'Rahilly and he said, 'OK, you want news, well you do it'; I felt terribly important. I'd never been a journalist, although I had read news back in Australia. 'You can pick a staff, two men on the south ship, two on the north, and you can become news director'. I took on those that were the most articulate with reading the news, I had to get people who could speak nice and clearly with a sort of mid-Atlantic accent. I had these guys, two on the north ship, two on the south, and I spent two or three days on each ship, flew in between and set it all up over six months and got it working very well. We called it Radio Caroline Newsbeat.

Newsbeat, bringing news to the nation, this is Radio Caroline Newsbeat, Fast and Factual.

You ask how we gathered the news – we stole it, yes we did. We had no telex or fax machines in those days, so I had my newsmen listen around the dial: Radio Asia, Radio Australia, BBC world service, South African Radio.

Graham Webb, DJ and Head of News

In Parliament on 12 November 1965, during a debate about the worsening situation in the Commonwealth country of Rhodesia (now Zimbabwe) which was threatening independence from Britain, it was suggested that Caroline could be asked to help the Government.

My Right Hon. and learned friend was asked about what we were doing to improve the audibility of broadcast services from outside. Perhaps the House will leave that with us. We have been on it for some little time. There are difficulties in this connection, and, if we have to borrow on the experience of an organisation known as Radio Caroline, we shall not hesitate to do so.[1]

Aware of the obvious point-scoring that could be had, Project Atlanta Chairman, Oliver Smedley, wrote to Downing Street offering the services of Caroline South and Ronan O'Rahilly contacted the Labour Party.

When Rhodesia declared independence, we picked that up on Rhodesian radio and broadcast it four hours before the BBC would even mention it. That was certainly a scoop for Radio Caroline.

Graham Webb

Nick Bailey would eventually join the Newsbeat team, but it took a while. Because of the standards set by Radio London's professional broadcasters, Caroline had started to demand more from the on air talent.

I was working for the Mermaid Theatre in London in the publicity department and getting itchy feet, and there was a chap in the box office who was a Tasmanian radio actor and he went off to get a job with Radio Invicta and then to Caroline as a copywriter. One day he came into the theatre and said that he'd actually moved onto the ship itself as a news reader. I prided myself on having a deep voice and as I was doing interval announcements at the theatre, I asked if there were any jobs going to let me know. He told me he was earning £25 a week and I thought that sounds pretty good to me. Three weeks later he phoned and said 'Were you serious about the job?' and I said, 'Well yes I was', he said 'They're looking for a couple of newsreaders, get down to Caroline House in Mayfair as soon as possible because they're holding auditions'.

So off I went, very confident, I took an audition with a gentleman called Graham 'Spider' Webb, an Australian disc jockey, he was head of news and he gave me a script, just one page of news, and I went in so confident, but he tore me down a strip. It was at the time of the Vietnam War and instead of saying Hi Phong harbour I said Hi PONG harbour. He said at the end, kindly, maybe just trying to get rid of me, 'Well you've got potential, but we can't employ you at the moment, go away and practise and get in touch with us in a few weeks'. I took him at his word, being rather naïve, I was only 19 at the time, I practised every night for several hours reading this one script of news into a tape recorder and eventually, when I felt confident, I phoned Radio Caroline back and spoke to Graham Webb, who by that time had forgotten who I was totally, but being the generous man that he was, said 'Come along and take another audition', and amazingly they'd had two jobs vacant and filled one post but not the other. Second time around it was a lot better and he said 'We've just got to play it to Ronan O'Rahilly, see if he approves, which he did apparently and out I went on the ship.

Nick Bailey, DJ and News Reader

Radio Caroline off Felixstowe, April 1964. (David Kindred)

Radio Mercur broadcast to Denmark from the tiny *Cheeta*. (Ingemar Lindgvist)

Bon Jour, home to Radio Nord. (Ingemar Lindgvist)

Allan Crawford's Rocket record label. (Authors collection)

Bon Jour or *Magda Maria* or *Mi Amigo* moored close to Radio Veronica off the Dutch coast. (Ingemar Lindgvist)

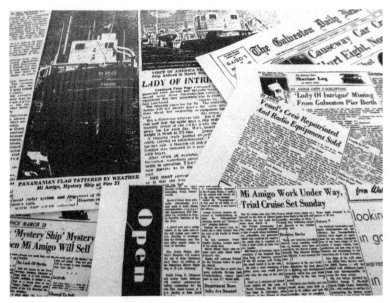

Mi Amigo was the talk of Galveston. (Authors collection)

The Danish ferry boat, *Fredericia*. (Nordjylands Kyst museum)

Caroline Kennedy disrupts proceedings in the Oval Office, with father John F. Kennedy and brother John Jnr. (Getty Images)

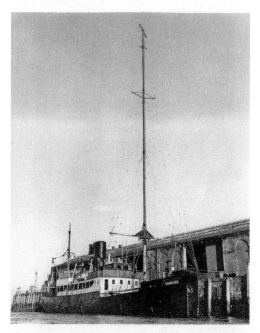

The *Fredericia* was now MV *Caroline*, fitted out in Greenore and complete with her huge new broadcast mast. (Bruce Fleming)

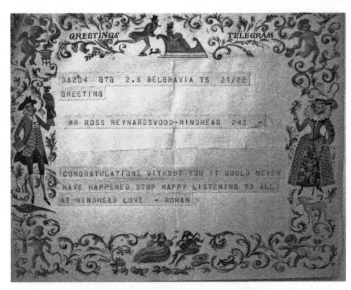

The telegram from a jubilant Ronan to Caroline financier 'Jimmy'
Charles Ross. Happy listening … Caroline was on the air. (Ian Ross)

Chris Moore

Simon Dee

Studio engineer, Ove Sjöström plays in the pre-recorded programmes and records for the announcers. (Getty Images)

'You're in tune to Radio Caroline on 199.'
(Alan Turner)

'Your all-day music station.' (Alan Turner)

The attempted name change. (Alan Turner)

Mi Amigo off Greenore, complete with new transmitting mast. (Colin Nicol Collection)

Mi Amigo finally anchors off Frinton. (David Kindred)

O'Rahilly and Crawford, two bosses, two ships, one business.
(Associated Newspapers/Rex Features)

It's in the air – The Tony Blackburn Show. (David Kindred)

Tender trips weren't always smooth sailing. (Carl Thomson)

Carl Conway

Tony Blackburn

6 Chesterfield Gardens, London W1.

Caroline Club literature.

TIME	COMMERCIAL	SCRIPT/TAPE	LENGTH	REMARKS	TRANS/TIME
12 noon	BULOVA WATCHES	SCRIPT-4 Live	5	T.S.F. 12 Noon	PN
	MUSHROOM ASSOC..	SCRIPT A 291	7	Net.	12:06 DK
	NEW MUSICAL EXPRESS	SCR 7090	45		12:12 DK
12.15	RICHMOND CIGS. CASSETTE # 7	TAPE VER 3 (CHUCK MISTER)	30	Net.	12:19 NK
	DUNN'S SEEDS.	SCRIPT A301	3c		12:27 NK
12.30	IRELAND HOLIDAYS	TAPE 2	360		12:34 DK
	NEW MUSICAL EXPRESS	SCR 7118	60		12:37 DR
	AGENTS.	TAPE 2	3c		12:43 DK
12.45	RICHMOND CIGS. CASSETTE #3	(F.M. VER/3 TAPE)	30	Net.	12:47 DK
	NOVUM.	A 296	3c		12:40 DR

Commercial log, signed by PN and DK, DJs Paul Noble and Doug Kerr. (Authors Collection)

Big L, Radio London from the former US minesweeper, *Galaxy*. (Dallas Willcox)

Caroline South runs aground. (David Kindred)

Tony Blackburn dries off after his rescue. (David Kindred)

Beached at Holland Haven. (John Steer)

Mi Amigo with Breeches Buoy still attached. (John Steer)

Mi Amigo, high and dry. (John Steer)

Mi Amigo, dangerously close to becoming a total loss. (Getty Images)

Mi Amigo close to disaster (David Kindred)

Coastguards are jubilant as *Mi Amigo* is re-floated.
(Associated Newspapers/Rex Features)

Cheeta II, the temporary home of Radio Caroline in the South.
(Colin Nicol Collection)

The *Mi Amigo* returns after her refit, with tender, *Offshore 1*, alongside. (David Kindred)

11

THE TOWER OF POWER

Operating costs were high and because of Caroline South's diminishing audience, advertisers were still choosing to use Radio London. Income, particularly from the south ship, was poor; Project Atlanta was running out of money. As autumn 1965 approached, there were attempts to resolve the situation. Contact was made with Radio City based on the Shivering Sands fort and a deal to amalgamate was discussed. City started to relay Caroline Newsbeat within their programmes and when they closed down for the evening they suggested listeners re-tune to Radio Caroline whose programmes continued into the night. At the time Radio London's management believed the *Mi Amigo* might be moving position further up the East Coast and there was newspaper speculation that a radio ship would soon be broadcasting from the Bristol Channel. Was the plan to transfer Caroline South's programmes to the fort, where operating costs were considerably less and allow expansion of the Caroline network and so increase income, or had relations between Project Atlanta and Caroline become so fraught that Crawford needed an alternative broadcasting option?

> I went to Reg Calvert and said, 'Now look, you've got a rotten transmitter, supposing we put up a really decent one and work together?' He was interested because he was short of money, so I flew out a second-hand transmitter from America via Holland and put it on the station. But in doing that a bit fell off into the sea. I couldn't blame anyone because they were operating with a make do crane.
>
> Allan Crawford[1]

I believe the request to join forces came as a last-minute bid from Atlanta who were rapidly running out of money and going to lose their partnership with Caroline. My father, unaware of the Atlanta money problems, agreed to go into partnership with them on the promise of Atlanta providing him with a new transmitter. They were to receive the income from advertising, pay the bills and wages, and pay my father a percentage of the profit. When the transmitter arrived, it was about thirty years old, the wrong sort, too big and took too much power to work. Part of it fell in the sea and had to be rescued, the transportation bill alone was around £600.

Susan Moore, Reg Calvert's daughter

I was employed by Radio Atlanta; they wanted someone who knew about transmitters and that was my speciality. They had a transmitter from the States which was a large 10 kilowatt device and it had been taken apart in the States and all of the cabling had got labels on. Ted Walters who was chief engineer at that time and me were told to go to Radio City, 'it'll be a doddle because everything's marked'. Well when we got there we found that one of the cabinets had been dropped into the Thames, the sling had broken because everything taken aboard the forts had to be hoisted up, and all the paper markings had come off. We never really did get that running after it had been soaked with seawater.

Carl Thomson, broadcast engineer

After a couple of months, Atlanta was not paying the bills, and cheques for wages were being returned. My father picked up the pieces, paid the bills and carried on. The bill for the transportation costs was batted backwards and forwards between Alan [*sic* – Allan] Crawford and my father as it was felt that the responsibility for purchasing an old and unsuitable transmitter was theirs. Nothing more was said for months about the 'partnership'.

Susan Moore, Reg Calvert's daughter

The on air tie-up between Caroline and City failed to go further; money, or lack of it, was the reason and it would appear that time was up for Project Atlanta. As 1965 came to an end, Planet Productions took full control of both Radio Caroline services and Allan Crawford and Atlanta relinquished control of the south ship.

Our company decided not to continue because of this roller-coasting of the income, the see-saw aspect, it was getting to be too heavy. We did get a further loan from Jarvis [sports promoter Jarvis Astaire, a Project Atlanta investor] who, when we reached this point, recalled the loan, which, of course, put us out of business.

Allan Crawford[2]

Oliver Smedley and I were sick and tired of being kicked around and Allan had proved himself to be a totally broken weed. At this stage Caroline was in the process of taking over completely. Project Atlanta had contributed a lot of money, something like £80,000 to install the equipment aboard Radio City, certainly Radio Atlanta never got it back – maybe it was £10,000. I was the underwriter to a very large extent, eventually the Atlanta shareholders were bought out by Radio Caroline. I don't think anybody lost any money. In that sense I certainly didn't, I think that the shares were eventually sold as tax loss shares. But I felt raging fury that the whole thing should have been handed over on a plate at a very disadvantageous arrangement and for that we were giving them the ship, the entire set up, all the expertise that had been accumulated over the years and it seemed totally unfair.

Kitty Black[3]

The radio dream of Allan Crawford had come to an end; Project Atlanta was all but bankrupt, and was forced to sell out to O'Rahilly's Planet Productions. Crawford eventually returned to record production and became very successful producing covers of hit songs on *Top of the Pops* LP's. Members, other than Crawford, of the Project Atlanta board would feature in dramatic events in the offshore radio business within months ...

a SUDDEN SWING
IN HIGH COMMaND

As Christmas 1965 approached, there were big changes on land, Caroline North was sounding good but the on-air sound of Caroline South was still inconsistent. During 1965 Caroline South had lost tens of thousands of listeners to Big L and, worse still, to the BBC Light Programme. Canadian Bill Hearne had become shore-based Programme Director by this time, but controlling the output of a radio station remotely wasn't easy. Word of the management changes and other concerns reached the ship by this memo.

> There's been a sudden swing in the High Command in Caroline House, which finds Ronan as Supreme Commander and Alan on the outs. Things are all just a little bit vague at this writing but it seems there was a big board meeting last weekend which wound up with these changes. He wants the station to 'swing' more than its presently doing. Well it has been my opinion for some time that the sound of the station is 'dropping off' and it was my intention to work on it after the New Year. There is a little too much 'individuality' instead of the team feeling and obviously the 'policy' which I went to great lengths to prepare is gathering dust … It also needs 100% co-operation of all the DJs aboard and, I regret to say it, if their co-operation is not forthcoming, we'll have to go looking for those who will adhere to format and policy.
>
> Bill Hearne, programme director[1]

More changes were to follow. To replace the position of joint Managing Directors, the Caroline board made financial man, Barry Ainley, General Manager for Planet Productions.

> Jimmy Ross said, 'would I go and run Radio Caroline?' I said, 'you must be mad, I know nothing about pop music.' He introduced me to John Sheffield, another shareholder, who told me that if I took on the job of running Radio Caroline, he would guarantee me a job in his organisation when the end came.
>
> Barry Ainley, Planet Productions, general manager[2]

Disc jockey Tom Lodge, who had sailed north with the original Caroline ship when the two groups merged, was deemed to be the person who could get the station sounding right and was transferred to the *Mi Amigo* as the search started for new DJs to join the team. The first to sign up was one of the few Englishmen with commercial Top 40 radio experience.

> I was working for a radio station in Los Angeles called KHJ, the number one radio station in LA. I was doing 6 till 9 each night and having a great life, then my draft papers arrived, and they said, 'Hey son, would you like to go to Vietnam?' I said, 'No thank you, I've still got a British passport'. I waited as long as I could; if I'd stayed any longer I would've had to go to Vietnam. I flew to Seattle, crossed the border into Canada and then flew directly to London. I got off the plane with £47 in my pocket and went immediately to Radio Caroline with my tape of the last programme I'd done in Los Angeles. The guy there said, 'We love the tape, come back after Christmas', so I got a room in a hotel in Baker Street in London, went back three or four days later when the office reopened, and a day after that I was on my way to the ship in the North Sea. I went from Los Angeles to the middle of the North Sea in five and a half days. It was the biggest culture shock of my life.
>
> Tommy Vance, DJ

The Caroline North ship was alone in broadcasting off the West Coast to the north of England. Other than the BBC, it had no competition for audiences in Liverpool, Manchester, Belfast, North Wales, Eire and southern Scotland. With offices at PO Box 3, Ramsey, Isle of Man and a mainland office at 61 Lord Street, Liverpool 2, all was well up north, although consideration was given to moving the ship in an attempt to improve the signal to the mainland. A date was set, but bad weather prevented the move, and nothing further came of the idea – the ship remained in Ramsay Bay. But the programmes continued to evolve as the disc jockeys now became known as 'Caroline's men of a new breed – the men who make radio active.' Their style of presentation became more 'hip and zany', and they now spoke with a distinct echo added to their voices. Jerry Leighton had joined Radio Caroline just weeks after her first broadcast and had sailed north when the *Frederica* moved to the Isle of Man and was the regular breakfast show presenter waking up millions of listeners in the north every day.

It was decided by the 'powers that be' that we were going Top 50, it was going to be pop, and the middle of the road shows were going to be phased out. Consequently, I had to build a 'pop like' persona, as did the rest of the team. 'Daffy Don Allen' wasn't 'Daffy Don' until we went 'pop', Bob Stewart became 'Baby Bob', I became 'Soopa' and of course, being the sixties, I spelt it wrong.

Jerry 'Soopa' Leighton, DJ[3]

All was fine onboard, at least on air, but it wasn't all plain sailing for Caroline North, the ship's dog bit the captain who had to go ashore by lifeboat for treatment. This dog wasn't the only creature on Caroline North.

One of the Dutch crew used to keep chickens on the back of the ship and I went up there one day and one of these chickens got out and flew straight over the back of the boat and landed in the water and this crewman was a real big guy who used to talk to his chickens, he really loved these chickens like kids. I was trying to think of a way to rescue it and this bloody chicken was bobbing up and down in the water looking incredibly bewildered, drifting off towards the English coast and there was nothing I could do. I was saying 'come here chook, chook, chook' and of course chickens can't use their feet to turn around. I thought of launching the boat so I went and saw the captain and I explained what happened and he roared with laughter and poured me a Dutch gin.

Mike Ahern, DJ[4]

mayday, mayday

The start of 1966 looked more positive for Radio Caroline. With two ships now under the control of Planet Productions, the focus was on improving the output and signal strength including the plan to fit a more powerful transmitter on the *Mi Amigo*. Despite the Government making threatening noises towards the offshore radio stations, the biggest challenge to Caroline's survival came on the night of 19 January 1966. The *Mi Amigo* lost her anchor, causing the ship to drift in strong winds and high seas. Walton-on-the-Naze coastguard had been taking bearings on the ship and, realising the problem, tried to make contact by lamp and radio, but failed. As Walton lifeboat was prepared to launch, conditions on the ship were more uncomfortable than usual.

> When there was rough water out there, we knew about it, with that high mast and being anchored at one end you're really saying, 'Go on, turn this thing upside down, I dare you.' Well, that's almost what happened. You had to hang on and you did things like strap pennies on the stylus just to stop them sliding across the records. I went out on deck as I'd been watching television and the pictures were so bad because of the poor signal on this particular night. We realised later that the programmes we were trying to watch were flashing messages to us saying 'excuse me, you're in deep trouble', but we couldn't see it because the TV aerial was all over the place. Two of us were looking at the lights of Frinton, which were always in a given position, and they seemed to be bigger on this particular

evening, and I said as much, and they were saying don't be silly. We thought the lights were coming towards us, but of course it was us going towards the lights.

Dave Lee Travis, DJ

We always used to joke about one day we'd run aground, and one day we did. I went to bed early because I was on the breakfast show and Norman St John came down and said, 'you must get up because we're going aground.' I thought he was joking, and then the captain came down and said, 'we really are going aground'. We all went out onto the deck and we thought we were quite a way out with these winds and waves crashing over the boat. I remember the captain shining this massive great light and literally just twenty or so yards away there were people walking along the seashore, I can remember him saying 'Mayday' in a very quiet voice and I thought, that's a bit too late, then there was a sort of crunching noise and we ended up on the shore in Frinton.

Tony Blackburn, DJ

It was scary. I shared a cabin with Tony Blackburn, who used to go to bed early so he was in good shape to do his Breakfast show. I ran down stairs and woke him. Initially he was none too pleased and I told him to grab a life jacket. As we reached the deck there was an almighty thud and we were aground. I don't believe that any of us were convinced that the *Mi Amigo* wouldn't soon break up. The crew told us to take cover as the Coastguard would be firing rockets with a Breeches Buoy attached. The first rocket missed and the second one hit the aft deck and the crew were able to secure it and set up our lifeline to the beach.

Norman St John, DJ

Ken Haggis was the assistant engineer for the Walton-on-the-Naze lifeboat. At the time, they had a reserve boat on station when the call came of a ship in distress.

We always thought we might get a shout out to the ships when the weather was bad, but it was a surprise when it came. It was a real stinking night; the wind was blowing a good 9 to 10. It was very, very cold and we thought she was dragging her anchor, then we suddenly realised she was coming in a great rate of knots. We had a bit of a problem getting launched; one engine wouldn't fire up. By the time we got close enough she'd hit the beach. Then we heard that the LSA crew [Life Saving Apparatus] were getting them off, we hung around waiting for the tug to come up and then we went back to Harwich because it was too bad for us to get back on the moorings. The LSA did a good job that night; it was the biggest job they'd ever done, getting them off with Breeches Buoy. They were very fortunate where they came in, onto the hard beach; one way or the other they'd have been on top of the groynes.

Ken Haggis, Walton Lifeboat Station

We came aground on the beach. We were genuinely so lucky as we could have been in some awful trouble. We landed, as luck would have it, between two sea walls. If we'd have gone 100 feet either way, we'd have hit this side on and the ship would have broken up and people would have died. It was that serious. We braced ourselves ready for the grounding and the whole ship tilted over, and you've no idea what it's like being in your home watching a fridge flying across the room at you. Then the Breeches Buoy was set up, we all ducked as this rocket was shot at the ship, and guess who came off first and landed in the arms of a waiting photographer? … Blackburn, cup of tea, towel over his head … it was an interesting night to say the least.

Dave Lee Travis

I turned the transmitter off as we thought we might be going into territorial waters. The ship was really moving in a strange way, when we beached there wasn't really a crash bang, but then it all started, the waves had nowhere to go so they were hitting us broadside. The coastguard shot ropes to the ship which we tied up just under the bridge. Tony Blackburn, Norman St John, Graham Webb ... and engineers Patrick Starling and George Saunders went off and that just left me and Tom Lodge. I told him to go and then I went to the captain to say all the English were off, did he want me to stay?

I came ashore with one leg in the Breeches, one leg out; I lost my slippers and socks in the surf and then walked up the beach. I thought they'd laid a carpet out, I didn't realise there was six inches of snow. We were all gathered together and interviewed by customs, then taken to a store in Walton and given clothing as we were distressed sailors; it was good quality stuff too. Then we went to a hotel, which was freezing cold, had a cup of tea and a scotch. We went back the next day and got some of our gear off.

Carl Thomson, broadcast engineer

The *Mi Amigo* was hard aground and being pounded by huge waves breaking right over her. With each wave the ship 'waddled', her stability not helped by the towering mast. The Wijsmuller tug, the *Titan* arrived next day and made several attempts to pull the *Mi Amigo* back out to sea, but without success. The story was making headline news but this was a worrying time for Caroline, there was a real possibility that the ship could be lost completely and with the station off air, Caroline South was earning nothing, at a time when finances were already dire. Further attempts were made to free her on the following high tides, but eventually, using cables and her own anchor, the captain was able to winch the ship off the beach and back out to sea. The hull needed inspection and repairs for any likely damage and the *Mi Amigo* was taken in tow to Holland.

We went across the North Sea towed by the tug *Titan*. We left at a tremendous rate of knots and the next morning I got up and noticed that we were barely moving. When I got to the transmitter room it looked as if a bomb had hit it, with pumps everywhere, we were taking in water. The plates had sprung and water was coming in like a 'good 'un'. All the pumps were running to try to keep her afloat. I put everything up high in the transmitter room, thinking that we might be able to hold it. The next day we approached Ijmuiden and as we came in, and I'll remember this to my dying day, there's a hill with a light-house on it, the whole of that hill was covered with people and as we went into the locks from the North Sea there were hundreds of people around to look at us come in. They towed us all the way up to the shipyard in Zaandam.

She was dry docked there, mainly rivets had been knocked out, but because she was made of iron and steel there was cor-rosion and a lot of areas that had gone thin, so they patched it up the best they could, to make it seaworthy. They lifted the transmitters out and fitted the new one. One 10 kilowatt even-tually went to the north ship to increase power there, so the south ship now had one 10 kilowatt and this new 50 kilowatt. We put the new transmitter in the hold and the 10 kilowatt at the bottom of the stairs.

Carl Thomson, broadcast engineer

With the *Mi Amigo* under repair, there was no service in the south. Fortunately for Caroline, the one remaining Scandinavian ship-borne radio station, Radio Syd, had recently stopped broadcasting from their ship *Cheeta II*, after increased political pressure from the Swedish Government and a build-up of ice in the Baltic Sea, which had forced the ship to move. It was planned to take the *Cheeta II* and the radio station to The Gambia and start broadcast-ing there, but meanwhile a deal was offered by the owner, Swedish businesswoman Britt Wadner, and the ship was used by Caroline as a temporary replacement.

I helped commission the *Cheeta II* for temporary use as Caroline South and stayed on board for over five weeks. The Swedish crew were great and we had a pleasant but construc-tive time urgently fitting the ship for medium wave broadcasts,

it had been broadcasting in FM to Sweden. There was much
to be done on the technical side: we shipped the transmitter
back from the *Mi Amigo* in Holland along with other equipment and got it all aboard. I remember how tricky that was
and can still picture the moment as we lowered the transmitter
away and cautiously eased the valuable and delicate bulk into
the hold. One slip and it could have been all over for Caroline
South. Then the complicated and highly technical puzzle of
how to design and install an antenna that would radiate effectively. There was no tall tower, as Caroline had. All that could
be done was to adapt what was there and that meant rigging
copper cables between the ship's masts fore and aft. It worked,
thanks to the brilliance of our technicians.

Colin Nicol, DJ[1]

Broadcasts from Caroline South during February and March
1966 were erratic, but eventually the technical issues on board
the *Cheeta II* were solved – only to be followed by a further
setback when the *Cheeta II* started taking on water. Once again
programmes stopped as she was towed to a shipyard in Lowestoft
for repairs.

The *Cheeta* was a stop gap, the crew were messing around with
something in the engine room and they opened a sea valve
and they couldn't shut it, water was pouring in, so a tug had
to come out from Harwich and tow us to Lowestoft for repairs.

Carl Thomson, broadcast engineer

After repairs and renovation had been carried out to the *Mi Amigo*,
she returned to the English coast, for a while, there were two ships
providing two separate Caroline south broadcasts. The *Cheeta*
continued on 199 metres with new DJs Robbie Dale and Tony
Prince telling listeners to retune to Caroline's new frequency of
259 metres, where the rest of the team were broadcasting with a
new higher powered transmitter and new jingles. Some unique

broadcasts were made as the DJs struck up conversation on-air between both ships, involving the listeners in the adventure.

> *Radio Caroline now has action on a new wavelength of 259 metres*
> *medium wave, so why don't you switch over the dial to the new sound*
> *of Radio Caroline on 259.*

The *Mi Amigo*, complete with its new powerful 50 kilowatt transmitter, was on the air, but issues with the aerial mast were still causing problems.

When we went to 50 kilowatts, the insulators started burning through, we had riggers out with new wires and insulators and that's the only time I saw people go up that mast in wellie boots and sou'westers in a gale to replace them. I was also on board when Tony Blackburn went up and tried to clear a wire that was causing us problems. Ronan offered fifty quid for anyone who would go up and everyone thought about it then looked up and thought no.

Carl Thomson, broadcast engineer

When I started on the south ship we couldn't transmit, there was something right at the top of the mast that was faulty and we couldn't get anyone out to sort it, so we were all sitting on the ship, bored crazy, thinking what can we do. So Norman St John said, 'let's get up this bloody mast and get back on air'. So Norman tried to go up first, but he soon came down. It was cold and very stormy and the mast was swaying all over the place and then Tony Blackburn had a go. Well, Tony went about half way and then he came back down, hands freezing, and then I had a go. You put this safety harness on and it has a clip, but there was a part of the mast where a new section had been welded on and at that point the rungs were thicker. The little clip on the safety belt wouldn't clip over the rungs, so the worst part of the journey up was the most dangerous because you had no safety harness.

I went up a few rungs and I was like jelly and with the swaying and freezing hands I thought I was going to drop off there any minute and I came down, by which time Tony had decided to have another go and this time he went all the way to the top and freed the rogue wire, he let it go, but it didn't come down all the way. Then I went up and got the wire from the point where it had got stuck again, and just at that point the tender came out with Ronan O'Rahilly on board. There was all sorts of yelling, telling them not to come alongside in case they knocked the ship because I was still up the mast.

Tony Prince, DJ

14

IT'S a CaSH CaSINO

Although the northern ship had broadcast without incident throughout this period, the loss of revenue following the
grounding of Caroline South to Planet Productions was huge,
and this coming shortly after Atlanta had been bought out. More
financial input was desperately needed, and it was music publisher Philip Solomon who came up with the cash and bought
into Caroline. He'd been responsible for a number of big hits
that Caroline had played, and helped into the charts: 'Here
Comes the Night' by Van Morrison and Them and 'Terry' by
Twinkle were just two.

> I was approached by Ronan O'Rahilly. he said, 'I need a lot of
> money'. I said, 'how much do you need?' and he said, '30,000.'
> In those days it was a hell of a lot of money, so I said, 'Alright,
> I'll give you the 30,000, but I want to be co-director with
> you', so we got together and I paid him the 30,000. Ronan
> had no idea of keeping money, he wanted to spend it. When
> I gave him £30,000 one of the first things he wanted to do
> was repaint the whole of Caroline because a mate of his was
> going to do the job. He was a very good ideas man but rotten
> at controlling money.
>
> Philip Solomon, director

Phil Solomon wasn't the only person to put money into Caroline
at this time. One of the most successful acts on his books was
the Bachelors; Solomon acted as their agent and his wife was
their manager. The repertoire of ballads from this Irish singing

trio appealed to a more mature audience, but their songs were regularly in the charts and they had been played on Caroline from day one.

> We got involved through Philip Solomon. He approached us and said he needed some financing, I believe that the station was in trouble at the time, and Philip, with a good financial brain, got involved. Another Irish colleague of ours was also involved – it was him, Philip and us, a three-way split. The good thing was that because of our financial interest we could get our stuff played all the time. Not many people knew that we were involved, that was the way Philip wanted it and that was the way he got it, we were silent partners. We expected to make money, but we didn't make any, we lost money. We put in around £3,000 each, that's all three of us, as The Bachelors. If we hadn't put money into Caroline I think it would have just sunk with the waves.
>
> Dec Cluskey, The Bachelors

The costs of operating Caroline were too high and the income too low, so drastic action was needed. The answer was to employ two top radio men from Canada to bring in extra advertising. Englishman Terry Bate excelled at sales, together with Alan Slaight, who'd programmed Canada's largest Top 40 station CHUM. Through a series of innovative advertising projects, this 'Dynamic Duo' started the money rolling into Caroline.

> It was obvious they had no idea how to sell radio, and the programming wasn't much better. I told them at a board meeting that they were running the biggest commercial radio station in the world, they had no idea – I still don't think Ronan realised that, even now.
>
> Terry Bate, head of sales

Bate employed a new sales team and ensured that serious effort was put into selling Caroline. He was also responsible for introducing a series of ground-breaking on-air competitions, including Caroline Cash Casino.

> *Within the next few minutes, some lucky Radio Caroline listener could win as much as £3,330 – so let's play Caroline Cash Casino, brought to you by these quality products …*

In the initial competition, listeners had to identify a mystery sound, but in subsequent episodes they were invited to solve a series of rhyming clues, featured five times a day during week-days, on both the north and south ships. With every wrong answer, a cash kitty was increased by £10 and to enter, a 'product proof of purchase' was required. Almost £30,000 in prize money was won throughout the ten competitions and several household names sponsored daily segments: Findus Frozen Foods, Weetabix, Alberto VO5 shampoo, Libby's tinned fruits, Galaxy choco-late, VP wines, Brands Quality Foods, SPC Fruit and Nabisco Shredded Wheat.

Because it was so successful, the cost to the advertisers increased each time, each existing sponsor had one week to renew for the next round. On one occasion Shredded Wheat had seen Weetabix just clearing the shelves and said we'll pay whatever to be part of it. I went to Weetabix and said its £26,000 this time and they delayed, so Shredded Wheat joined in. Then Weetabix were desperate for me to find a way of them coming back on air, so I introduced 'Partners in Profit' for them. We had another competition involving Helix tooth-brushes, I asked how much of their product was on sale at any time and was told around 800,000 units, their campaign was so successful they didn't renew; I don't think they had any more toothbrushes available.

Terry Bate, head of sales

Caroline Cash Casino was really big all week, and some-one thought up the idea of having a similar thing for the weekends. Every hour, on the hour we had a ten-minute sponsored programme with a couple of records, it became 'Weetabix Partners in Profit' and it was produced in Caroline House. I was also the caller of the bingo numbers on a thing that comedian Charlie Drake did called OGNIB which ran on Caroline North and that was also produced in the basement, which is where I was tucked away.

Colin Berry, news reader/commercial traffic

Carolyn Irvine worked in Caroline House as secretary to the press officer, Frances van Staden, and knew much of what went on behind the scenes. She remembers the huge response to Caroline Cash Casino.

The Dynamic Dup, these Canadian wiz-kids were brought in at a huge cost, I don't know how much, but it was crippling for the company, but Cash Casino was such a popular competition. We had ten sacks of mail each delivery. Everyone had to come downstairs and sort all this mail into individual sponsors, so they could be shown the response.

Carolyn Irvine, assistant press officer and secretary

We loaded sacks and sacks of entries and took them up to Welwyn Garden City and then dumped them at the Shredded Wheat factory to show them just what response they were getting and how successful the competition was.

Terry Bate, head of sales

15

THE SOUND OF THE NATION

The real magic of Caroline for the listeners and certainly for those on board was the fun that enveloped *The Sound of the Nation*. Listeners were intrigued by what went on behind the scenes and listening in to your favourite DJs just made the link with Caroline very special. Emperor Rosko had a style that had certainly not been heard in the UK before when he joined the station in 1966.

> *Great Cassaboo, have I something for you mummyo and daddyo, glad to have you on the show!*

I was already a disc jockey on Europe 1 in France and I was on stage with Sam the Sham and the Pharaohs at the Olympia Theatre and the road manager of the tour and I were chatting and he was telling me about Caroline, saying it's a pirate boat and they're looking for DJs of class and quality, 'why not make a tape?' The following week I got a phone call from this guy called Ronan O'Rahilly who said, 'hey, come and join the boat, we'd love to have you'. For the princely sum of £70 a week, I packed my bag, got to London and then out to the ship.

The time we stole the jingles from Radio England was a good time. This new ship arrived, it was backed by the Texans and an unknown Johnnie Walker was one of their 'stars' and they were anchored about 2 miles away from us. This big beautiful ship turned up and started doing test transmissions, and on Caroline we would sit around and listen to what other people were doing in the hope that we might embellish … steal … circumvent anything they were going to do. We were listening for several nights and they'd just play their jingles and leave dead air on either side, so of course we got the recorders working about the third night. These were the days when jingles really meant something, they were the all new, ultra expensive PAMS jingles, made in Texas. They were going to go on air the next day and we took all their jingles – since it was so close we could record them in very good quality, well as good as pirate quality could be, and we edited out all the names referring to Radio England and added Radio Caroline and then went on air the next morning at the same time as them, using their jingles with Radio Caroline in them. Of course they went absolutely berserk, there were law suits threatened. I think Ronan O'Rahilly had a good laugh for a couple of days, but then I think he sent a memo saying, 'OK, enough guys'.

Emperor Rosko, DJ

Mark Sloan joined Radio Caroline for two spells, initially as a news reader on board Caroline South and later on the northern ship as a DJ.

The *Mi Amigo* was a nice ship to be on. I'd been on the forts so I was used to the rather primitive ways of life. She was comfortable and had creature comforts on board, although she was small and at times during high seas she behaved like a submarine, the seas broke over her. I found because it was so small and compact that everybody lived together as a family, including the Dutch crew. On Sunday morning the Dutch captain would assemble everyone in his cabin, say a little prayer and then get out the Dutch gin. Then we'd have a proper Sunday lunch, so everyone would have their lunch apart from on air jock and news reader. We'd play monopoly, cards or chess and we'd play for rations, we were given one case of beer and two cases of Coca Cola or 7up and we'd see how we could convert the soft drinks to beer. Then we'd get a whole stack of beer, but wouldn't drink it all at once; we'd pick a particular night and then have a party, on occasions there were hangovers on air.

Tom Lodge used to run a regular Canadian parachute training session. He'd bought this book and it involved us doing press ups and star jumps up on the roof while those down below were sleeping or doing their programme, anything that would disrupt a programme was fine. Emperor Rosko had this mynah bird called Alfie; he would be part of the show, talking in the background while Rosko would do all his stuff on air. So while he was ashore we put a tape in with the bird teaching it to swear and say things like 'Rosko's a fink'. Of course, when he returned from leave his bird was ruined because it kept swearing on air.

Mark Sloan, news reader and DJ

The biggest memory for me would be the first night on board. The captain and the crew all gathered at a dinner and went through the safety instructions for me, the new boy, and what would happen in the event of an emergency. 'The Dutch crew will have the final say in what will happen and you'll be given your orders by them and you might be asked to man a lifeboat,' and dinner continued and, of course, I'm looking around, very wide eyed, and the nasty buggers kept me up and gave me a few drinks. I went to bed very late; I'd been asleep for about an hour and a half and suddenly bells started going off.

I dropped out of my bunk in just underpants, in the middle of the North Sea at three o'clock in the morning, freezing cold, to be told, 'Quick get up on deck, there's an emergency, no time for your trousers, get up there.' I got pushed out of the cabin and everybody, the whole ship's compliment, were going upstairs, and I got up on deck and this Dutch crewman said, 'This is yours, number 1 lifeboat, get up on top.' So, I went to the highest part of the ship and was told to 'Stand by that wheel and wait for your instruction.' Ten minutes later

I can't hear anything. No one's running around anymore, but I thought I must not leave my post. It must have been twenty minutes, I was freezing cold, standing on the deck of this ship in the middle of the night in my underpants, still holding onto this wheel, and there was nobody about. I started calling out and eventually I went downstairs, and I heard this muffled laughter and then there were just cries of laughter as the whole ship had done this to welcome me on board at three o'clock in the morning.

Dave Lee Travis

Going back in time on the Sound of the Nation, it's a Caroline Flashback

Canadian Keith Hampshire presented *Keefers' Commotion* every afternoon, but later took over the breakfast show, which became known as *Keefers' Uprising*.

We set fire to Mike Ahern's carpet slippers. He liked to wear them all the time and one afternoon he was taking a nap, we snuck into his cabin, took his slippers and soaked them in lighter fuel, set them on fire and then floated them out to sea. Then we woke him up and said, 'Mike, quick, quick you must come and see this', so he jumped up, out of the cabin and up the stairs, onto the deck watching his blazing carpet slippers sailing away.

Keith Hampshire, DJ

Join me again tomorrow when I'll have another three solid hours of finger snapping, toe tapping, knee knocking, thigh slapping, knuckle cracking, finger popping, leg pulling, wrist twisting, tongue tangling, foot stomping rock and roll music, brought to you by me, Keefers, spelt with an F.

The American, Canadian and Australian DJ's had all worked on radio stations in their home countries before joining Caroline, but for the British DJ's most of them had no radio experience; they were making it up as they went along.

> We were learning a trade. The profession did not exist; pop radio, commercial radio, in Britain, it didn't exist, and we were making it up as we went along. So, we were learning, and we were getting paid for it and we were getting some form of stardom as well. It was a great time.
>
> Jerry Leighton, DJ[1]

During March 1966, Caroline's Tom Lodge interviewed The Beatles for a promotional 'flexi-disc' release for pop paper *Disc and Music Echo*. The recording, more a selection of silly answers to unprepared questions, was available to *Disc* readers and Caroline listeners and featured interviews with other top stars of the day. When The Beatles toured American during August 1966, they were accompanied by three offshore radio DJs: Jerry Leighton from Caroline North, Kenny Everett for Radio London and Ron O'Quinn from Swinging Radio England. Reports of the progress of the Fab Four throughout the States were phoned or cabled back to the UK and then sent out to the ships for broadcast.

> I never met Jerry Leighton and still don't believe he was on the tour. I have read that he was on it, but it would seem that I would have bumped into him somewhere along the way and I didn't. We were given free access to the group back stage before the shows and we were allowed to speak with them whenever they had time during the tour. They were always most gracious to Kenny and me. I placed phone calls back to the office every couple of days, I also fed reports via phone to a newspaper and to some American radio stations. We did not share the questions or the interviews we did with each other. Remember, while we were friendly we always remembered we were competitors.
>
> Ron O'Quinn, Head DJ, Swinging Radio England

Even though O'Quinn and Leighton never met, he was definitely reporting for Caroline, as the reports were read out regularly on both Caroline North and South. When a new Beatles' single or album was released, both Caroline and London claimed to have the exclusive first play. DJs would make a point of announcing their station's name over the introduction, in the middle and over the fade of the record, to prevent others from recording it and playing it as their exclusive.

It wasn't just the major, established artists that were played on Caroline, any new band or artist making their way onto the station's playlist was often on their way towards a huge chart hit. Their management would often take out advertisements in the music press announcing that their record was a Caroline SureShot!

16

OH, MISTER BENN,
YOU'RE A YOUNG MAN

Despite the friendly rivalry on air and the carefree sounds of
happy DJs playing the hits of the day, behind the scenes offshore
radio was big business and the less glamorous side of it spilled
out into the public gaze in June 1966, when Radio City on the
Shivering Sands fort was silenced by a boarding party. Major
Oliver Smedley and Kitty Black of Project Atlanta were concerned that what they still saw as their property was about to
be included in a deal with Radio London, who were about to
take control of the fort and the equipment on it. The property in
question was the transmitter supplied to Reg Calvert of Radio
City some months earlier. In Atlanta's eyes, it was a valuable piece
of equipment that still belonged to them; others saw it as useless,
after part of it had fallen into the Thames.

A group of Thames dockers were enlisted to board the fort and
prevent Radio City from broadcasting in an attempt to retrieve
the equipment. Kitty Black led the boarding party which arrived
at Shivering Sands in the early hours of Sunday 19 June 1966.

> Oliver [Smedley] said we are sick and tired of being kicked
> around by everybody else. 'Why don't we do a little bit of
> blackmailing ourselves? Why don't we go out, occupy the
> tower, prevent Calvert from carrying out the deal and make
> him cut us in on whatever arrangement?' Well, I was undoubt-
> edly young and foolish and it seemed like great fun; I had
> always been slightly browned off by the fact that I'd had to
> pledge my entire fortune in support of this project, and had
> never had any of the fun.

We all converged on Chatham and we went on board a tug with twenty riggers from the dockyard, led by a man called Big Alf. I decided that the best way of passing the time was to knit some golf stockings for a friend of mine and so I cast on the first stocking as we cast off from Chatham. At something like three in the morning we arrived off the Radio City base. Oliver said to me, 'Do you want to come with the first wave?' so we chugged along to the iron ladder up to the radio tower, shinned up this thing and the hatch was open at the top where everybody was asleep. We went inside and the riggers took possession of the transmitting station and, little by little, the crew woke up as I ran from the different towers, there were five of them linked with catwalks, and we finally got back to the main tower where they were all living. We explained that we didn't mean them any personal harm, all we wanted was the crystal which was the single item that enabled them to transmit. One of the DJs handed me an object which I proceeded to put into the pocket of my anorak; in the meantime, our lads had pulled out the wires of all the transmitting equipment from various sockets and having done all of that we climbed down the ladder and got back on board our boat, and so back to Chatham in the small hours, by which time, of course, I'd finished my golf stocking.

Kitty Black[1]

What followed made headline news around the world; a confrontation took place between Reg Calvert, owner of Radio City and Oliver Smedley at Smedley's cottage in Wendens Ambo in north Essex. Calvert was shot dead and Smedley was arrested and charged with his murder.

> *Thirty seven year old Reg Calvert, manager of many pop beat groups,*
> *including the Fortunes and owner of the offshore radio station, Radio*
> *City was shot dead in a country mansion near Saffron Walden Essex*
> *early this morning ...[2]*

Magistrates at Saffron Walden sent Smedley for trial at Chelmsford Assizes, but the charge was reduced to manslaughter; he was acquitted after it was judged that he shot Calvert in self-defence.

> When Atlanta finally failed, Smedley offered to find a backer for my father to go into partnership with him. He couldn't find anyone. When he heard about the partnership deal that my father had with Radio London, he decided, as he'd lost everything on the Atlanta project, to take over Radio City and blackmail Radio London and my father for £5,000 and 50% of the profit. Allan Crawford said he should not involve Radio Atlanta as he was totally against what Smedley was doing. Neither Phillip Birch, from Radio London, nor my father agreed to pay the blackmail ransom.
>
> Susan Moore, Reg Calvert's daughter

Throughout the trial much had been exposed of the seedier side of pirate radio. The bigger stations, such as Caroline and London, tried to distance themselves from these events immediately. As the fort invaders left, Radio City resumed broadcasting with Calvert's wife, Dorothy, taking charge, but this incident, more than any other, forced the Government into legislating against the offshore radio stations. The events around Radio City were discussed in Parliament on 22 June 1966.

> There has been a tendency perhaps to dismiss pirate radio as a matter of no great importance and no great significance, as something which is a passing episode, but the extraordinary and tragic events of the past 24 hours have perhaps impressed everyone, the Opposition as well as the Government, that piracy is piracy in whatever aspect it occurs. We have seen the hi-jacking of a pirate station, Radio City, and the taking over of that illegally occupied tower by another group equally illegally occupying it. We have seen this culminate in the shooting to death of the chief of one of the pirate ships and the captain of another accused of murder.[3]

The Postmaster General had responsibility for authorising all broadcasting in the country. At the time of the dramatic events surrounding the Shivering Sands Towers the position within the Labour Government was held by Tony Benn.

> I remember on one occasion I was listening to the radio in the morning and Radio Caroline was there and I heard the voice of somebody saying, 'Oh, Mister Benn, you're a young man', I was then in my thirties, 'and you've got young children, why shouldn't people listen to light music?' and on that I had total sympathy. The problem was that it was not done in a way that conformed to domestic or international law. I've never denied it was a very popular station, that was never the problem; as far as I was concerned, the problem was how they were stealing the copyrights and interfering with other stations, that was the only problem, nothing whatever to do with the output of the station, which was very enjoyable.
>
> Tony Benn, politician

These events surrounding Radio City were seen as the beginning of the end of Britain's pirate radio boom. Within weeks of the Shivering Sands episode, Edward Short, who'd since become Postmaster General in a Government reshuffle, announced the Government's intentions of introducing a bill to outlaw the stations before the summer recess.

The fans of the offshore stations became more vociferous, encouraged by the radio stations, who could see their business being curtailed. Various organisations were formed to lobby politicians and public opinion. The FRA (The Free Radio Association) and the Campaign for Independent Radio were two such groups. Ronan O'Rahilly announced that any such bill would be a contravention of Human Rights and any attempt to close the stations would be fought in the European courts. The Fight for Free Radio was on.

17

LeT Me Marry You ...

Despite the threat of approaching political action, the summer of 1966 is remembered as the heyday of the Sixties pirate stations. The songs in the charts sounded fabulous, many recorded by British artists, their success highlighted on the very stations that the Government was trying to abolish. Britain was an exciting place to be – these were the days of the Swinging Sixties.

Both Carolines, north and south, had entered a settled period with a fabulous sound, a huge audience and healthy income from advertisers, and the Caroline DJs were becoming as popular as the artists performing the songs they were playing. Caroline South was now competing equally with Radio London and Caroline North still had little competition. Although the hits continued, there was a presence of country and Irish music on the northern station, acknowledging the differing musical tastes in the north of England, Scotland and Ireland. Both ships kept the hits coming, whatever the weather; calm seas and sunshine, or howling winds and huge, relentless seas.

I remember the gale-force winds, thunder and lightning and waves that sloshed across the decks in a way that made you really glad that your skin doesn't leak. Thirty-five degrees side to side, at the same time the bow and stern were in competition to see which end could be higher above the waves. All this of course aggravated with the frame bending leverage that the 180ft of mast at the whim of 60 or 70mph winds would give. When the bow was high on a wave, the anchor chain was riding high, but as the wave lowered the bow, the chain followed more slowly. The bow would then begin its next ride up with another wave ... the chain still falling would finally loose it's slack and the tug of war would bounce the ship. Disc Jockeys would become ping-pong balls. Our dining table was bolted to the lounge floor, taking a meal required you to hook your legs around the table legs, your arm around your plate and your hands around your cup, racing the storm tossed chaos with your fork to get the food from plate to mouth.

Gord Cruise, news reader

Rough seas weren't just confined to the Irish Sea, despite the protection from sandbanks in the southern North Sea; Caroline South would also experience horrendous conditions, especially if the wind was from the north-east.

There can be no doubt that on a fine, calm, day it was the most beautiful place on earth, but when it was rough it was almost unbearable. We kept on broadcasting and sometimes had to crawl to the studio. A bucket was kept there as many of the guys in these conditions suffered from sea sickness but we all kept going. The hardest thing was to keep the needle on the record, we used to put a two bob coin on the stylus head to hold it down. The *Mi Amigo* was 470 tons and used to bob up and down like a cork. When the sea was coming from the front of the ship it would climb right out of the water, then there would be a sickening thud as it caught the anchor. It was a real task just staying upright.

Norman St John DJ

The newspapers thrived on stories concerning Radio Caroline and events of 22 September 1966 resulted in a truly good news story that went around the world, as DJ Mick Luvzit got married to the sister of fellow DJ, Ray Teret, on board Caroline North. A sea captain conducting a marriage on board a pirate ship was a story that didn't come around too often.

We had one particular captain who was a joy. He'd invite us up to his cabin and open up the ship's rations, the whisky and the ciggies and we'd all cram into his cabin with a guitar and we'd have a sing song and drinks flowed till dawn, he was a wonderful captain. One night he said, 'Mister Prince, why don't you let me marry you?' I said, 'because I don't fancy you' and he said, 'No, I'm serious, I am the only captain with this company who has a licence to marry people at sea, you have a girl-friend?, I'll marry you'. I told him I wasn't ready for that yet, but then it struck me; Canadian DJ Mick Luvzit was courting fellow DJ 'Ugly' Ray Terret's sister. I ran to his cabin, and he's trying to get some sleep and I woke him up saying, 'Mick, I've got a wonderful idea, propose to Jan and marry her here on Radio Caroline, you'll be world famous'. The next morning he'd given the idea more thought and spoke to the captain and within a few weeks the marriage of the year took place on the ship. It was pictured in every newspaper from here to Australia, this DJ getting married to another DJ's sister on the good ship Caroline. The day of the wedding was fantastic, we'd got all these guests on the Isle of Man, all these boats waiting to make it a big occasion, families and pop stars, all kind of groups waiting to come out, but they couldn't find us because it was foggy. We had the fog horn going and we were all out on deck looking for boats, but it finally happened and the couple were married, what a wonderful thing to be a part of.

Tony Prince, DJ

The wedding ceremony took place in the saloon of the MV *Caroline*, as Dutch Captain Martin Gips officiated over the service. It was carried out under Panamanian law in Spanish and English, and broadcast live on Radio Caroline. In 1964, when Caroline first came on air the Panamanian Government claimed that they'd withdrawn the ship's registration after British Government requests, but at the time of the wedding it became obvious that the ship was still registered in Panama. Government memos show that enquiries were made to ensure the marriage was legal.[1]

18

PAYING FOR PLAYS

Long-serving Caroline DJ Tom Lodge left the station in the autumn of 1966. He claimed that after Philip Solomon had become involved, his 'play what you want' instruction to the DJs, was being challenged and Tom was convinced that his musical format had turned Caroline's fortunes around.

> There was a guy called Tom Lodge who they made chief DJ, he caused a real stir because he was so good. He negotiated just one week on the ship at a time and he could take his wife on board. Well that did it, all the other DJs didn't like it, they said there were stockings and underwear hanging up everywhere and they got very upset. Ronan would say 'yes you can do this' to stop him from leaving and Philip would come along and say 'on yer bike'. He was getting £100 a week, which for that time was amazing; when he went, he left very quickly. New DJs coming on board were getting £25 a week and they'd keep coming in saying 'can we have a rise?' but Philip wouldn't give them anything.
>
> Carolyn Irvine, assistant press officer and secretary

One new DJ to make his mark was Johnnie Walker, who jumped ship from Swinging Radio England to Caroline. Radio England had opened in a blaze of publicity, but with its brash, quick-fire American sound had failed to capture a sizeable audience; Walker had been one of the few English voices heard on Radio England.

> My first love was always Caroline. I took a tape in and asked if I could have a job, I waited around in the reception area at

Chesterfield Gardens for about an hour. Terry Bate took a tape up to Ronan. He heard it; he liked it. Terry came back and said, 'Right, when can you start? Can you be on the boat tomorrow?' It really was as quick as that. So when I went out there I was just filling in for people on leave and then I took over the nine to twelve programme, it became the *Johnnie Walker Show*. The music I was playing was R&B and the Motown stuff, which I really loved. It seemed the natural thing to do was to play as much of that as possible on Radio Caroline and the night time was a brilliant time to be able to do that.

Johnnie Walker, DJ

Radio Caroline had made its mark by playing new music. Although going through a number of formats since its first broadcast, the DJs, with guidance, had always chosen the music they were playing, but that was about to change after a huge upheaval in Caroline House.

When I first joined, Ronan was the boss and then Philip Solomon became more involved: One day there's this great big row, a huge row and every one could hear it, banging and thumping and screaming, everyone was terrified, wondering what on earth was going on? Philip Solomon had bought a percentage of Radio Caroline and he'd understood that he'd got the ships and the whole set up, but in fact Ronan had been very clever and all he'd bought was a percentage of the airtime. From that day onwards, my job changed completely, he said, 'Right, if this is all I've got then everybody is going to pay. Unless a song's in the Top 50 then everybody else will have to pay', even the Beatles when they first bring a record out and it's not in the Top 50, everyone had to pay £100 a week and so it was my job to set up a system. I think it was four or five times a day they would be played and that started a lot of controversy, because people would sit and listen, waiting for their song to come on and if it didn't come on then all hell was let loose and it was very unpleasant.

Carolyn Irvine, assistant press officer and secretary

We did a deal with the record companies and the managers and agents that we would give them so many plugs per week for £100, this was a new company policy brought in so that Caroline could give the smaller independent record companies a proper chance to 'plug' their records and artists. The next thing is that Ronan starts creating hell. So we have a directors meeting and they throw him out and I took over. At that stage I said to Ronan, 'if you behave yourself and not interfere with my playlist I'll let you back', so that was how I began to control it.

Philip Solomon, director

We did this playlist which we sent out to the ship and the DJs went absolutely berserk, as far as they were concerned this was their job being totally demoted. They could no longer be free thinkers and play their own fabulous music, which was why we were so famous. They all got up in arms out on the ships and from that day Philip Solomon never set foot in Caroline House again.

Carolyn Irvine, assistant press officer and secretary

This new policy took on even more relevance after November 1966, when Philip Solomon started his own record label. The Major Minor record label featured recordings from a wide-ranging variety of artists, many completely unsuitable for a pop station such as Caroline – Irish folk band, The Dubliners; comedian Freddie 'Parrot Face' Davies and The Raymond Lefevre Orchestra all had regular plays on Caroline and sounded very strange when heard alongside The Who or Jimi Hendrix. Fortunately, some artists with genuine chart potential were also signed by Solomon, notably Ulster singer songwriter David McWilliams and his excellent songs were played frequently. 'The Days of Pearly Spencer' was played endlessly, but strangely it failed to enter the national charts.

'Days of Pearly Spencer' was by David McWilliams. He was a young man who came from Northern Ireland and I liked some of the material that he'd written. I introduced him to music publisher Dick Rowe and he said the man to record him would be Mike Leander, so I gave him to Mike and we produced this record which was wonderful. The Dubliners were very big, but I would say the biggest act that I had were the Bachelors, I had eighteen hits with The Bachelors.

Philip Solomon, director

Despite some songs of dubious quality getting regular plays on the radio, there can be no denying that Caroline and the other pirate stations opened up the pop music industry for countless new artists, producers and record labels. Although a number of the new labels were associated with bigger companies, most of the recordings were from independent record producers: Page One, Deram, Immediate, Reaction, Strike, Direction and of course, Major Minor, all had their share of hits, thanks to plays on pirate radio.

The Marmalade label hosted a release by the Roaring Sixties, who had been the successful Sixties band, the Ivy League, led by singer/songwriter John Carter. The song was called 'We Love the Pirate Stations' and understandably received plenty of radio plays, although not on the BBC!

We'd heard pirate radio and we loved it, we listened to it all the time and when they tried to close it down, we thought we must do something about this. It was probably a protest song of its day. The BBC banned it.

John Carter, musician and writer, The Roaring Sixties

Although the DJs were expected to follow strict management directions when it came to the playlist, they still had one of the most exciting jobs around. The conditions at sea were often extremely uncomfortable and the money wasn't as good as on Radio London but the benefits outweighed the disadvantages.

My first impression was that I'd come to a lunatic asylum. My second impression was that everyone was incredibly friendly.

There was no back biting, there was no bitching, there didn't seem to be any politics and we had an endless supply of Heineken beer. I found it a fun place to be; I had a good time while I was on Radio Caroline. Two weeks on, one week off and during the one week off, I did gigs in Chislehurst caves and various places like that. I made whole lotta money and met a whole lotta women. I loved it.

Tommy Vance, DJ

Caroline co-promoted a number of music nights with various clubs and venues, including the Chislehurst Caves in south-east London. A one-off advertising campaign soon became an on-going partnership with regular 'disc nights' attended by Caroline DJs and top recording artists.

We were running dances every Friday and Saturday night with local bands and a rep from Caroline came along and said he could do a good deal for us if he could put some of his lads in. We agreed and we had two of their DJs every Friday and Saturday night and a lot of the bands that they were promoting playing down here, for very little money. They produced some magical bands, Jimi Hendrix played down here twice for about £60 a night and we managed to pull in the biggest crowd we ever had, we had a thousand people in here, absolutely packed to capacity for a single artist and he was a brilliant act.

They produced a tape for us and put it out thirteen times a day, seven days a week, it was amazing, it was just like turning on a tap, people came from miles around, thousands of them. There were queues out to the road and we had to take on extra staff, it was brilliant advertising, it was certainly effective.

Jim Gardner, Chislehurst Caves

Since Caroline North first arrived off the coast of the Isle of Man, she'd broadcast on a frequency close to 199 metres, but as 1966 came to an end, a series of overnight test transmissions resulted in a move to a frequency that was close to 259. Both

Radio Caroline services were now announced as being on the same frequency, but little of the output was shared. Other than commercials that were booked on both stations and competitions such as Cash Casino, each Caroline had its own unique sound and approach to broadcasting. Caroline, like the other offshore stations, also broadcast a limited number of religious programmes which produced good income, but at a cost, such programmes were a turn off for many listeners.

19

THE FIGHT FOR FREE RADIO

The Government continued with their plan to rid the air-waves of 'the pirates' and a number of radio stations, including Caroline, looked at ways of evading the proposed law by using foreign crews, DJs and advertising. It was reported that Ronan O'Rahilly had spent more than £10,000 adapting HM Fort Roughs (Roughs Tower) off Harwich for use after the new Act was passed. The Roughs was another wartime defence fort which, unlike similar forts that had been used for radio stations, was outside territorial limits and ideally suited as a future supply base for Caroline South. Newspapers were told that the plan was to turn the manmade island into a health farm for exhausted people in the entertainment business; Ronan O'Rahilly also disclosed plans to turn the lower, darker, damp part of the tower into a mushroom farm!

> I spent a day and a night there not long ago, you go into such a deep sleep. This is partly due to the sea air and partly due to the rhythm of the waves.
>
> Ronan O'Rahilly[1]

> The idea of a health farm was mine; I just said it when the press got hold of it. We were going to put TV towers up, radio, the lot on there. We had two guys out there, holding it, but something happened and one got burnt and they had to come ashore. Roy Bates got to hear of it and put his people on it.
>
> Terry Bate, head of sales

There'd been a Caroline presence on the Roughs Tower since August 1965,[2] when Bill Scadden landed two men on the tower with supplies. Possession was maintained by Ronan O'Rahilly's men throughout 1966, but on 23 December they were forcibly evicted by a raiding party organised by Roy Bates. He had operated Radio Essex on the Knock John Fort further down the coast which *was* within British waters and had been forced to close. An agreement between Bates and O'Rahilly was then made to share the fort, but when the Caroline men had to leave the Roughs because of illness, Bates refused to let them back. Several attempts were made by O'Rahilly's men to recapture the fort, and on 24 June 1967 petrol bombs and shots were fired at them from the tower. One man was left dangling from a rope-ladder after their boat was attacked and forced to withdraw with the wheelhouse burning, the lifeboat was called to rescue the stranded man. Ronan O'Rahilly said he was confident that he would regain control of the tower, but the Bates family went on to declare the tower the Independent State of Sealand and they still control the structure today.

There was a similar fort, at the Sunk Head that was also outside territorial waters. It had been the base for Tower Radio in 1966, but that station wasn't viable. Any possibility of it being used in the future ended on 18 August 1967, when a detachment of Royal Engineers boarded the fort and prepared explosives that were detonated during the afternoon of 21 August, destroying the structure. The huge explosion was heard all along the Essex coast as hundreds of tons of concrete and iron were fired high into the sky.

As the 'summer of love' got underway, the date was announced for the introduction of the Government's Marine etc, Broadcasting Offences Act. The pirate stations were to be outlawed from midnight on 14 August 1967. Radio Caroline confirmed that its two ships would continue to broadcast after the law was introduced, but on board the ships, there was much speculation as to what might happen. Australian DJ Ian MacRae remembered an event just a few days before the Act became law:

It was quite late, I'd just finished a shift and I walked out on the deck of the *Mi Amigo*. It was a calm, placid night and a fog had come in. I heard the throb of approaching engines and I thought, 'this is a big ship coming our way'. As the lights came out of the fog I thought, 'I hope he knows we're here'. He did; it was a Royal Navy ship. I heard the engines reverse and I was convinced that we were in trouble, 'they're gonna tow us in' I was thinking, 'and I'm the only guy really up and about on Caroline, apart from the fella on air'. This guy was up on the bridge and had a loud hailer and he said, 'Ahoy Caroline.' I said, 'er, yes, hello', 'Can you play the lads "A Whiter Shade of Pale?"' I thought why not … and away they went. Never saw them again.

Ian Macrae, DJ

Politicians on the Isle of Man battled for exemption to the bill to enable Caroline North to continue. The radio station had become a very popular asset, promoting tourism and business on the island, but the people of the island were angry at what they saw as London overruling their right of autonomy. For a while it looked as if the might of the Westminster Government would be defeated by the island's historic Tynwald parliament, claiming that one state could not make a law for another, but ultimately the bill was passed and became law for the Isle of Man also on 1 September 1967.

It would now be an offence for any British subject to broad-cast, work for or advertise on, promote or assist any vessel, aircraft or structure that was involved in broadcasting to the British Isles from outside territorial waters. As an Irish-American, Ronan O'Rahilly and Philip Solomon, who'd become an Irish passport holder, wouldn't be directly affected. O'Rahilly maintained that Caroline's future looked good, beyond 14 August.

As far as the public is concerned they will think there has been no change, but in fact supplies will be coming from other places than Britain, advertising will be coming from other countries than British, they cannot be British companies, but I would say in a year's time Caroline will be stronger than ever.[3]

In a year's time we will be choc-a-bloc with advertisements
for Japanese transistors, South African oranges and many other
products that have nothing to do with Britain.[4]

The time had come for those working for Radio Caroline to
stay or go. Until now Caroline had operated legally, albeit using
loopholes in various laws, to stay afloat, but now British staff
had to decide if their convictions were strong enough to defy
the law.

> It was a time when everyone concerned still believed that
> Ronan remained the boss, me included. I had taken on a lot
> of new responsibility regarding the day-to-day running of
> the south ship. It was Ronan who gave me the job of senior
> DJ. It was also a time when Phil Solomon and Ronan where
> at loggerheads over programming and money. Both Ronan
> and Phil knew that some of the team would back down
> and be out the door when faced with exile or a spell in jail
> should they return to the UK. In his final analysis Ronan, the
> shrewder of the two, recognised his severe shortage of funds
> would get the Caroline organisation and himself nowhere. He
> knew Phil had money in the bank and that Phil would want
> to call the shots in the immediate future. It was Money bags
> verses Ronan Radio.
>
> Robbie Dale, head DJ, Caroline South

The board members of Planet Productions resigned on 1 August
1967 and Caroline House in London was closed down, as an
office was set up in Holland.

> They all got their money back and a few dollars more, I think
> there was £600,000 left at the end and that went to Mid-
> Atlantic films which was Ronan's film company and went to
> make the film *Girl On A Motorcycle*. I set up the office at Singel
> 160 in Amsterdam.
>
> Terry Bate, head of sales

Most of those working in the London headquarters left Caroline
and moved on to other jobs, although some were offered the
chance to stay with the organisation.

> I did commercials, sometimes about ten different commercials
> a day, and voice overs, and that is why I was lucky and stayed
> on land. I was there until the very end and they said, 'would
> you like to come to Amsterdam with us?' but I thought, 'I
> don't know, if I go over there I've finished with my career in
> acting and television.
>
> Carl Conway, DJ

> As the Marine Offences Act approached I was given the
> opportunity to go out to the ship along with Robbie Dale
> and Johnnie Walker, the offer was to read the news and do the
> occasional music programme, it just didn't appeal to me, it was
> a very hard decision, but I said no.
>
> Colin Berry, news reader/commercial traffic

In the days leading up to the Marine Offences Day the Caroline
South DJs Johnnie Walker and Robbie Dale appeared at a
number of events where they were encouraged by the response
from huge numbers of supportive fans. They'd made it clear that
they intended to stay on.

> I remember a very big party, it was very emotional with a lot
> of bands here just for the hell of playing for the farewell party.
> The lads who were going back to the boat were well the worse
> for drink by the time that it all finished, yes it was very emo-
> tional and sad, because we'd all had a tremendous time for a
> couple of years, and that was it, off they went and we've never
> seen them since.
>
> Jim Gardner, Chislehurst Caves

caroline continues

On Monday 14 August, Walker and Dale left England to go to the ship for the last time, legally. But when they arrived on board they were shocked to find that most of their colleagues who had planned to stay and defy the law had changed their minds and were returning to shore. The two DJs, together with news reader Ross Brown, were faced with running what had, until now, been a twenty-four-hour radio station between them.

> Johnnie and I had been teamed up on the same shift for some time, gigging and partying around the night club scene in London. For me, I may have fallen in love with the fantasy of being exiled, it didn't bother me at all; it was another adventure. The last thing that I expected was to be greeted by a united front of DJ staff wanting to get off the boat that day. I expected some would jump ship but not all of them. I found it hard to understand; they were giving up this great opportunity to participate in something very special. By leaving they could be seen instantly as cowards in the eyes of some listeners, rats leaving a sinking ship.
>
> Robbie Dale, head DJ, Caroline South

Disc Jockey Roger Day had been a Caroline presenter prior to the Act and would return to the station later, but on this day he went ashore – he had to renew his passport!

> They did point out, 'you know you'd be risking a heavy fine and a period in jail?' and I said, 'yes, it's a matter of principal.

They can do what they like to me; they're not gonna scare me off.' We were on our own and we had every listener there was going, it was fantastic. We must have had the largest commercial radio audience ever, 'cos all the Radio London people would have flicked on to us, because, basically there wasn't anything else, just the old Light Programme in those days. You just felt that everybody was with you, particularly after the Marine Offences Act became law.

Roger Day, DJ

One by one all of the remaining pirate radio stations closed down with the exception of Caroline North and South. The most financially successful station of them all, Radio London, closed at 3 p.m. on that Monday afternoon, 14 August, playing 'A Day in the Life' by The Beatles hours before the Act became law.

Big L time is three o'clock and Radio London is now closing down.

As Big L's listeners re-tuned their radio to Caroline South, in search of pop music, on that Monday afternoon Robbie Dale went on air and paid tribute to Radio London and marked its closure with a one-minute silence.

Millions of Radio London listeners have just joined us as a sister station in commercial broadcasting has just closed and, once again, Caroline is alone.

The decision to continue broadcasting past August 1967 was Ronan O'Rahilly's. I was totally supportive of his decision and his determination to continue. We were concerned, to a degree, about the seriousness of the ramifications that we could face, but I was convinced that the Wilson Government wouldn't move against the ships aggressively. Public opinion was on our side, there was an amazing buzz in the air and the excitement was unbelievable.

Robbie Dale, head DJ, Caroline South

I thought, if Radio Caroline is going to keep on going I wouldn't want not be a part of it. There was definitely a principle, here we have something that is not doing any harm to anyone, and all that baloney the Government put out about blocking emergency frequencies and all that, it was all hogwash, it really was. So I thought it was a very important point of principle. The ship was never illegal, it was not illegal to do what we were doing in international waters, if we did it within the national waters of England then obviously it would be, so I thought, if Radio Caroline is going to carry on I definitely want to be a part of it.

Johnnie Walker, DJ

As midnight approached the last legal British commercial was played, for Consulate cigarettes, and Johnnie Walker prepared for his first announcement on the renamed Radio Caroline International. Accompanied by the Caroline theme by the Fortunes, 'All You Need is Love' by The Beatles and the civil rights anthem, 'We shall overcome', Johnnie Walker spoke to the huge audience, eagerly listening to see if Caroline would be true to their word.

> *This is Radio Caroline it is now twelve midnight … Radio Caroline would like to extend its thanks to Mister Harold Wilson and his Labour Government for at last, after over three and a half years of broadcasting, recognising this station's legality. Its right to be here, its right to be broadcasting to Great Britain and the Continent, its right to give the music and service to the peoples of Europe, which we have been doing since Easter Sunday 1964 and we in turn recognise your right as our listener to have freedom of choice in your radio entertainment and of course that Radio Caroline belongs to you. It is your radio station, even though it costs you nothing and, as we enter this new phase in our broadcasting history, you, naturally, have our assurance that we intend to stay on the air, because we belong to you … and we love you – Caroline continues.*

Because of the delay in the introduction of the law on the Isle of Man, commercials continued to be played and supplies delivered legally until 1 September for Caroline North. Much to the delight of journalists, the Caroline North team were involved in a football match in St Helens against a Post Office team, just days before the Act became law. It was the Postmaster General who had responsibility for ridding the airwaves of the 'pirate' stations. Hours before the new law came into force, Ronan O'Rahilly visited the ship to give words of encouragement to the remaining DJs, led by Canadian Don Allen. A few new recruits also went out on that last tender from Ramsey to be faced, like the south ship, with a departing crew of DJs not prepared to stay on once the new law was introduced. It was Don Allen who made the first announcement at midnight on 1 September 1967 on Radio Caroline North.

> *Good evening ladies and gentlemen. It's now twelve midnight on Radio Caroline North, broadcasting on 259 metres in the medium wave band. You're listening to the continuing voice of free radio for the British Isles, Caroline North, national and international. It now gives us great pleasure to play for you the Manx national anthem, 'Oh Land of Our Birth'.*

A great tribute to us was the IOM steamer SS *Manxman*, which brought hundreds of fans to take a look at the MV *Caroline* on the afternoon before we entered into so-called illegality. Mark Sloane took the roving microphone on deck and gave a commentary of this event, heavily punctuated by the sound of ships whistles from both the *Manxman* and the *Caroline*. With fewer DJs our shows were increased from three to four hours, so in effect four DJs and one radio engineer were running the station. The ship's crew, provided by Wijsmuller, had been reduced to about five: the captain, a marine engineer and three seamen, which included a cook and steward. The tender now came from Dundalk, about 70 miles away, in the Irish Republic. The journey to Ireland was never pleasant; the vessel was originally an inshore fishing boat and lacked accommodation for passengers and was heavily weighed down with extra

fresh-water tanks below deck and large cylindrical fuel tanks
strapped either side of the wheelhouse.

Martin Kayne, DJ

Support staff were still needed on land, Carolyn Irvine was one of
the few to move from Caroline House and stay with the organisation. She was to look after the north ship and was now based
in Ireland.

When I went out I was living in a hotel, I had a section of an
antiquated record company office in Grafton Street, Dublin. I
was still filling out the playlists for Philip Solomon and I lasted
about a month, then told Philip I was leaving, he was very
angry. I did help him to find somebody, trained them up and
then left.

Carolyn Irvine, assistant press officer and secretary

For six weeks Radio Caroline International had the airwaves
to herself. Following the legislation to outlaw the radio ships, a
new pop music service was to be provided by the BBC. Radio 1
would fill the void left by the pirates according to the politicians,
but not until 30 September 1967, when former Caroline DJ Tony
Blackburn introduced the first *Radio 1 Breakfast Show*. With a
mixture of pop and middle-of-the-road music presented by an
assortment of former pirates and established BBC entertainers,
such as Jimmy Young, the new BBC radio station was seen by
many as frumpy and boring and without the fun and spontaneity
of the pirates.

Caroline continued, but with many obvious 'plug' records
and endless references to recordings on the Major Minor label.
Surprisingly commercials continued as before for many big
name products, including Horlicks, Pernod, Peter Stuyvesant
and Consulate cigarettes, together with new commercials
for international companies like Ford, Coca Cola and Schick
razor blades. Ronan O'Rahilly had claimed that advertising
foreign products would enable Caroline to continue. Some of

the smaller companies that had advertised in the past also had
their commercials broadcast, publicly these companies complained, but Ronan O'Rahilly insisted that all the commercials
had been paid for. As it was now illegal for British companies
to advertise on Caroline, it was thought that by running a campaign of confusion, the authorities would be unable to spot any
'paid for' ads amongst the 'spoof' ads that Caroline continued
to broadcast, although it's doubtful that money ever changed
hands for any of the ads heard after 14 August. The commercials
were being played from old tape cartridges onboard the ships,
recordings from American radio stations and even commercials
obviously recorded with a microphone from the television in
the ship's lounge.

> We expected the advertising to stop, but it didn't and our
> advert kept coming out thirteen times day, seven days a week
> for another four months, which put a lot of people's backs up.
> We had lads from the Home Office down asking serious ques-
> tions and threatening death and disaster, but there was nothing
> we could do about it; they were out on a boat and we couldn't
> contact them. All their offices were shut down; there was
> nobody from Caroline in the country.
>
>   Jim Gardner, Chislehurst Caves

> *With offices in Amsterdam, Paris, New York and Toronto this is Radio*
> *Caroline International on 259 metre medium wave, the continuing*
> *voice of free radio.*

All contact with the UK was banned for those involved with the
Caroline ships and the DJs had become outlaws, unable, legally,
to return to the country. The official base for the station was
Amsterdam; the Northern ship had an office in Dublin, but both
Ronan O'Rahilly and Philip Solomon still had their offices in
London and regular contact with the ships continued via clan-
destine radio links. Small boats from the Essex coast were also
making occasional deliveries to Caroline South.

They used to come out from Frinton and Walton and places like that on boats and occasionally when we needed some supplies. In fact we didn't even need to ask for them, we'd just give some sort of hint on air and out would come steaks and things and papers and various bits and pieces. We'd also get a lot of visitors coming out to the ship. It was a great pleasure. One interesting event was when a fishing boat turned up and brought records and news of what was happening ashore and cash for everyone, a little bonus from Phil Solomon.

Robbie Dale, head DJ, Caroline South

It was the hardest time in terms of living, in terms of supplies, in terms of getting time off in Holland, but in terms of broadcasting and being involved with Caroline it was just the most exciting time, they were Caroline's finest hours.

Johnnie Walker, DJ

Those tuned to the Johnnie Walker show were able to communicate with the DJs by taking part in Frinton Flashing. The whole Caroline crew would often take to the decks and hold a conversation with their listeners parked in cars on the Greensward at Frinton-on-Sea, 3 miles away and in sight of the *Mi Amigo*. Once identified by attracting the attention of the DJs by continually flashing their car headlights, the occupants of a particular car would then be invited to flash out letters of the alphabet to spell their name and the car they were in. For the exercise to work properly, a car containing groups of young men would be teamed up with a car containing young ladies, and even if you weren't involved it was great fun to listen to. Two flashes for 'yes' and one for 'no'!

There were uncertainties about the full powers of the Marine Offences Act. Granada TV's 'World in Action' team attempted to film aboard the *Mi Amigo*, but the captain of their chartered ship was forced to anchor some way off the Caroline ship while frantic negotiations went on with officials on land to confirm whether the TV team would be breaking the law by boarding Caroline.

The uncertainty followed a warning that they'd be unable to return to a UK port. The stand-off resulted in front-page newspaper headlines, giving Caroline another welcome burst of free publicity. There were also threats from Caroline that tapes exposing 'the secret life of Prime Minister Harold Wilson' would be broadcast, but that story quietly went away.

It wasn't all fun on board though. Rough seas delayed tenders, resulting in longer spells on board than anticipated, shortages of supplies and having to play some dire 'plug' records in amongst the gems took its toll on the on-air crew.

> In the days after 14 August Mother Nature seemed to be against us. We had a terrible winter and it was like Caroline had been forgotten. So I sat up one night and I wrote this positive dream of Caroline actually winning and sailing up the Thames and being welcomed as a legitimate radio station. I think I went over the top on the sort of Churchillian acting performance and I find it a bit embarrassing now, but at the time it was just a good morale booster for us on the ship and the listeners and we played it regularly just to emphasise something positive. It became known as Man's Fight For Freedom.
>
> Johnnie Walker, DJ

As Christmas 1967 approached, there were signs that all was not well aboard Caroline. Supplies and new records were failing to get through; the American charts were highlighted in an attempt to give the programmes a fresher sound as it became more difficult to keep ahead of the British charts. Johnnie Walker, renowned for telling his audience 'how it was,' let his discontent be known on air.

> *We are almost out of water. The supply tender has not been near for almost two-and-a-half-weeks. We need supplies, especially eggs. I have been stuck on this ship for a month: no letters, no contact with my parents, no hot water, no decent wash and no contact with people.*

Fellow DJ, Andy Archer, shared Walker's distaste of the 'plug' records, but unlike the station's star DJ, wasn't in a position to do anything about it.

One evening I was walking on deck when all of a sudden I saw flashes of phosphorescence in the sea which was as calm as a mill pond. I then spotted black Frisbee-like objects flying out of the studio window that were causing the disturbance in the water. As I reached the open studio window, Johnnie's head appeared. 'That's it, I've got rid of the f★★★ing lot of them'.

In one foul swoop, Johnnie had successfully de-cluttered the ship of every 'plug' record on board! I don't know exactly what was said to him, but I do remember that the rest of us were eternally grateful for his bravado. It meant, for a few days at least, we had the freedom to play whatever we wanted until a new batch of replacement 'plug' records arrived on the next tender. Johnnie was our greatest asset, a fact Philip Solomon was well aware of. I suspect if one of us lesser mortals had been foolhardy enough to take the same action, we would have been ceremoniously keelhauled.

Andy Archer, DJ[1]

I was lucky to have an insider at Major Minor, Joan Thurkettle, she later became a reporter with LBC and ITN, but at the time Joan worked for Phil in the London office, putting together play lists and writing threatening memos to go out to the ships. It took some time but I finally convinced Solomon that giving Johnnie Walker some responsibility would have him realise Caroline needed not only star jocks but team leaders in the radio business. I think we finally convinced him that 'pay for plays' was the only way to survive and put food on the table.

Robbie Dale, head DJ, Caroline South

Other than the 'official' messages, news of everyday events on the ship was also getting ashore to the Amsterdam office, which was being run by a demure, middle-aged English woman, Nan Richardson. Her husband, Don, was an engineer on the ship and she claimed that they were so close as to be telepathic. On their return to shore, the DJs would be amazed to find that Nan knew of events on board before they got to the office. The explanation was later discovered, Don, in the middle of the night after Caroline had gone off air would send his wife details of all the day's events over the powerful 50,000 watt transmitter, millions of listeners, or even Government officials could have eavesdropped and found out exactly what was happening behind the scenes.

The possibility of jamming Caroline's programmes was again investigated by GPO officials as the Government attempted to curtail their activities, although the radio station itself wasn't illegal; it was the activity surrounding it that was against the new law.

> If it is accepted that a sterilisation of the offending transmissions could be achieved for the majority of users by laying down an adequate interfering signal in large centres of population, the desired result could probably be achieved …[2]

Caroline had survived for almost six months since the new law had been introduced; those thought to be running the organisation were interviewed by police and Home Office officials. Ronan O'Rahilly was asked if he ran Planet Productions from the UK.

> *Negative, I don't exist really. I'm not being negative. The company does not really exist nowadays; it was taken out of the country.*
> Ronan O'Rahilly[3]

Philip Solomon was interviewed in his London office and questioned about the link between Major Minor records and Caroline. He was asked why every record he produced was advertised on Radio Caroline and Major Minor was mentioned about forty times a day.

I give them (records) to agents in Holland – I have agents all over the world – and he places them … It's up to him.

Philip Solomon, director[4]

Original shareholders were also interviewed; they all said that they were no longer involved and those who'd owned shares had sold them 'for two shillings each to a man from the Bahamas'.[5] Transcripts of Caroline programmes were made, including mentions of records on the Major Minor label and observations of boats seen close to the *Mi Amigo* were recorded, but no criminal charges were brought.

We tried every avenue to continue, we were controlling it in England and the Government didn't like it. I was investigated; they were going to put me in jail, so I moved the operation to Dublin. There was a man there called Charlie Haughey, he later became the Taoiseach [Head of the Irish Parliament] and he was very sympathetic to us and if there was anything he could do to damage the British Government he was happy to do. He said, 'Run your operation from here. Every time the British Government ask for us to pass a law I will get one of my people in parliament to put a private members bill in and it means the British request will go to the bottom of the pile again'. We ran it successfully from Grafton Street in Dublin and then I got a bit fed up with it.

Philip Solomon, director

21

CUTTING THE CHAIN

Despite attention from the authorities and the bad weather, it was lack of money, or certainly lack of payments being made, that brought an end to the programmes of Radio Caroline in the Sixties. As the transmitter was switched off at 2 a.m. on Sunday 3 March 1968, Andy Archer, unknowingly, had presented the last programme on Caroline South.

> I remember the last programme I did was from midnight to two. Carl Mitchell, who normally presented the programme, was off and it was the one programme that we all enjoyed doing because after twelve we didn't have to play plug records. You could play some fantastic songs and it was a real pleasure to go on and have free choice for a couple of hours. I'd played some pretty good music on that last night, but just as a bit of a joke I played the number one record of the day to finish, which was 'Cinderella Rockafella' by Esther and Abi Ofarim, which is probably one of the worst records ever made, I suppose it was the last record played on Caroline. I went to bed and then in the morning we were all woken up when this huge tug tied up alongside.
>
> Andy Archer, DJ[1]

The Wijsmuller tug *Titan*, tied up alongside the *Mi Amigo* and, at around the same time the crew of another tug, the *Utrecht*, boarded Caroline North. On the south ship, Roger Day was preparing for his breakfast programme.

I was getting ready to do the breakfast show and I heard this throbbing engine alongside, nothing unusual, but I wondered 'what's going on there?' It was just after five I guess – I used to go on air at six. It was the Wijsmuller tug *Titan*, which was in the area and just happened to call in, or so I thought. This was nothing unusual as their friends and workmates, our crew on the *Mi Amigo*, also worked for Wijsmuller. I knew some of them; I said 'how are you?' and they said 'ah, Englishman, we're towing you to Tokyo.' I was getting the studio ready to go on air at six and these rather beefy chaps who had been my friends until then came in and ordered me out of the studio. I said, 'Why, what's happening?' 'We have to go to Holland for a refit,' was the reply. We weren't allowed in the studio, they cut the anchor chain and we were towed to Amsterdam. Everybody was crying their eyes out because we knew it was the end, although we all tried to put on a brave face.

Roger Day, DJ

As preparations were being made to tow the *Mi Amigo* away from her mooring off the Essex coast, similar events were taking place off the Isle of Man. Disc jockey Roger Scott had arrived on board just days earlier.

Being a Saturday we had the *Don Allen Country and Western Jamboree Show*, and then the station closed down for the night at 10 p.m. We were woken when the tug came and there on board were these burly Dutch guys saying, 'That's it, that's all', they locked the studio and took the crystal out of the transmitter and it was all over. They cut the anchor chain and we embarked on a journey past Wales and around Land's End and we ended up in Amsterdam on the following Saturday. None of us knew what the future held.

Roger Scott, DJ

This was the saddest time of all; it was the most inglorious end there could ever be. We'd heard rumours on the boat that something had gone wrong with the financial structure of Caroline. The Dutch company that made the continuance of the ship possible in terms of the crew, diesel oil for the generators, food, that sort of thing, hadn't been paid for quite some time and they reached a point where they thought, 'well it doesn't look like we're going to get paid at all so the only way to recoup our losses is to nick the boats'. At 5.30 in the morning there was a massive banging on the door of my cabin, 'wake up, wake up, they've come to tow us away' and I'd only got to bed a couple of hours before. I got out of bed, went upstairs half asleep and there's something like fifteen large, threatening Dutch sailors on board, who just said, 'we're sealing up the studios and that's it, you're finished'. We thought well maybe they've come to take us to Amsterdam to be serviced ready to come back out again. But in that case they would have taken the anchor chain and put it on a buoy so that we could reconnect when the boat came back, it was a massive anchor and it's a huge operation to put that anchor down in the sea, but they just cut the chain and let it fall in the water, I knew then that was probably it. They towed the boat across the North Sea, down the canal into Amsterdam. We hung around there for a few days, hoping to find out what was going on, nobody seemed to know, but for me that was the end, the end of the dream.

The worst thing was that I knew there were thousands of people turning on their radios and not hearing anything and fiddling with the tuning knob and thinking 'what's happened to Caroline, has it shifted frequency, is it just off for a couple of hours, will it be coming back?', and them not knowing what was happening, that was the most awful thing. For us to be there one minute, happy and doing the programmes as we'd always done and the next day, dead silence. I was terribly upset about that, that we didn't have a chance to say goodbye, or, terribly sorry but we have to go off the air, thanks for everything in the past, but … that's it., but suddenly just to disappear like that without any warning or explanation was the worst part about it for me.

Johnnie Walker, DJ

The *Mi Amigo* was first to arrive in Amsterdam amid much speculation as to what had happened. The newspapers were asking 'Is this the end?' Statements from various people connected to Caroline suggested that work needed to be done to the ships and they would return to sea. There was a belief that the financial crisis could be resolved but, as with everything connected with Radio Caroline, the situation was unclear. Days after the arrival of Caroline South, the north ship arrived and was tied up alongside the *Mi Amigo*.

We arrived in Amsterdam via the canal, when we got there the south ship was already there. There were no wildly cheering crowds and we must have had amazing egos because I remember this being something of a disappointment that people weren't out to welcome home the Caroline North ship; it was a very low-key arrival. Remarkably, there was this guy, I think he was an agent for Ronan, and he had some money for us, so we got paid off, that was very positive, I don't think any of us were expecting that and then that same day I flew back to London.

Roger Scott, DJ

It soon became clear that the Caroline ships would remain impounded in Amsterdam. Wijsmuller had been very much a part of offshore radio in the UK. They'd been involved before the start of Radio Caroline, yet it seemed that they had brought the dream to an end. Robbie Dale knew more of what was going on behind the scenes than others on the ship

Phil's failure to pay the Wijsmuller brothers was what some would call a business tactic that went badly wrong. At the time I felt that I had Phil Solomon's ear but no influence with his cheque book. He could be cool under pressure, as sweet as pie, then in his next breath would calmly fire everyone including me or shout, 'get out of here and never come back'.

In hindsight, the usually tough guys at Wijsmuller were somewhat sympathetic in their understanding of the plight of the Caroline ships and demonstrated this by extending credit way beyond a few months. I suppose they also considered the feelings and stomachs of the Dutch crew, many of whom had given service on other company ships and tugs in the Wijsmuller group.

Whilst ashore in Holland, I met the Wijsmullers, passing on Phil's promise of payment. I pleaded with Phil several times to pay something to the brothers. More than once Phil gave me his assurances that he would pay within days, a week at most. It's important to remember, it was Phil Solomon who had stepped up and paid the entire cost for the *Mi Amigo* refit some time earlier.

Phil had big bucks invested in the so called 'pirate' radio business; he wanted to see the return of his money as quickly as possible and he knew time was running out fast. When the brothers ordered the tow in of the ships the 'outstanding monies' as Phil would call it, was what the brothers had lost and this was the only chance of earning it back in the future. The money was in his bank, but the logistics of taking the ships out again was beyond Phil Solomon's reason, according to him the brothers Wijsmuller were impetuous.

Robbie Dale, head DJ, Caroline South

Ronan O'Rahilly had done such a terrible deal with the people providing the trawlers [Wijsmuller] that were going out to feed it and take the men on and off the boats, that it was very hard to make money. I had regular meetings with Johnnie Walker and Robbie Dale. I liked them very much, Robbie Dale was one of my friends – but I got 'browned off' with it, I backed out and I said, 'you've got my money'; I've had good value out of it because I made a lot of hits.

Phil Solomon

The ships were both towed to a remote area of Amsterdam harbour, their future uncertain, but within days an attempt was made to get Caroline back on air, making a fresh start from another ship. A trusted team were enlisted to be part of a new Caroline, with negotiations to buy the former Radio 270 ship, the *Oceaan* 7 which was still moored in Whitby, where she had lain since 14 August 1967, when Radio 270 had closed. With financial assistance from the Free Radio Association, the plan was to relaunch Caroline from the fully fitted radio ship that had been used off the Yorkshire coast until the anti-pirate law was introduced. The team travelled to Yorkshire and were very close to sealing the deal. Andy Archer was one of the chosen few.

Ronan put his close friend and confidante Jimmy Houlihan in charge of the operation. Jimmy was a giant of a man, a former boxer, nightclub bouncer and had worked for the unscrupulous London landlord Peter Rachman in the early 1960s. Despite his somewhat dodgy past, Jimmy was a gentle soul and the only person in London I think Ronan really trusted. Disc jockeys Don Allen, Roger Scott, Mark West, radio engineer Ray Glennister and me found the ship lying on its side on the muddy river bank with its mast extending over a hedgerow and into a neighbouring field. We had to wait until the tide turned and she righted herself before we could climb aboard. With the exception of Mark West, who had previously worked for Radio 270, we were all surprised by its size – not much bigger than Radio Caroline's tender *Offshore One*. The living quarters for the disc jockeys and crew were situated in just one large room. There was a long table with benches either side, a dozen bunks lined the walls, two tiny studios, a galley, the transmitter and engine room and that was it. Ronan was in continual telephone contact with Jimmy, he was keen to get the ship out to sea as soon as possible before the authorities got wind of our plans, but speculation was rife in the town about the return of Radio 270 and it wasn't long before our cover was blown, the deal fell through and we went back to London.

Andy Archer, DJ[2]

Two years before his death I asked Phil Solomon why he thought Caroline had closed in 1968:

'I haven't a clue … I honestly couldn't answer that. I think they needed a new bottom of the boat for one thing.'

'There've been suggestions that bills to the tender company weren't paid. Were you aware of that?'

'No, I was not aware of that.'

'Were you involved with any attempt to get Caroline back on the air?'

'No, I was so busy with other things that I treated it as a chapter in my life that had finished.

Radio Caroline was finished, her listeners reluctantly tuned to BBC Radio 1, although some were able to listen to Radio Veronica. Despite the programmes being broadcast in Dutch they were playing English pop songs and it was an offshore pirate radio station, and to capitalise on this, former Caroline DJ Robbie Dale was hired by Veronica. Meanwhile the Caroline ships were left abandoned and rusting away in a secluded Amsterdam back-water at the mercy of vandals and thieves.

22

TeLeVISION, WHO DO YOU THINK YOU are KIDDING … ?

One year on from the closure of Radio Caroline and a one-hour *Caroline Revival Hour*, featuring music and historic recordings, was presented by Caroline North DJ Don Allen on 2 March 1969. Airtime had been hired on Radio Andorra by a free radio group. The hope was that this programme could lead to regular Caroline-style broadcasts, but the signal was almost inaudible in Britain and as the programme went out at 2 a.m. UK time; the audience was small.

Many land-based pirate radio stations sprang up around the country, most were low powered, amateur 'hobby stations' operated by radio enthusiasts, usually at weekends. These operators risked prosecution in order to continue 'the fight for free radio', but some, like Radio Jackie in South London, were more professional and more tenacious. The Dutch offshore station Veronica became a haven for many Caroline listeners. With legal commercial radio some years off, Veronica was the only daytime alternative for those listeners who felt that tuning into the BBC was like throwing in the towel, but when, in April 1969, even Johnnie Walker joined Radio 1 it seemed that the pirate dream was over … or was it?

Reports appeared in a number of newspapers with claims that Caroline Television was about to start beaming programmes from a Super Constellation aircraft flying at 20,000ft above the North Sea. Two aircraft had been bought, according to publicity, for nearly £1 million. A pre-recorded pop programme was planned, to be broadcast at 6 p.m. every evening, followed by films until 2 a.m. Ronan O'Rahilly and George Drummond, both directors of Mid-Atlantic Film Holdings Ltd, were said to be behind the project; Drummond was a wealthy friend of O'Rahilly and an heir to a Scottish Drummond banking family. At his request Mr Drummond met with the Minister of Posts and Telecommunications, John Stonehouse, and other Government officials in December 1969 to discuss the project. Mr Drummond claimed that he and two American partners were behind the project, that £600,000 had been invested in the enterprise, an aircraft was available in the United States and broadcasts to the UK from international airspace would start over the Christmas period. He claimed that American advertisers were willing to back the project as they believed the Government wouldn't act against Caroline TV.[1]

With Christmas approaching, officials went to great lengths to prepare for the broadcasts and to do all in their power to curtail them. Embassy staff around Europe searched for the foreign airfield that would house the aircraft. The possibility of jamming the broadcasts was discussed in great detail; experts in America provided technical details of similar equipment used in US military experiments and press releases were prepared rebuking the project. Foreign flight plans were to be scrutinised, the UK's defence radar system was on standby to identify any aircraft used and military aircraft were to intercept any flights.

Despite the belief that the broadcasts would fail, the threat was taken very seriously – but the Christmas broadcasts failed to materialise.[2]

Radio Veronica had been on air off the coast of Holland since 1960 and was accepted as part of daily life in the Netherlands, but in January 1970 a new radio ship anchored close to the *Norderney*, Veronica's ship. Radio North Sea International (RNI) broadcast from the multi-coloured *Mebo 2*, the best equipped radio ship yet, bristling with a variety of transmitters and modern studio equipment. But RNI struggled to establish itself, despite former Caroline DJs Roger Day, Andy Archer and Carl Mitchell joining the station. A variety of frequencies, suffering from or causing interference and an ill-judged move to the English coast, resulted in the British Government taking the extreme measure of jamming the radio station, something that hadn't even been done in wartime. The jamming signal made listening to the radio station difficult, but not impossible. The regular pulsating bleep could be partly avoided by turning the radio away from the direction of the jamming signal, and the radio station's short-wave and FM signals were unaffected. As the 1970 general election approached and the jamming continued, RNI became involved in the politics of the time and just five days before the general election, Radio North Sea changed its name.

> *Stand by for an important news development ... The unbelievable has happened, welcome to the return of Radio Caroline International.*

The Caroline jingles were used again, together with the 'Fight for Free Radio' recordings from 1967. A parody of the television theme from Dad's Army was also played frequently as war was declared on Prime Minister Harold Wilson and the Labour Government.

> *Who do you think you are kidding Mister Wilson, if you think Free Radio's done? We are the boys who will stop your little game; we are the boys who will make you think again.*

Ronan O'Rahilly became involved with the pro-Conservative Party campaign and took part, together with Simon Dee, who had just lost his top TV show, in a well-attended 'free radio' rally. Organised by the Campaign for Independent Radio, there were estimates of 3,500 supporters present at the rally, which was held in London on the weekend before the election. Hundreds of thousands of leaflets depicting Harold Wilson as the communist dictator Chairman Mao were distributed from campaign buses covered in banners and on air the propaganda continued incessantly, as listeners were urged to vote for Conservative MPs in marginal constituencies.

The link with the Radio Caroline name came when we spoke
to Ronan O'Rahilly. He said, 'something has to be done, we
must get involved politically, we must do something to stop
this illegal jamming', and so we decided that we would ask the
young listeners to vote Conservative, and reminded them that
one of the platforms that they were going for was for commercial radio. Ronan wanted to oversee the entire operation
and asked if we would change our name to Radio Caroline,
because Caroline meant much more to the country, so we
became Radio Caroline for, I believe, ten days.

Larry Tremaine, programme controller and DJ[3]

The Conservative Party went on to win the election. Later both
Simon Dee and O'Rahilly were questioned by police about their
involvement in the campaign, but no charges were made. Two
days after the election the radio station reverted to Radio North
Sea International.

Just days later Caroline TV was again in the news, this time
with claims that the first broadcast would start at 6 p.m. on
Wednesday 1 July 1970. John Lennon and Yoko Ono were to feature in the first programme according to newspaper reports. But
once again Caroline TV failed to appear.

We are most disappointed. In 1964 we sat down one evening
and waited for a completely new radio service to take to the
air, it happened right on cue. Tonight we sat down and waited
for a completely new television service and nothing has happened. We shall go on trying of course.

Ronan O'Rahilly[4]

It was real enough, we had landing rights in France but there
was much pressure on at the time regarding the Common
Market. There was an option on the aircraft and there were
backers. I'd got a £1 million deal from a major American cola
company lined up, but it didn't happen.

Terry Bate, head of sales

As 1970 came to an end, broadcasts were heard from Radio Free Solent at a time when the BBC local radio station started broadcasting. A former motor torpedo boat moored in Chichester harbour, the *Eidolon*, was boarded and found to contain 'radio' equipment. The owners, Mid-Atlantic Films, claimed it was a mobile film unit.

By 1972 there were two offshore radio ships serving Europe: Radio Veronica and Radio North Sea. They were both broadcasting legally off the Dutch coast; there was no Dutch anti-pirate law at this time. However, relations between the two stations had become volatile during 1971 when members of the Veronica management had been imprisoned for their involvement in planting a bomb on the *Mebo 2* in an effort to stop RNI from broadcasting. But by 1972, in an attempt to present a united front, their relationship had improved and both organisations were now providing separate Dutch programmes, RNI also continued to broadcast an international service every evening with a team of English DJs, a number of whom had served on the British pirate ships in the Sixties.

23

UNSEAWORTHY AND BARELY HABITABLE

On 29 May 1972, the two former Radio Caroline ships were put up for auction. Both ships had been ransacked and were in a near-derelict state after being abandoned four years earlier. The MV *Caroline* was sold for 26,500 Dutch guilders (about £3,150) and was taken to Ouwerkerk, in Zeeland, where she was scrapped, work that finally finished in 1980.

The smaller ship, *Mi Amigo*, went for 20,000 guilders (£2,400) and was bought by a ship broker for an unnamed client. Peter Chicago had been involved with land-based pirate radio stations in London after the closure of Caroline in 1968 and was now working as a radio engineer for RNI. He was keen to find out more about the ship's new owner.

I was told that the Caroline North ship had been bought by a scrap dealer, but the *Mi Amigo* was going to be turned into a museum. I went to track the ship down and met a Dutchman who introduced himself as Gerard van Dam who proudly showed me around HIS ship and explained about the museum idea. When I told him that I was the chief engineer on the Radio Nordsee ship, he took me into his confidence and said the idea really was to get the ship ready to broadcast again; could I take a look at the radio transmitters and tell him what the possibility was of getting them working? I had been on the ship before it had been sold and had a very bad impression of the general state of things. This time, with a bit more light, it became obvious that although a lot of small components and pieces had been broken and taken off, the basic parts of the transmitter were all there and the more I looked the more obvious it became that they could be put into operating condition again.

A few weeks later I turned up again on the boat and this time Gerard introduced me to a grey-haired old gentleman whose face was vaguely familiar. It turned out to be Ronan O'Rahilly, again very interested in knowing what the state of the transmitters was and what would be required to put them into operating order … well, that's where it started. Gerard promised to have the boat dry docked and Ronan was trying to organise as much money as possible to make it all happen and in the meantime there was a group of volunteers on-board, some English, some Dutch, trying to keep things ticking over, most of them believing more in the museum idea than the broadcasting idea.

Peter Chicago, broadcast engineer

Radio fans were invited to visit the ship for payment and were asked to help with the clean-up. The charges ranged from 5 guilders for a brief visit to 185 guilders for a four-day stay, including the chance of sitting in the studio. The challenge to raise the funds needed to get the *Mi Amigo* in a seaworthy condition and back on air had started.

I wasn't at all hopeful that anything would come of this; it seemed like a lot of well-meaning amateurs doing only superficial work, nothing that was going to change the status of the boat and more importantly no sign of it being dry docked. Gerard proudly announced that the ship had been in dry dock. I looked outside the boat, but there was no real evidence that anything had changed – the slimy green watermark was in exactly the same position as it had been before, but Gerard was very definite: it had been dry docked; it was all ok. Later, I turned up on the boat and was told that we were going, so I put my stuff on-board and, sure enough, a tugboat turned up and we started heading out to sea. I remember, we got about a mile outside Ijmuiden and the tug captain stopped and said his licence only permitted him to take us 1 mile offshore. We were horrified, this was no good at all because once we were

off the coast the Dutch authorities would realise the intentions
were to broadcast and unless we were safely outside the Dutch
limit they would obviously insist that we go back inside again.
Needless to say this was a ploy for money; the man wanted
a lot more money if he was to take us the extra 2 miles. I
remember Gerard had to leave the ship and go ashore and I
think he borrowed the money from his mother, but somehow
the funds were found, we were taken that extra 2 miles and we
dropped our own ships anchor. Once the tugboat disappeared
we all stripped down to our underwear, dived over the side and
went for a swim to celebrate the fact that we were out there
and free.

We were off Ijmuiden for probably a whole day before
a fishing boat arrived to tow us down the coast towards
Scheveningen; we anchored about a mile and a half from
each of the other radio ships. We had no working power generators so we were struggling around the boat at night with
oil lamps and torches. I noticed that if I held a florescent light
tube near our aerial feeder it lit up with the power being
transmitted from the Radio Nordsee transmitters half a mile
away and because they were operating at about 50 kilowatts
it was inducing a sufficiently high voltage. So we taped this
tube up and it was the only external light that we had on
the boat. Somebody on their ship was observant enough to
realise that as they switched their transmitters off, our one
external light went out, so they were kind enough to keep
them on all night in order that we had some light to get
through the night.

                              Peter Chicago, broadcast engineer

For the first time in four years the *Mi Amigo* was back at sea, but
certainly not ready to resume reliable broadcasts; she was unseaworthy and barely habitable.

The *Mi Amigo* was almost a wreck; the cabins were in a terrible state, we had no decent mattresses on the beds, none of

the kitchen equipment really worked and no working power generators. We were out there with a ship in an unknown condition, we didn't know the state of the hull [and] it became obvious it had never been dry docked, but we were just so excited to have the ship out at sea and we put in an awful lot of work and really got the ship turned round. I think we spent about three months solidly working, getting port holes to fit and getting the water system running properly and getting the power generator sorted out.

Peter Chicago, broadcast engineer

Every effort was put into restoring the *Mi Amigo* while erratic test broadcasts and non-stop music programmes could be heard, but with no reference to the ship's name or Radio Caroline. Money was scarce and the payment of bills was avoided, except to all but the most persistent creditors. Former Caroline presenters, Andy Archer and Chris Cary, who'd previously been known as Spangles Muldoon and Herb Oscar Anderson, were both back on the ship.

We were just about to go on air and the anchor chain snapped. We had a spare anchor, but while we were putting that down the boat was thrashing around and the aerial mast came down, but it wouldn't leave the boat. It took us the best part of two days to get it free; we had like a 200ft pole laying parallel across the deck, some of it in the sea and you'd never seen so much wire and cables all across the ship, it was quite dangerous to be out there. There was a stub of about 50ft left so we erected an aerial to the flag pole at the back and got a signal out.

Chris Cary, DJ[1]

As the ship returned to the airwaves, programmes in Dutch and English were announced as coming from Radio 199, but soon this was changed to Radio Caroline. Gradually improvements were made to the signal and the programmes during this period.

Since the enforced closedown of Caroline in 1968, Ronan O'Rahilly had become involved with producing films and music management. *Gold*, billed as 'a movie about the new American Dream', was one of his projects, featuring music by the American band the MC5 and the former Major Minor artist, David McWilliams. The movie was certainly 'of the time' and was promoted heavily on Caroline.

Programmes continued over Christmas 1972, but on 28 December Andy Archer told listeners that a Dutch naval vessel and a launch with former crew members aboard were close by. The marine crew hadn't been paid and had gone ashore. Returning, armed with iron bars and revolvers, they boarded the ship, cut the anchor chain and towed the *Mi Amigo* back into Amsterdam.

> *We're having a lot of trouble out here. There's a fight starting on the deck over something … so we may have to go off the air, we'll continue with music until then …*

The English people were there, mainly, for fun. We might get paid and we were getting fed, whereas the Dutch crew guys wanted to be paid. Every time these guys came off they were given some money and told there was more to come, but each time this happened the amounts owed just kept increasing until there was no chance of the outstanding debts being cleared, so they made plans to take the ship.

Chris Cary, DJ[2]

With the ship impounded, frantic negotiations took place between Ronan O'Rahilly, representatives of the crew, police and harbour officials. Enough money was raised to pay off the hostile crew and with a mix of good luck, coinciding with a public holiday, and chance, the ship escaped detention.

The police said 'you can go'. We were quite surprised because there were still a couple of writs on the ship at the time and also the harbour authority in Amsterdam had said there were two holes in the ship that needed repair before we could leave.

We went through the locks along the canal and got out to Ijmuiden where the inspector from the Dutch equivalent of the Board of Trade came down and wanted to be shown the repairs. Unluckily he put his foot through the silver paper that was jammed into this hole and he went mad. We had to get a welding team on board who patched up two plates and carried out the work very quickly. A certificate was produced, the chains were taken off the wheel and at about 4 a.m. we set sail again. We got the anchor down and we were back on air later that same day, 2 January 1973.

Rob Eden, DJ[3]

Programmes resumed from the *Mi Amigo*, with commercials for shops and small businesses in Holland bringing in some money. A Dutch evangelist booked airtime and a number of contra-deals helped to provide much-needed replacement parts and equipment, although broadcasts from the ship were still erratic. An office was opened in The Hague, though this also served as a meeting place for some of the decidedly odd characters who were attracted to the radio station at this time. There were some unusual performances from the presenters too.

We spent most of our time stoned out of our heads and otherwise on another planet, but at the same time we managed to paint certain things, fix things, and make stuff work. It was a mixture of mayhem but determination and we created a liveable environment. My cabin became known as the Hippy Hilton. There were times when we were without a generator with the bilge full of water and oil slopping around and no power, for two whole weeks there were just two of us on board.

Norman Barrington, DJ

Serving the European continent from the North Sea – this is the new Radio Caroline.

Money was still a significant issue, but an opportunity that would change the fortunes of the organisation presented itself in April 1973. In one of the worst storms in living memory, the Radio Veronica ship was blown ashore on Scheveningen beach, leaving her unable to broadcast. Veronica needed to be on air as the Dutch Parliament were due to debate the future of the off-shore radio stations and a huge supporters' rally was planned in The Hague.

The use of the *Mi Amigo* was offered to Veronica and money changed hands, enabling repairs were made to the ship's generator and a huge effort was made by all on board to ensure the *Mi Amigo* was capable of broadcasting the Veronica programmes. It did so, successfully, for the next ten days. Caroline DJ Norman Barrington was the technician responsible for operating the studio equipment during the live news bulletins and playing out the Veronica programmes, which were pre-recorded on tapes, as they were throughout Veronica's entire fourteen years at sea. The money raised from the Veronica deal would buy Caroline a new aerial mast, designed and built at sea over a period of three months, with sections ferried out until it eventually towered 180ft above the ship.

We had riggers out on the ship, who built all but the last two sections of the mast, but then one of the top sections came crashing down to the deck and they left, saying it was impossible to do anymore. But to give the mast its strength we needed those sections on the top to fit the supports to. In the end three of us had to drag the last pieces up and as the ship moved we were on an unsupported aluminium mast over the sea. I had the job of bolting the last section and connecting the guy wires. I was then elected to go out on the cross trees, again over the sea, to connect more wires for support. I wanted a cigarette when I was up there, so they had to light it and hoist it up with a rope, by the time it got up to me it had almost burnt to the end.

Norman Barrington, DJ

Improvements continued to be made to the ship and the broadcast equipment and by June 1973 two strong signals were heard coming from the *Mi Amigo*. Engineer Peter Chicago had managed to adapt the equipment to allow two different signals to be broadcast via the one mast; it meant that a Dutch service, able to legally accept advertising, and a separate English service could broadcast at the same time, as Caroline One and Two. From Monday 4 June 1973, there was, once again, an all-day English service from Caroline, until yet another major generator failure took both stations off the air just a few weeks later.

Everything was incomplete and 'work in progress', but the air was charged with enthusiasm. The overall message was 'Caroline is back, and it's gonna be big time once again' We ran separate tests as Caroline 1 and Caroline 2 on both 259 and 389 metres for about a week, the glorious weather encouraged us to work hard to get the ship ready.

On the Sunday afternoon our daily tender came out and there was a meeting where we decided to start regular broadcasts at 6am next morning – the Dutch 'easy listening' service was ready to go, so we thought we may as well start Caroline International, we even had three adverts too!

I was asked if I would do the breakfast slot as I could do 'wild & frantic' presentation, so on the morning we re-launched Caroline from a studio that had a pair of Garrard SP25 disco turntables, a mixer from a nightclub and an old Grundig domestic reel to reel tape recorder sitting on the floor under the desk. The only thing that was professional was the microphone.

We had been having problems with the generator for days and it suddenly slowed right down, causing the lights to flicker and dim during my link: 'This is Caroline International, and if you don't believe me listen to this … that f***ing generator has f****ed us up again', fortunately the transmitter had tripped out just in time to prevent my words being heard by

thousands, you just didn't swear on the radio, not in 1973 and
certainly not at 7 p.m. in the evening.

Paul Alexander, DJ

Repairs were again needed and just one transmitter was used
when the station returned to the air. Two radio transmitters
needed extra power and extra fuel to operate them, that cost
money and money was still scarce.

I was in a car with Ronan and he asked if I had £30,000. I said
no, but then as we were going down St James' we saw George
Harrison and picked him up. Ronan said, 'I need some money
George' and he asked, 'how much?' '£40,000,' said Ronan and
he wrote a cheque out.

Terry Bate, head of sales

Musical tastes in the 1970s were varied; some of those on the
ship wanted to recreate Caroline in the style of the 1960s pop
station, others wanted to play more adventurous album tracks –
albums were outselling singles at this time and few of them were
heard on the radio. Disc jockey Johnny Jason joined the team at
this time and made the transition to an album music format after
working on Top 40 radio in Australia.

When I first arrived I met this very long-haired guy who
turned out to be Dick Palmer, the captain. He said, ''ello, I'm
the captain'; he wasn't quite the sort of captain I was expecting, you must remember that I'd seen nothing like this at all.
I'd come from Australian radio which was very normal, zippy
top 40 radio, formats and stuff and I had this Aussie accent and
I was frightfully ... well you know, I really wasn't prepared for
that sort of thing ... obviously I'd been through the '60s so I
knew all about long-haired hippies – I had long hair myself
– but to be confronted by this guy in greasy overalls saying
''ello, I'm the captain' ... really ... I thought, crikey, what sort

of set-up is this? All the people on the ship turned out to be quite eccentric.

Johnny Jason, DJ

At the start of July 1973, a new radio station was heard from the *Mi Amigo*. Radio Atlantis was run by a Belgian business-man, Aadrian van Landschoot, who hired a transmitter for three months to broadcast a pop music service to Belgium. He had involvement with a number of Belgian singers and recording art-ists and saw a radio station as a way to promote their material. The programmes were recorded on tape in Holland and were played out from the ship throughout the day, with Caroline's English programmes during the evening.

Meanwhile there was an opportunity to experiment with a new progressive music format as Radio Seagull replaced Radio Caroline. In 1970 a small group of music fans had hired time on the European transmitters of Radio Monte Carlo, and started Radio Geronimo. The programmes featured alternative music, album tracks from artists such as Frank Zappa and Captain Beefheart; musical tastes were changing and experimental albums that were very much 'of the time' were selling well.

Ronan approached Barry Everitt and Hugh Nolan who'd been running Geronimo and he thought it would be a good idea for them to reproduce what Geronimo had been doing on Caroline. It suited me too because I was on the side of playing alternative rock, so I was quite pleased when they came out with their remit because I was a perfect fit for Radio Seagull which was what it became called. Ronan didn't want to call it Caroline because he was worried that the experiment might not work.

Norman Barrington, DJ

These next six hours are especially dedicated to Ronan, who is the driving force behind us and also to George Harrison and friends … and I think George Harrison is about the nearest thing to Radio Seagull …

Throughout the summer of 1973, Radio Seagull was introducing new music to its loyal listeners, but this radio station couldn't have been more different to the pop music of Caroline from the 1960s, this was 'hippy radio.' As the summer came to an end so did the contract with Radio Atlantis who had obtained a ship of their own, this coincided with the *Mi Amigo*'s latest mast collapsing, so once again the ship fell silent. However, Caroline had found a new radio partner, with money! Representatives of a successful Belgian waffle maker asked for a meeting with Ronan O'Rahilly; they wanted to start a radio station for Belgium and South Holland.

They said they wanted to buy the *Mi Amigo* but Ronan would never sell the ship, but he saw an opportunity to make a lot of money by renting out the transmitter during the daytime. At first Ronan was sceptical about it all but he was persuaded to come to Holland to meet their boss, Sylvain Tack. The meeting was held in a restaurant on the top floor of Amsterdam's smartest hotel. Tack didn't speak English and Ronan didn't speak Flemish but after hours of negotiation Tack finally signed an agreement, which was written on one of the hotel's paper napkins. As they were leaving, Tack announced that he was going to hire a small plane to take a look at his investment; well this was the last thing Ronan wanted to hear as there was no transmitting mast on the ship. Realising that the deal would be off if Tack discovered this, Ronan came out with a classic line, 'You can't do that, it will be too dangerous. If you take a small plane anywhere near the ship, the radiation will act like a magnet and it will crash into the mast'. Tack's main source of income was a factory producing Suzy Waffles which were full of fat and sugar. On a visit to the factory after the deal was signed, Tack showed him the production line and insisted Ronan try one. He quickly declared, 'This is quite wonderful. I've never tasted anything so delicious in my life'. When he returned to the office in The Hague he told me that the Suzy Waffle was 'the most f★★★ing disgusting thing I've ever tasted. I should have won an Oscar for my performance.'

Andy Archer, DJ[4]

Yet another mast was erected at sea, built onshore by an engineer who made farm gates, it had been commissioned by Radio Atlantis for use on their new ship. However, as with many events surrounding Caroline there are differing versions as to how it came to be on the *Mi Amigo*: either, Atlantis failed to pay for it once it had been completed, or, Caroline snuck in before them and hijacked it, quickly getting the sections out to sea. This extremely heavy, over-engineered mast was to remain standing for more than ten years. On 1 January 1974, Radio Mi Amigo came on the air sounding very professional. It had catchy jingles, with a mixture of recorded programmes and live broadcasts from the ship; it soon challenged RNI and Radio Veronica for a sizeable chunk of the Dutch and Belgian audience. There were plenty of commercials too, including regular ads for Suzy Waffles and a pop magazine called *Joepie*, which station owner Sylvain Tack also had an interest in.

More importantly for Caroline, the new radio station was bringing in money. Radio Seagull also returned to the air in the evening, after the daily closure of Radio Mi Amigo, but within a few weeks the station reverted to Radio Caroline and gradually became a little less bohemian, although still very different to any of the mainstream, land-based radio stations. The Stonehenge Free Festival was promoted heavily on air and programmes featured recorded interviews with various characters who claimed to know the meaning of life. It was around this time that the term 'anorak' was first used to describe a group of offshore radio fans. Several fans had made the journey out to see the *Mi Amigo* off the Dutch coast, dressed appropriately for a chilly day in May 1974. Disc jockey Andy Archer remarked during his programme, live from the deck, that he'd never seen so many anoraks in one place. The term has become universal to describe an enthusiast, of any persuasion.

From a point at sea to the circles of your mind – this is the new Radio Caroline.

For a commercial radio station an unusual product was promoted endlessly, love. Caroline was into LA, Loving Awareness, opposing DA, Defensive Awareness. The idea revolved around being nice to each other, promoted by Ronan to the presenters. Some presenters appeared uneasy talking publicly about love, others immediately subscribed to the theory. American DJ Mike Hagler created some superb production pieces promoting the ideal, these were played frequently.

LA – it's the only way.

24

Caroline Comes Home

The Dutch Government announced in July 1974, that they would, at last, join the majority of European countries and introduce a law to outlaw the offshore radio stations, including Radio Veronica, which had been broadcasting off the coast of Holland for fourteen years. Veronica, Radio North Sea International and Radio Atlantis announced that they would close, but Caroline was to continue, once again prepared to evade the law and joined this time by Radio Mi Amigo. Two days before the law was introduced the *Mi Amigo*, accompanied by a tender, left the Dutch coast and returned to England, this time to a position 12 miles off the coast and out of sight of the prying eyes of authority. The *Mi Amigo* anchored in the Knock Deep channel, away from major shipping routes and protected on three sides by sandbanks, but when the wind blew from the north-east those aboard the radio ship had an uncomfortable time.

You're tuned to the voice of peace and good music, coming live from the North Sea all through the night on 259 metres medium wave, the voice of Radio Caroline.

As in 1967, a number of Caroline DJs decided to leave the organisation, but soon more recruits were ferried out to the ship. The Radio Mi Amigo team, including owner Sylvain Tack, moved their entire operation to Spain; the address for contact with both radio stations was now in Playa de Aro in Gerona. Programmes were recorded in Spain on cassette and sent to Belgium via coach and then taken out to the ship. Under the Belgian anti-pirate law it was illegal to advertise, but passing on information was within the law, consequently many of the advertisements heard on air were read from newspapers and magazines. Some commercials, such as the catchy jingle for 'Goudhaantje' pre-cooked chicken, were recorded and sold as a 45rpm record, sung in Dutch and featuring an instrumental B side on this 7-inch single. It was available in record shops, and received airplay on Mi Amigo. Airtime was booked on small legal radio stations in Spain, broadcasting to Dutch tourists, but by some coincidence those same tapes managed to find their way to a radio ship broadcasting to the Low Countries from an anchorage off England. Tenders left from various ports in Holland, Belgium, England and France, but the authorities were keeping an eye on them. Successful prosecutions under the Marine Broadcasting Act were made in September 1975. DJ Andy Archer became the first to be fined and there were also prosecutions for promoting and advertising the radio station, even for displaying a car sticker and wearing a Caroline tee-shirt. More prosecutions and investigations would follow periodically on both sides of the North Sea. Sometimes supplying the ship became difficult with watches made on small boats leaving the East Coast, as a concerted effort was made by the authorities to capture those involved.

Occasionally police boats or launches chartered by the Home Office would circle the *Mi Amigo*, usually on calm sunny days, with officials taking photographs of the aerials and the crew. The Caroline crew would then parade around the deck with bags or album sleeves over their heads to avoid recognition, although some were happy to be photographed. Female presenter, Samantha, was happy to show more than others for the official photographs. But these challenges were inconsistent; with intensive efforts to make life difficult for those on board, followed by long periods of inactivity and toleration of the broadcasts.

But a number of prosecutions followed an incident in November 1975, when the *Mi Amigo*'s anchor chain broke and the ship ran aground on the Long Sands in the Thames Estuary. Listeners were kept informed of the ships predicament.

> *And as most of our listeners now realise we have got problems at the*
> *moment. We broke our anchor chain this evening and since then we've*
> *been drifting in a south or south-westerly direction and we're approach-*
> *ing the point where we're going to enter British territorial waters, so for*
> *that reason we're now going off the air.*

An emergency anchor was put down, but coastguards were concerned that the *Mi Amigo* was in a position that was a danger
to shipping. Various tugs, at different times, stood by the stricken
radio ship, apparently to offer assistance, but the crew of the
Mi Amigo were wary of using them, fearing that if a tow was
accepted, they might be taken into port and so offers of help
were declined.

Jon Cowell was the second engineer aboard the tug *Sauria*,
based in Felixstowe that was sent out to relieve the Gravesend tug
Sun XXII, which had been the first to attend *Mi Amigo*.

> We turned up at same time as a small fishing boat that had
> been chartered by The Home Office. On board was a typi-
> cal 'Whitehall man', hat, case and brolly; he came aboard the
> tug and warned us not to approach the Caroline ship or there
> would be consequences for them and us.
>
> Our captain, Alan Ricketts, was in radio contact with our
> office, where a representative of Caroline was speaking with
> our Managing Director. An argument developed between the
> land and the Home Office man and eventually Dick Hazell,
> our MD said to our Captain, 'I would like you to escort this
> man off my tug'. He returned to the smaller boat and they pro-
> ceeded to patrol up and down the Knock Deep between the
> two vessels. Then our Captain received a 'link' call on the radio
> from the Home Secretary himself – giving specific orders
> that our tug would be arrested, together with *Mi Amigo*, if we
> offered it assistance, and we'd be forced to tow the ship back to
> the Pool of London. Our skipper, very bravely I thought, said
> 'no way, if I don't want to tow them in, I won't'.
>
> Jon Cowell, Crew member of Tug *Sauria*

Next a Port of London vessel, *Maplin*, arrived and the captain of the *Mi Amigo* was asked for permission to come aboard; he declined. Quite what the intentions of the PLA crew was is uncertain but the situation around the *Mi Amigo* at the time gave cause for concern to all on board.

During this time the transmitters on the ship had been turned off for fear of being within territorial waters, but five days later a ship chartered by the Caroline organisation arrived and hurriedly towed the ship to a position some way from the *Mi Amigo*'s usual anchorage, fitted a new anchor and chain and sailed off. Assuming they had returned to international waters transmissions resumed from the ship, but Radio Caroline's ship *was* within British waters. On the afternoon of 14 November 1975 the *Mi Amigo* was boarded by British police officers.

A scuffle and raised voices were heard as the Radio Mi Amigo programmes were interrupted by police officers and the station went off the air abruptly.

> *'Everything's off … You can see we've got no music.'*
>   *'Will you switch that off please?'*
>   *'No, why? … Listen there is nothing wrong.'*
>   *'Switch it off.'*
>   *'Listen mate, you can see there is nothing playing here.'*
>   *'Get out of the … tape recorder … don't cut …'*

I felt sure that they would just secure the boat and tow the whole ship into an English port, and then obviously charge the people on board with broadcasting from within the territory, but I felt sure that was going to be the end of the radio station.

Peter Chicago, broadcast engineer

The *Mi Amigo* was left at anchor but the captain, engineer Peter Chicago and two DJs were taken from the ship to Southend, where they were charged with offences under the Marine

Caroline on her way to make history, 1964. (Authors collection)

The end for Caroline North as the ship is towed to Holland March, 1968.
(Hans Knot collection)

Mebo II, Radio North Sea International and Caroline for a few days in June 1970. (Hans van Dijk)

Mi Amigo off the English coast once again 1975. (David Kindred)

Mi Amigo weathered many storms, 1977. (David Kindred)

Love, peace and good music live from the North Sea. (Marc Jacobs)

Looking a bit rusty, 1978. (Hans van Dijk)

Mi Amigo, her days were numbered 1978. (Hans van Dijk)

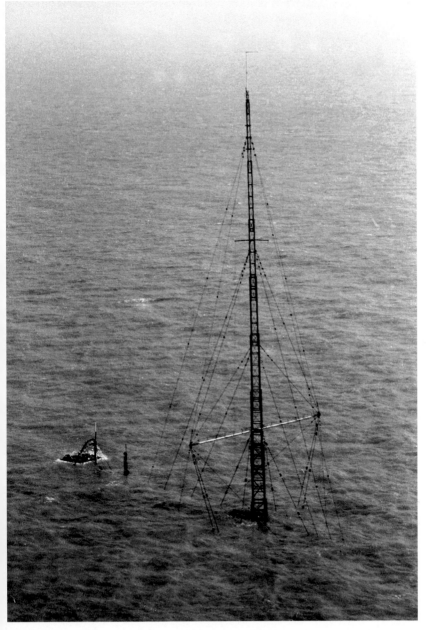

Mi Amigo's mast stands defiant, March 1980. (David Kindred)

Ross Revenge in dry dock, 1983. (Carol Maszka)

Lady in Pink, conversion to a radio ship continues in Spain. (Carol Maszka)

The 300-foot high mast is attached.
(Carol Maszka)

Eurosiege: *Laser 558* heads off to deeper waters, August 1985. (Leendert Vingerling)

Ship adrift and held on a temporary anchor, as emergency supplies arrive, February 1986. (Authors collection)

Not for the feint hearted, 300 feet above the North Sea. (Dennis Jason)

Everything's fine on Caroline. A beautiful summer's day at sea, August 1986.
(Authors collection)

Transfer to tender ship *Bellatrix* for the journey home. (Richard Buckle)

One small step. In calm seas *Bellatrix* tender ties up to the *Ross Revenge*, April 1987.
(Authors collection)

Watching you, watching me. Government officials keep watch on a visiting boat, August 1986. (Authors collection)

The twice-daily visit from the *Olau* ferry, 1987. (Fotolite)

Aground on the Goodwin Sands, November 1991. (Michael Fresco/Associated Newspapers/Rex Features)

SOS – Ship aground, November 1991. (News UK Ltd/Rex Features)

Caroline finally gets to London, Docklands RSL Broadcast, August 1997.
(Dave Roberts)

Caroline's stars of the '60s reunite for Docklands broadcast. L–R Tony Blackburn, Tom Lodge, Ronan O'Rahilly, Johnnie Walker, Mike Ahern, Pat Hammerton. (Shutterstock)

Ross Revenge finally escapes from Tilbury, under tow for the voyage to Bradwell, August 2014. (Authors collection)

All aboard, another Caroline North broadcast from the River Blackwater, October 2018. L-R: Ray Clark, Dave Foster, Nick Jackson, Kevin Turner, Johnny Lewis. (Alan Boyle)

Ross Revenge in calm waters. (Stacey Belbin, Lady Grace boat trips, Mersea Island)

Offences Broadcasting act. When the cases were heard before Southend Magistrates Court, fines were issued to the ship's captain and DJs Simon Barrett and Michael Lloyd, but the magistrates also issued an order that should the *Mi Amigo* ever enter British waters again the ship and its contents would be impounded. The case against Peter Chicago was adjourned, but he was later fined £100 for repairing and maintaining illicit radio equipment.

Following the court order to seize the *Mi Amigo*, Essex Police drew up a contingency plan of action if she ever entered British territorial waters again, but there was some confusion about the exact legal position, logistics and costs, should the situation arise.

> ... the illicit broadcasting station on board the *Mi Amigo* has been an embarrassment to us and the measures we have had to take to try and enforce the law have been expensive. If therefore an opportunity occurred to enable us to put an end to the problem we would be open to criticism if we failed to take advantage of it ...[1]

Should the *Mi Amigo* enter UK waters in the future, it was the duty of the police to execute the court order, even if the ship was in distress. The plan involved chartering a tug, which together with a police launch would go out to the vessel ... weather permitting. The *Mi Amigo* would have been towed to Southend and then onto London Docks.

> ... If she is in a reasonable condition she will be taken up river to a secure berth in the Royal Docks to await final disposal.[2]

Johnnie Walker's dream of Caroline sailing up the Thames in his 'Man's fight for Freedom' speech might have come to fruition.

Despite the risk of prosecution, there were always boatmen willing to support Caroline and earn a good price for taking supplies and personnel out to the *Mi Amigo*. Boats of varying sizes and conditions of seaworthiness would leave small ports and rivers on the North Sea coasts. Stuart Russell joined Caroline as a teenager and soon found that getting out to the *Mi Amigo* was far from plain sailing.

We set sail from Ostend in Belgium on a particularly bad day. The wind was blowing a Hooley when we went down to the harbour and the skipper said, 'we go now, don't worry, by the time we get there its calm'. I asked, 'how long will it take then?'

'Oh, twelve hours, in this weather, maybe fifteen', said the skipper with a broad Belgian accent.

So after about three hours the sea state is horrendous, the crew are in the galley cooking and stewing, there were fish smells and diesel smells. I'd just had enough of it, I went out onto the deck and was suffering from severe seasickness and seriously considered just jumping off. I was hauled back in and tied to a chair that was fixed to the floor, I just could not move and spent the entire journey to the radio ship, tied to the chair.

On another occasion I went out on this small wooden boat. Inside the boat was a radar and downstairs a cabin light, neither would work at the same time. If the radar was on you had to feel your way around the boat and if the lights were on you had no radar. Often when we went out from the English coast we sailed under the cover of darkness and we needed a few lights on, so the radar was usually off, which meant that every time we used this particular boat we hit a sandbank. If we'd been to sea for more than three hours and hadn't hit a sandbank then we'd start to worry, we'd get out to the ship and the returning crew members would ask, 'how many sandbanks did you hit on the way out then?' On one particular occasion this guy ploughed so quickly and deeply into a sandbank we were there for seven hours, we just couldn't pull ourselves off, low tide came, even a rising tide – I think eventually we dug ourselves off that time – this guy really was a character, he's probably still going around hitting sandbanks now.

Stuart Russell, DJ

The *Mi Amigo* was now fifty years old, she'd been at sea for more than five years continuously, before that she was abandoned in Amsterdam and it had been more than ten years since she'd been in dry dock. Because the original vessel had been cut in two and lengthened she had weak points, made worse by steel and iron reacting together. Electrical reaction between the sea water, the hull and the electronics on board had further weakened the ship. Dents, holes and gouges from countless collisions with supply tenders were evident on all sides of the ship.

The *Mi Amigo* was rusting away, the steel plates of the hull were wafer thin and holes regularly appeared. Leaks in the hull were common; these were patched as well as could be at sea.

> The procedure was to knock a pointed wooden peg into a hole, you took a risk because you could make the hole even bigger, but you'd hope to stop the water coming in then you'd put concrete over the peg, it wouldn't set until the water stopped. I came out to the ship once and the deck looked like a building site. We had to go off the air for a number of days at one time because we were out of fuel. Eventually this Dutch or Belgian boat came out with a full load of fuel but the sea was so rough their boat was crashing into ours and knocked a hole in the side and damaged the railings – we shouted at them to go away despite being out of fuel. The water pump broke when I was out there and we decided not to repair it because we used too much water, so from then on we just had fresh water for drinking, all washing from then on was with sea water. Often shortages were due to tenders not coming out; we'd go to the bottom of the freezer for forgotten food; I remember meals of boiled rice and pickled onions.
>
> Martin Fisher, engineer and DJ

Those who worked for Caroline continued to have great faith in the *Mi Amigo*, and everyone remarked on how homely, comfortable and safe she felt. There was a real belief that she was special, almost protective, and proud of her task as she continued doing the job she'd been adapted to do nearly twenty years earlier.

There was something about the *Mi Amigo*, we always felt safe on board. The ship and radio station had a great history and we all felt proud to be working on this compact ship that had defied the authorities for so long. We doubled up as crew, so this would involve oil and filter changes on the ships generators, pumping fuel around the ship to keep her balanced, chipping the hull, painting the ship. As far as the radio station was concerned there would be playlist meetings, shows to prepare and religious tapes to get ready. Life was very relaxed so we all paced ourselves to the lifestyle on board. I learnt to pump fuel, how to turn massive transmitters on and off, maintain generators – I impressed myself at how I was adapting to a world that was alien to me. Once on the ship we all knew that we would be spending the next twelve weeks or more at sea, so we just got on with it. The days of crews, hot and cold running water and an endless supply of cigarettes no longer existed. There was not a lot of money within the organisation, so we had to make do and mend most of the time.

Nick Richards, DJ

But there were times when even the most loyal Caroline staff members had their faith in the vessel stretched to the limit. The southern North Sea can be as rough and cruel as any elsewhere in the world and a ship at anchor, unable to run for the shelter of a harbour, is totally at the mercy of the weather.

As the ship pitched up and down there were times when the floor moved up and down so quickly it would leave you up in the air. On the bridge you'd be watching the mast going so far to the left or right and waiting for it to come back up and praying that it'd correct itself and come back the other way. I remember once we'd had supplies out, including a huge can of mustard powder and the sea got up very quickly. We were relaxing in the mess room when suddenly the ship lurched over at an alarming angle, the chairs slid to one side and we all fell in a heap on top of each other as we heard this almighty crash, the galley was awash with water, broken china and smothered in mustard.

Martin Fisher, engineer and DJ

We had no working engine and no crew on board, just a handful of radio presenters. Our main fear on a stormy night was for our anchor chain, as without it we'd be at the mercy of the storm. On one occasion we gripped on for dear life as the ship took on angles no vessel should ever experience. I opened the starboard hatchway door onto the deck to check on the gas bottles and equipment stored on deck, there was nothing left. Everything had been torn away and the noise from the wind outside was unbearable as I struggled along the heaving deck. I looked out across the sea and was rooted to the spot as I saw a massive rogue wave approaching, it was huge and dark and lumbering towards us. I kicked the metal handle down with my foot, as I pulled the door open and clambered back inside the ship as she took the full force of this monster wave. The *Mi Amigo* started to roll slowly to port as she reeled under the onslaught and water started to pour in around the door. I heard crashing from the galley as the wave breached the hatchway from the deck and there was a thunderous crash from the mess room as the television fell from its stand and hit the floor with the tube exploding. The roll to port continued and I fell across the corridor, the angle now too steep to stay upright. Water continued to flood in and was cascading down the stairway as I saw several faces staring upwards in terrified disbelief. I realised that the ship might not be coming back from this roll and waited for the watery onslaught: I prayed hard in what I thought would be the ship's last moments.

Stuart Russell, DJ[3]

There were fun times as well; the seas 12 miles off the coast can sometimes become unbelievably calm, it seems impossible to imagine that conditions could change to gale force winds and horrendous seas. But with plenty of free time, a relaxed, chilled out calm could be prevalent on board for weeks on end. A small number of people from differing social backgrounds were in close captivity, everyone dependant on the other in times of emergency and all aware of the Caroline ideals of survival and continuance of a unique radio station. Pranks and adventures were commonplace to prevent boredom setting in.

> One day the tender brought us out a rubber dinghy and an outboard motor, so we went for a tour, about 3 miles away there was a sand bank where the water was only about a foot deep. We had a game of football surrounded entirely by the sea and all you could see was the *Mi Amigo* in the distance, it was amazing, like walking on water. There was a buoy warning shipping to keep clear, so we climbed on it. It was just like being at primary school, just one big adventure.
>
> James Ross, DJ[4]

I got up one day, it was a nice day and Chicago had the rubber boat in the water and fishing rods, 'want to come fishing?' he asked. I was tired from working through the night so I said, 'no thank you', so off he went on his own. Later we saw him some way off the ship and noticed he was frantically trying to start the outboard, it wouldn't start. We wondered what to do, but the tide was about to change so we ignored him for a while thinking he'd drift back with the tide, which did happen, but then he drifted 200 yards past the ship in the other direction – we did contemplate leaving him there going back and forth on the tide, but thought we should get help. We called the coastguard and told them we'd seen someone in distress in a rubber boat. Next a rescue helicopter arrives, picks him up and we thought he'd be taken off to land, but they came to the ship and with some amazing control a winch man came down with Peter. I rushed downstairs and turned the transmitters off, it's not good to have a wire cable close to a high-power aerial, and we found a bottle of scotch for the crew. They'd asked Peter where he was from 'I left my ship' he said. 'Which ship?' 'That one,' he answered. They said it was easier to return him than taking him back and doing all the paperwork. We lost the rubber boat though; we heard it had been washed ashore, but nobody was brave enough to go and claim it.

Martin Fisher, engineer and DJ

The music played on Caroline was from albums, rather than Top 40 singles, although to a certain extent it depended on which DJs were on the ship as to whether it had a rockier, heavier or lighter style. Regular listeners could usually tell who was on board from the music that was being played, but playing album tracks gave a huge scope of musical opportunities.

This is Europe's first and only album station – Radio Caroline.

You had a completely free choice although anything seen as too commercial was frowned upon. We would play Blondie, but not Abba, that was too commercial and others would be playing that, and I think the listeners appreciated that. We were saying, this is the cool music that you should be listening to, forget the commercial stuff, other people can do that – I think that was one of the great strengths of the station, we chose wisely. There were plug records at the time, you had an album in the studio and you were expected to play at least one track during your show. If it was something that didn't fit even Caroline's broad format we made an ad from it to use across the day.

Martin Fisher, engineer and DJ

Love is the word and Caroline is the station – Caroline and Mi Amigo, sailing away on an ocean of love with you.

The concept of Loving Awareness continued throughout the Seventies, with jingles and promotions played regularly. In 1976, an album by the Loving Awareness Band was heavily promoted, with tracks played in every programme; it was a very good album. The session musicians who made up the LA Band went on to become Ian Dury's band, The Blockheads. Journalists were led to believe they might be about to witness the return of The Beatles at two press conferences held simultaneously, in Amsterdam and New York, to launch the album, and as the band were presented, a banner was unfurled behind them proclaiming 'The Beatles'. The journalists were not impressed.

Ronan was our manager and in Ronan's head there were Beatles connections. He sent us to Palm Springs in California for six weeks and we made the Loving Awareness album. We had this big press conference in Amsterdam linked to the States. He dropped this sign behind us saying, 'The Beatles'. We didn't even know it was there until we saw the video afterwards and we went 'who dropped that sign?' I think it backfired hugely, he was trying to equate us with the Beatles which he should not have done.

Mick Gallagher, musician, Loving Awareness Band

What is Loving Awareness? Well it's really a very simple concept, if you're nice to people then they will end up being nicer to you and I think if we just got that across then the idea worked – if it made people think, even if it made people cynical about it then it worked to a certain extent. The concept and the idea possibly suffered a bit from being seen as a legacy of the hippy era, but I don't see that as a bad thing. Love and peace is the message.

Tom Anderson, DJ

Loving Awareness is Free … is Free … is Free … is Free.

Throughout the Seventies, various medium wave frequencies were used for broadcasts from *Caroline* and *Mi Amigo* – 199, 212, 259, 319, 389 – and depending on the financial situation; two separate all-day English and Dutch services had operated. Throughout 1976 and much of 1977, Caroline listeners had enjoyed an all-day music service; Europe's first and only album music station, with DJs such as Tony Allan, Mark Lawrence, James Ross, Ed Foster and Samantha. But money was scarce, making it difficult to finance tender trips out to relieve the crew remaining on board. For a while, on-air pleas were made for listeners to donate towards the running costs of the station, but this involved sending money to Spain. Little cash was raised and the announcements soon came to an end.

For several weeks in 1977, Stuart Russell and Roger Matthews were the only DJs on the ship, attempting to present a full day's output.

> Roger and I were on the ship for four months, minus one day, it was frightful. Money was short, as always, and we saw tenders from France but never with an English crew change. Eventually, rescue came and we left the ship. I went to London and was told I was sacked because I had played the Motown story album. I'd done that purely because there were no gaps between the songs, as on a normal album, and it gave us a chance to get out of the studio for a short while before continuing with our twelve-hour shifts. Gratitude for all our hard work, in some of the worst storms of the winter, was never forthcoming.
>
> Stuart Russell, DJ

As another hard North Sea winter approached, the chances of Radio Caroline, or the ship from which she broadcast, surviving seemed unlikely. The authorities certainly thought so:

> We have received reports from several sources recently that the *Mi Amigo* is rapidly becoming unseaworthy and with the onset

of autumn and winter gales there appears to be every reason to
believe that, for one reason or another, the vessel is going to be
within UK territorial waters.[5]

A number of prosecutions in France and Belgium brought
continuing difficulties with supplies and there was talk of
establishing a blockade over a four-week period; the idea was
to force the *Mi Amigo* into port. Dutch authorities had investigated the cost, which would needed to have been borne by
Britain, Netherlands, France and Belgium, but at 150,000 guilders alone for the hire of four fishing vessels to prevent supplies
getting through to the radio ship, the operation was deemed
too expensive.

While the *Mi Amigo* remains in International waters we are
unable to put a stop to these broadcasts.[6]

The *Caroline Newsletter* was published, featuring articles on
various topics, not just about Caroline, and included listeners' letters. It was available from a British Post Office box address, but
authorities wrote warning the publishers against using a British
address, and later in the year the printer was visited by Scotland
Yard and warned not to continue printing the magazine. The
Caroline Roadshow was started as an opportunity for Caroline
fans to meet the DJs, but more importantly to bring in much-
needed cash for the station. These record shows played to large
crowds in halls and social clubs throughout the South East. The
Barry St James Roadshow was based in East Anglia and already
successful before advertising on Caroline.

I had a very big, very loud rock disco and was asked if I'd
like to get involved with The Caroline Roadshow. We were
playing all the rock bands that were in the charts at the time
and the response was huge, especially in the bigger towns
like Cambridge, Ipswich, Bury St.Edmunds. Everywhere
was full; we sometimes had to turn up to 500 people away.

Some of the money made went to buy food to feed the crew on the ship. We never had any grief in more than five years, although we were always looking over our shoulder, we were called The Caroline Roadshow, not The Radio Caroline Roadshow.

Barry James, Roadshow DJ

25

SHIP IN DISTRESS

By autumn 1978, conditions on the ship were getting worse; the equipment was constantly failing and there were frequent shortages of food and fuel. Generator problems led to erratic broadcasts and complaints from Radio Mi Amigo's advertisers. The Dutch had become disillusioned with the Caroline organisation and without notice, partway through the daytime transmissions on 20 October 1978, Radio Mi Amigo abruptly left the air. The Dutch DJs left the ship and went ashore. The relationship between Caroline and Radio Mi Amigo had come to an end; the radio ship fell silent, with no broadcasts at all, not even from Radio Caroline, for several months.

Radio Mi Amigo eventually returned to the air from a new ship of its own some months later, but never regained the success of the previous four years.

Meanwhile, conditions on the Caroline ship had become wretched. Power was only available for a short period each day to allow a meal to be cooked from the meagre supplies. The ship's generators were worn out and irreparable, and even if they had been working properly there was no money available to buy fuel to operate them. There was no heating or running water on board either.

A new, powerful generator was eventually put onto the ship, further damaging the vessel in the process, as plans were made for another group to replace Radio Mi Amigo. Radio Delmare had previously broadcast from two of their own ships off the Dutch coast, but both had needed assistance from the coastguards; the crews had been rescued and the ships escorted to shore. Now their plan was to unite with Caroline and rent the transmitters on the *Mi Amigo*, in a deal similar to that of Radio Mi Amigo. But ultimately, Radio Delmare failed to broadcast from the *Mi Amigo*.

In January 1979, the now silent radio ship was again in distress and an SOS was made for assistance. The ship had been taking on water in heavy seas. Usually the pumps could be used to keep leaks in check, but now, without power, the ship was flooding and had developed a list. As the lifeboat arrived, the crew abandoned the *Mi Amigo* and it seemed that she was sinking. Newspaper reporters spoke to the rescued DJs, who told stories of the water being way above the bilges and filling the studio. Those rescued included DJs Tony Allan, Tom Hardy and Roger Matthews. Wilson, the ship's canary, named after Prime Minister Harold Wilson, was also brought to safety. The lifeboat coxswain spoke of 25ft waves and gale force 9 winds. As the crew were landed at Harwich a message was passed on to supporters that it might be possible to save the ship if a salvage squad could get on board quickly.

Peter Chicago managed to get a boat to go out to the *Mi Amigo* the next morning and got aboard before the authorities could tow her away. Peter was alone on the ship for more than twenty-four hours before we went out with some new pumps. Water had come in from several leaks in the ships plates around the engine room at the stern of the ship. Some of us fixed them using concrete while the others on the ship set about clearing the cabins, the record library and the English studio below decks which had flooded to about half way up the starboard side. What made the mess worse was the water that seeped through the whole ship was mixed with oil and diesel. After about twelve hours we had pumped the whole ship as dry as we could and from then on we set about washing all the records in fresh water. There were about 3,000 of them; I remember Tony Allan did most of that. The rest of us started painting. We had very little diesel, water or food on board, and only gas for cooking, the rest of the time the ship had no electric power, our night lighting was with Hurricane lamps, they tended to go out in storms. We had been told to get the ship ready to go back on air around Easter 1979. Good Friday was very calm, but nothing came out to us and much the same on the Saturday, which I remember as being so calm that two of us went in for a swim. We had dinner that evening about 7 p.m. and we thought nothing's going to happen this Easter now. Then around 8ish we heard a ship's hooter. We went out on deck and a rather large boat was coming along side, Chicago came on board and announced that we were going back on air in the morning at 10 a.m.

Stephen Bishop, DJ

Over the years Easter Sunday had become an important day for events surrounding Caroline, with the station's anniversary always marked on the day. As loyal listeners tuned in to Caroline's frequency they were welcomed by the familiar powerful hum of the transmitter on stand-by, minutes later the recorded sound of seagulls signalled yet another return to air.

> *This is Caroline on 319, you're all day music station … this is us, we're back …*

Disc jockey Tony Allan played the Chris Rea song, 'Fool If You Think It's Over': was it dedicated to the Caroline listeners or the British authorities? Caroline was back on the air, this time with a new Dutch language radio service, confirming that Radio Mi Amigo had left the ship.

To bolster revenue, a number of American religious programmes were introduced to Caroline. The Dutch language service operated throughout the daytime hours, followed by the 'God tapes' and then Caroline's English service would take over and broadcast through the night. The religious tapes were sent to the UK and passed on to the ship for broadcast. Each programme asked listeners to contact them via their American address, but an address in London was also announced. The response was varied, but all letters sent in were forwarded on.

> Some programmes received less response than others, so letters were written in the US, sent over here, to be sent back to the various religious organisations, so they had British postmarks. But the letters, rather than just saying how enjoyable and uplifting the programmes were, would be more intense, with the writer getting carried away, saying things like, 'I'm visiting different parts of the world and I want to spread the word of the Lord as I go, and any help that you can give me in this field would be wonderful'. Now one of the addresses used was my own and I remember coming home one day to a huge box containing one hundred bibles and a note saying they were for me to distribute to the poor people of Africa so that they could also spread the word.
>
> Bill Rollins, land liasion

Ever since Radio Caroline's first broadcast, when ship to shore communication was withdrawn, various methods had been used to pass messages to and from the ship. A system of code numbers was used to get information to those on shore. The numbers were changed regularly but those in possession of the latest list would be aware of any shortages or problems on the ship. The output of Caroline was constantly monitored onshore: avid fan, Buster Pearson from Benfleet in Essex, and his team never failed to record all occurrences for compilation in *Monitor* magazine. Buster also knew the onshore contact telephone numbers to report any incident of concern.

> There was a list from 1 through to 100. Numbers 1 to 10 were usually indications that all was well on board. Other numbers would tell of things we were running short of or problems that were causing concern. The higher the number often meant that the problem was more serious. I do remember coming into Ramsgate harbour one Christmas Eve when we were

intercepted and detained for questioning and one of the crew had a copy of the current code list in his pocket. When he realised the possible consequences of this falling into the wrong hands, he tore it into small pieces and offered it round as chewing gum and we each swallowed several lumps of wet paper in the course of duty.

Nick Richards, DJ

And tonight's numbers are: Numbers 59, 60, 42 and 25 …

Communication was also made via shortwave radio at prearranged times. The messages were coded, but anyone knowing where they were coming from could soon work out their meaning.

Everything here is 100 per cent, a bit of a stormy day yesterday, so I didn't get much work done. Glad to say I was out on the fields today and had a look at the old fences, none of them came down, so no damage done at all.

The old tractors running OK, smaller engine that is, no problems at all with that one. Still having one or two problems with my foreign next-door neighbours, but hopefully that'll be sorted out before long.

Problems with the hi-fi equipment upstairs probably have to take that into a shop to be repaired by a professional before long.

All in all it's been a bit of a nice day today. Got a bit of a dinner party tonight, so I'm going to have to go out and get some food before long, otherwise there'll be a few disappointed guests.

Translated, it meant: The aerial stays are intact despite strong winds. The smaller generator is running fine, but we're having a few problems with the Dutch on board. We have on-going problems with the studio equipment which will need to go ashore and please send a tender soon as we need food.

As 1980 was heralded in by the DJs on board the *Mi Amigo*, there was speculation on air as to what the new decade held in store for Radio Caroline. Since the return of the joint Dutch and English service, conditions on board had failed to improve. If anything, they were getting worse: the ship was worn out and the studio equipment was in a similar state. As winter came to an end the crew were looking forward to better weather and calmer seas, but the waters of the Thames Estuary can become very rough at any time of the year and when the winds blow from the north-east, as they were on 20 March 1980, conditions in the Knock Deep channel had become extremely uncomfortable. With just four men and a canary on board, the *Mi Amigo* was once again a ship in distress, battling for survival in a force 10 gale.

We had a small tender visit the ship, it was more of a tapes, let-ters and light food visit than fuel and water, but there were a number of people who were well overdue for a break on land, so we agreed that those who stayed on board would maintain the Dutch and English services on the understanding that a full tender would be out to us in a few days. There were four of us left on board, we were stretched but just got on with it. Thankfully most of the Dutch programmes were on tape so Dutchman Ton Lathouwers, who had recently joined, was able to take care of those, leaving Tom Anderson and myself to look after the transmitters, generators and balancing our precious supplies of diesel oil. Tom and I removed the large inspection covers from the main tanks one night when we went off air. There must have been around fifty large bolts securing each plate, it took a while to do but once they had been taken off we could climb into each tank and scoop up fuel with tea cups and transfer it to a smaller tank which would keep us on air for another day or two.

On the day of the sinking, I had gone to bed exhausted at around 8 a.m. I was woken by Tom at lunchtime; he told me to get dressed as the ship's main anchor chain had broken. The ship's engine was completely out of service, so our best hope was to get the emergency anchor over the side to stop us drifting any more. There was a large length of chain stored in old oil barrels along the deck and the anchor itself was tied to a frame. The idea was to cut the rope and the chain and anchor would slide into the sea, but because both had been exposed to the sea air for years, they had corroded and become attached to the ship. It must have taken a full forty minutes to release them, but eventually we stopped and became aware that the ship was resting on the sand bank, so we waited to see what might happen when the tide began to lift the ship. We didn't have to wait too long to find out. The entire ship gave a deep dark thud as we seemed to bounce in slow motion on the sand bank. We had opted to play tapes of continuous music that night as trying to do live shows would have been impossible. Each hour we read out the code numbers to inform our office of the drama happening at sea. The lifeboat from Sheerness was standing by and we were in contact with the Coastguard via our ship to shore radio on the bridge.

Nick Richards, DJ[1]

Thames Coastguard reported that contact was made by the *Mi Amigo*, informing them that she was dragging her anchor and required assistance to fix her position. The weather at this time was east-north-east force 9, with a heavy sea and swell, visibility 3 miles. She had no echo sounder and a faulty compass, therefore her own estimated position was very suspect. Radar showed a report of a stationary echo, three cables from the north-west Long Sand beacon, this more likely position was some 10 miles south-west of the vessel's own estimated position.

'*Mi Amigo*: We do not wish, repeat, not wish to leave the vessel, over.'

'This is Thames coastguard, roger, I appreciate that, but in terms of safety the lifeboat will stand by you, over.'

'Thames coastguard, *Mi Amigo*, yes thank you for that, over.'[2]

There were some long periods that evening when nothing seemed to happen, we just kept checking the most vulnerable parts of the ship for water and repeated the sequence of numbers on air, hoping that help would arrive in time. I had been on my way to the bridge and passed the main engine room when I noticed that the bilges in that area had now got a significant amount of new water in them. We had one last diesel pump that I had been saving should we discover a new hole. I ran and got it and began priming it. Typically it refused to start when we needed it most. Just as I was about to give up, it burst into life and began to pump the water out of the generator room and into the sea. I let everyone else know about the new problem we had and went to make a coffee. Something told me to go and check that area again, but the water was now coming into the ship faster that we were pumping it out. I went back into the engine room to see if there was anything else I could do. When I came back into the main section of the ship I could hear our theme song, 'Caroline', by The Fortunes fading away. Tom and Stevie had closed the station down, explaining that we were about to go onto the lifeboat. A voice said, 'someone turn off the transmitter' and as I was nearest I climbed down the steps to the area where the three transmitters were housed. I felt that this just might be the last time I would be doing this for some time, so I deliberately left a long pause before switching it off.

Nick Richards, DJ

The final announcements from the *Mi Amigo* were spoken by Stevie Gordon and Tom Anderson.

> *Well, we're sorry to tell you that due to the severe weather conditions and also to the fact that we're shipping quite a bit of water we're closing down and the crew are at this stage leaving the ship. Obviously we hope to be back with you as soon as possible, but we'd just like to ensure you all on land that there's nothing to worry about, just for the moment we'd like to say goodbye. Tom?*
>
> *Yea, it's not a very good occasion really, I'll have to hurry this because the lifeboat is standing by, we're not leaving and disappearing,*

> *we're going onto the lifeboat, hoping that the pumps can take it, if they*
> *can we'll be back, if they can't … well I don't like to say it …*
>
> *I think we'll be back one way or another.*
>
> *Yeah, I think so.*
>
> *From all of us, for the moment, goodbye and God bless.*

Moments later we were on the starboard side of the ship, attempting to jump onto the lifeboat. This took a lot longer than we thought as the ship was sitting awkwardly on the sand bank and the skipper of the lifeboat passed by our ship as close as he could with the waves lifting his vessel too high or too low. Eventually each of us were jettisoned from the *Mi Amigo* and caught by the lifeboat crew and quickly placed below deck. We stood by for about twenty minutes after which the hatch opened and we were informed that 'All the lights have just gone out on your ship' … a knowing look flashed between our faces; we knew that the sea had probably now engulfed the ships main generator. That was when we decided we were beaten and took the option to head to the UK and face whatever the authorities had waiting for us. Once on land we were greeted by a number of police cars and we were taken to the police station and were told that we had to wait for officials from the Home Office who were on their way from London to interview us. Eventually we were all contacted and told that no further action would be taken unless we were foolish enough to become involved in any similar illegal operations.

Nick Richards, DJ

The rescue by the Sheerness lifeboat was carried out under extreme conditions in force 10 winds. The lifeboat had to make thirteen approaches to the ship before everyone was safely aboard. The coxswain had to take direct action several times to prevent the lifeboat either landing on top of the *Mi Amigo*, or being crushed beneath her hull, as seas took her 20ft above the lifeboat and then 20ft below. The coxswain of the *Helen Turnbull*, Charlie Bowry later recalled the moment when the canary was pulled to safety, 'its eyes were popping out of its head'. Mr Bowry was awarded the RNLI's silver medal for his part in saving the crew of the *Mi Amigo*. Once again Radio Caroline was making headline news around the world, but surely this would be the end?

As day broke, it was seen that the *Mi Amigo* had finally succumbed to the North Sea: she was under water. The roof of the wheelhouse was just visible, but the 180ft high tower was still standing defiantly above the waves, in fact the mast survived until 1987. There was talk of raising the ship from the sands that were already starting to engulf her. Realistically this would never happen, but the same could have been said about Caroline's chances of returning to the airwaves.

26

WE'LL BE BACK

With Caroline off the air, her loyal listeners were forced to turn to Radio 1 or the local commercial radio stations that had started up during the previous decade. Some questioned if there was still a need for Caroline, but within the Caroline family anyone with those thoughts were keeping them to themselves. Within weeks, efforts were underway to raise money for another ship. The search for investment went to America and Canada while the search for a new ship started closer to home.

> We were looking for another ship to replace *Mi Amigo* and contacted Greenpeace. They were in the business of buying ships and they suggested we look at a big factory fishing vessel, *The Lord Nelson*, which was in Hull. It was a very impressive ship. Ronan, Rob Eden and I travelled up to Hull, and the taxi driver who took us from the station volunteered that he'd actually been a member of the crew, so he was able to show us around. At first sight it looked fairly suitable, so we contacted someone who ran a dry dock and asked for a rough price to overhaul the ship and make her ready for sea. He couldn't give us an exact price but told us he'd recently carried out that sort of work on a similar ship and it had cost around £30,000. That was the *Ross Revenge*. He then told us that this ship would suit us better, but he did have a vested interest in pointing us in that direction as he was never paid for the work he'd done. 'It owes me £30,000,' he said.
>
> After a little research, we discovered that she was in Cairnryan in south-west Scotland, a port where shipbreaking

took place. We went up to take a look, and we saw from a distance the Ark Royal aircraft carrier and a small fishing boat next to it that looked rather insignificant. It was painted in grey and didn't look very attractive, or very big, and our initial impression was disappointment.

We were able to get on board as there was nobody on the ship and it wasn't locked up, but we could see that it was in fairly good condition. I remember going down into the engine room with Ronan, and I was a bit daunted by the size of the engine and all the machinery, having been used to the machinery on *Mi Amigo*. Although recognisable, the pumps were enormous; they stood taller than I did. The engine was huge – I said, 'It looks a very good ship but how will we handle any of the machinery.' Ronan replied, 'Don't worry about that, everything's the same, it's just bigger.'

Ronan seemed to think this was the ship and paid a local man to keep an eye on her, even though we were unable to make contact with the present owner. Ronan was then able to trace the banks handling the mortgage on the ship: they were owed money; payments were in arrears. Ronan asked if it were possible to buy the ship from the bank that held the papers, but they were reluctant to sell, and the owner remained elusive – nobody could find him or contact him.

Then there was a big storm. *Ross Revenge* broke her mooring lines in the harbour, and it was only because the ship was being watched that our man was able to get assistance and the ship was saved from disaster. After this, Ronan went back to the bank and said, 'If it hadn't been for us your ship would have been wrecked and your investment totally lost. We do want to buy the ship, but how much will it cost to buy?' He managed to get a price, but far less than she was worth. It was very, very strong at the bow, the shape of the boat was right, it would be a very stable boat and very suitable to take a tall mast, which of course was what we needed, and the accommodation was more than adequate. It was a superb ship.

Ronan was quite enthusiastic and said, 'right we'll get the boat'. Of course, we didn't have the money to go straight out and buy a boat. Ronan's department was raising the money, and this is a skill which Ronan has perfected over the years, but there was never really going to be any definite timetable on raising the money and when the boat would be bought. Ronan sent me over to America to look for transmitters and to buy the broadcasting equipment and at the time that I left to go to Dallas, we still hadn't purchased the boat. Ronan never had any doubts that we would find the money and that this would happen. I was a bit sceptical and keeping my fingers crossed, but it was while I was in Dallas and lining up the transmitter equipment, that I got an ecstatic telephone call from Ronan saying, 'Peter we've got the boat – it's bought and paid for' and shortly after that I got another call to say that the boat was ready to go to Spain and a company had been found in Spain which would build the mast and fit it to the ship.

Peter Chicago, broadcast engineer

The new Caroline ship was a former Icelandic trawler, built in Germany in 1960 as the 1,000-ton *Freyr*. Registered in Reykjavik for just three years, the world's largest trawler of her type was bought by the Ross fisheries group. Grimsby became her home port as she made countless record-breaking catches and during the Seventies she was embroiled in the Icelandic cod wars, but as the deep-sea fishing industry became subject to fish quotas, she was laid up, surplus to requirements. The *Ross Revenge* was a superb ship and capable of working in seas anywhere in the world.

In true Caroline style, various companies of dubious means were involved in the acquisition of the ship with one company transferring title to another, making the trail of ownership impossible to follow. Northfleet Enterprises of Liberia, Simor Establishments of Lichtenstein and Grothan Steamship Lines of Panama were all involved in the trail.

News stories of the imminent return of Caroline appeared regularly, even though there was serious financial wrangling between investors, causing constant delay to the financing of the project. Several Caroline stalwarts were set to return to the station and were just waiting for the call. Legendary American DJ Wolfman Jack was signed to record regular programmes and a British radio legend, Johnnie Walker, was to headline yet another against-the-odds return for Radio Caroline. The ship was to be painted pink and, in tribute to John Lennon, would be renamed *Imagine*.

I'd heard that there was going to be a new Radio Caroline and I'd been working in America, but my marriage broke up while I was in the States. My wife and daughter had come back to England and I just felt it was time to come back home when I heard that Ronan was in New York planning a re-launch of Radio Caroline and I thought, 'wow, what a fabulous way to come back to Britain, to suddenly re-appear on Caroline'. So, I went to New York and had a chat, they said, 'yeah, brilliant, fantastic', came back to England, got a bunch of guys together, got records organised and we just waited for the word that the boat was ready, but all we got was excuses, or 'it's not quite ready yet' and it turned out to be the usual Ronan Caroline thing, a lot of hot air and not much reality. Eventually, after spending a year and a half doing nothing but waiting for it to come back, I realised that it wasn't going to happen, not then, and I needed to get a job.

Johnnie Walker, DJ

There was a serious disagreement with the Americans who had put up the money to enable the project to go ahead, the whole project was halted and we spent about a year and a half in Spain. When we finally had the money to clear the shipyard bills, it was just like a dream come true. I'd spent about a year and a half on the boat, beginning to wonder if it was ever going to leave Spain.

Peter Chicago, broadcast engineer

The *Ross* went into dry dock in 1982 for the first time and Ronan was insistent that 'The Lady' should be painted pink. The Spanish shipyard workers had to mix it specially because pink wasn't a colour that was called for much in a shipyard, but having reached agreement on the cost, the ship was painted pink. Various patches were painted in different shades; every time they had a new pot of paint the shade of pink changed. There was a Norwegian captain on board and when he saw the first coat of pink paint go on the ship, he packed his bag and walked out without telling anybody, leaving a note saying, 'I refuse to be captain of a pink ship'. That delayed matters as we couldn't leave Spanish waters without a captain on board, also that week we had to be inspected by the Spanish Marine authorities. The commander and his wife came on board while the pink paint was still wet, she was in high-heeled shoes and very tight red slacks and, this being a working ship, there was no easy way to get on board, so she had to clamber on over the railings, at which point her trousers split down the seam, she was very embarrassed about it. The commander, in his very smart white pressed uniform, left the boat with pink stripes on his trousers, he wasn't very pleased, but we needed his approval before we could leave dock. So that's as far as we were going, out of the dry dock, but no further, at least not in 1982.

Carol Maszka, crew member

After the delays caused by the complex financial issues, the point was reached where shipyard bills had finally been paid and the *Ross Revenge* was ready to leave Spain for England, with a new captain, crew and some of the DJs on board. The ship's name was never officially changed to *Imagine*, as originally planned and she remained *Ross Revenge*. Engineer Peter Chicago still had work to do on the transmitters and the studio. During the early stages of conversion to a radio ship, the studio was fitted inside a portable cabin on the back deck. Wisely it was removed before going to sea and subjected to the gale force winds of the North Sea.

It was so exciting to be leaving. An American girlfriend of
mine came over from Texas to be with us as the boat was
leaving and she decked out flags between the masts. The ship
really was a spectacle as we left Santander and because it was
in August, the beaches were full of trippers. There were bath-
ing beaches on either side of the estuary so we had a huge
audience as the ship sailed majestically out to sea. There was
a sightseeing boat that normally did trips around the bay that
Ronan chartered and he was on the bows of this ship following us as far as he could with the small ferry getting buffeted
by the big waves as it headed out into the open sea. It was just
such an exciting moment; we were towed from Santander to
England. It would have been exciting to have done it under
our own power, but we were able to relax and enjoy the journey; there was no pressure, no worry about whether we'd get
there and we were able to enjoy almost a cruise. The Bay of
Biscay, which can be very rough, was absolutely clear; the
water was a lovely deep blue and it was just a wonderful voyage
between Santander and the English coast. In fact, we could
tell when we got into the English Channel because the water
went from this beautiful clear blue to a sort of greeny, yellow
colour and the closer we got to our intended anchorage up at
the Knock Deep the murkier the water got until we kind of
looked over the side and said ' yes, it looks like we've arrived',
but it was a fantastically exciting time. The first day there was
almost a flotilla of small boats that came out; you could step
from one boat to another all around the *Ross Revenge* – it really
was a very exciting time.

Peter Chicago, broadcast engineer

We were very lucky with the voyage over to the UK, we
had another Norwegian captain and a first mate who was an
experienced Irish captain, both of them had experience of
the Bay of Biscay and they were full of horror stories about
how bad the seas could be. When we finally did leave, on
3 August 1983, the forecast gave high pressure for three days,

but we lost two of those days waiting for permission to leave, but we did have a good voyage; the weather was good until we arrived off the English coast. It was a lovely trip over, we saw some whales jumping about in the water when we were getting closer to England, we were full of excitement because the voyage was finally happening after well over a year of delay and the atmosphere on board was really delightful, really good fun.

> Carol Maszka, crew member

A team of DJs had been preparing to broadcast for many months but, like Johnnie Walker, several of them had dropped out of the project because of the long delay. Tom Anderson had been the last person heard from the *Mi Amigo* and had returned to Caroline for the relaunch. Disc jockey Robin Ross was also sent to Spain to join the ship.

I arrived in Bilbao late at night with just a slip of paper saying 'Shipyard, Bilbao'. I remember the freezers were full of tuna and asparagus; we had it toasted and curried. The disc jockeys on board then included Tony Gareth and Dixie Peach. We also had Raffles, the ship's dog; Chicago had rescued him from the harbour in Spain.

> Robin Ross, DJ

Raffles the ship's dog was to stay on board for several years until his health was affected by life at sea. He was then brought ashore, quarantined and spent his retirement with Peter Chicago, a real old sea-dog.

I remember being seconded into the final months of fitting out in a little shipyard tucked up the river near Bilbao. We were eventually towed out from Spain and dragged up to the North Sea. Lots of people were quite interested in this vessel with a large mast being towed along, including a French destroyer which shadowed us for about half a day. When we finally got to

our location we didn't even have a working studio – I was still
building them, Peter Chicago was still installing all the equipment – but we were there.

Tom Anderson, DJ

Caroline veteran Andy Archer had been heard on Caroline in the
1960s and '70s; he returned for another spell as part of the new
Caroline team. The newspapers were again full of stories about
Caroline's return and ITN were aboard to record a lengthy piece
for Channel 4 television news.

Test transmissions with regular announcements were made
throughout the day before Caroline's official return to the air. The
signal was very powerful and extremely clear; Radio Caroline
was using a sound processing unit called Optimod, made by an
American company, Orban, it was the first of its type to be used
in European radio and was later used by many other radio stations after they'd heard Caroline's signal.

*You're listening to a test transmission from Radio Caroline on
319 metres, 963 kilohertz, our programmes commence at twelve
noon tomorrow.*

Former Capital Radio producer Anne Challis had been
employed by Ronan to oversee the music format of the 'new'
Radio Caroline. Many, including Ronan, were expecting to
hear a 'Gold' service, with some new tracks interspersed, something that would have been unique for British radio at this time.
However, what emerged, to the disappointment of many, was
a 'sort of watered-down album format'. Not for the first time,
or the last, internal disputes over the music formats of Caroline
would cause consternation.

As Tom Anderson's voice had been the last heard from the
Mi Amigo, it was decided that he would present the first official
programme, starting at 12 noon on Saturday 20 August 1983. But
that first show wasn't the programme that many had hoped for.
The music and presentation had gone back to the laid-back style

of the previous decade and the first songs were from the Sixties, followed by a selection of obscure album tracks.

> *Good afternoon ladies and gentlemen and welcome to Radio Caroline on 319 metres, 963 kilohertz, I'm Tom and for the next hour I'd like to take you on a couple of musical journeys through the past two decades.*

It was a rather inauspicious start. Various plans were made and then somebody came up with bright idea, 'oh well Tom, you were the last voice heard on the old *Mi Amigo* before she sank, you ought to be the first voice to go on, however, you're going to do it like this', which really didn't go down very well with me, because it really wasn't what I wanted to do. I personally would rather forget that actual opening broadcast, although within a few days everything went fairly smoothly, but the actual, very first broadcast is barely something I'm proud of.

Tom Anderson, DJ

The programmes from the new Caroline soon settled down with a number of DJs, now known as music presenters, spending regular stints on board; Carl Kingston was one of them:

My friend, Peter Tait, was offered a job. His friend, Dale Winton, was supposed to be joining Caroline, but could not go and Peter got the job. He suggested I make a demo, quickly post it to him and he would take it to the ship and get Annie Challis [programme organiser] to listen to it, which she did. She called me and the rest is history. I joined Radio Caroline and all that was promised to me was that I would get paid, as I had a wife and two children at home, and that promise was kept and I was paid for all my work. Conditions were great on the ship and I worked with Andy Archer, Robin Ross, Tom Anderson, Simon Barrett and Dixie Peach at the start and of course Peter Tait, who called himself Peter Clark on air. The format was 'Europe's First and Only Album Station'. I left Radio Caroline after some months, but I have nothing but happy memories; it was a dream come true to work on board Caroline. It was a major highlight in my life so far.

Carl Kingston

Also joining the Caroline team at this time was a very young Paul McKenna:

I still tell people that it was my greatest real-life adventure. I can remember it like it was yesterday – that day in 1984, when I was 20 years old and I went to a little laminating shop in Covent Garden, which was the secret London HQ of Caroline and met the amazing Ronan O'Rahilly. I didn't feel like I was just joining the most famous pirate radio station in history, it also felt like I was now part of a freedom of speech movement. It was so exciting! Caroline changed the course of history significantly for the better and I had no idea it was about to change my life as well. Soon I made the clandestine journey to the ship, meeting first at a pre-arranged train station and then hiding on a fishing boat that took a group of us DJs to the mighty *Ross Revenge*, anchored eighteen miles off the coast.

After we got aboard, it soon became dark and then the generator stopped working. I looked at the lights of the other ships nearby, who we could see, but who couldn't see us, which I found somewhat daunting. Luckily, a trip to the bowels of the ship soon fixed the generator, which was a relief! There was a wonderful sense of camaraderie amongst everyone on board, plenty of humour and much anoraking. I remember one night some of the others decided, whilst I was having a bath, to lock me in the bathroom. I had to climb out of a porthole and down the superstructure of the ship. I wanted to get them back, so I filled up a bucket of water, sneaked up to the laughing group outside the bathroom door and soaked them. A water fight then ensued all over the ship until the wee small hours.

I loved being on the air on Caroline. There was a big record library and a fantastic studio, plus we had total free choice in the music we played. I was aware that we had a massive audience all across Europe. Every day on board was so much fun.

Paul McKenna, DJ

With Caroline's return, interest was again shown in the ship by the authorities. A boat returning from the *Ross Revenge* was boarded on the River Deben in Suffolk; DJ Andy Archer was on board and was charged under the Marine Offences Act, all those onboard were suspected of being illegal immigrants.

Grant Benson was another disc jockey who joined the radio station at this time. Like many, he had limited radio experience, having previously been involved with land based pirate radio.

When my first month's shift came to an end I was almost reluctant to leave the *Ross Revenge*, but I hadn't seen my family for some time and so on a very calm autumn evening, I climbed on board the tender boat, an ex-RAF rescue launch, to make a clandestine journey back to British soil.

The sea was exceptionally calm, almost completely flat, and somebody noticed that on the horizon, there were the lights of a small, apparently stationary vessel. We thought no more of it as we made ourselves comfortable and prepared for the four-hour journey home.

The tender was a very comfortable boat with bunks and a galley and the next thing I knew it was dawn and somebody was waking me with a cup of tea. We had entered the River Deben, but had to wait a while for the tide to come in and the river to be deep enough for us to reach our mooring.

But just as the crew were preparing to secure the vessel to the jetty, a police launch swooped by and we were boarded by a dozen uniformed officers. They instructed our captain to tie-up the boat and we were all told to wait in the galley. In true British fashion I offered to make everyone a cup of tea, accepted by all – both 'heroes and villains', and after a few minutes we were told we were being arrested on suspicion of being illegal immigrants!

I remember thinking what were the odds of being arrested on my first trip to Caroline?

We were bundled into a police Ford Transit and taken to Ipswich police station. I was locked into a warm, single comfortable cell, served breakfast and fell asleep. An hour or so later they took me to the interview room and showed me statements made by some of my colleagues. The statements detailed how we were all broadcasters and crew members of Radio Caroline.

In true sixth form lawyer style, I feigned surprise saying that I was somewhat confused, having first been accused of being an illegal immigrant and now a Radio Caroline disc-jockey. I told the officer that I thought it was probably in my interest to get some independent advice before making any comment.

My interrogator seemed to take this in good spirit and half an hour later I was told I was free to go. I never heard any more from the Ipswich constabulary.

Grant Benson DJ

Caroline had been back on air for a number of months and still no advertising had been heard. Already there were complaints from some of the more recent crew members of broken promises over payments. Commercials eventually appeared at the start of 1984, for a number of American products including Jordache jeans and Wifa ice skates; neither product available in the UK at the time, *Newsweek* magazine was also advertised extensively. Into 1984 and the *Ross Revenge* lost her anchor and was adrift for some time in the North Sea, but now there was another radio ship in the area; the *Communicator* was home to Laser 558, and despite a troubled start the American DJs and non-stop hit music heard on Laser, made a huge impact on British radio listeners, with millions tuning into the all-day pop service.

You're never more than a minute away from the music on Laser 558.

All the hits all the time – Laser 558.

Radio 1 and local commercial stations rapidly lost audience to Laser, but so too did Caroline. Laser wasn't to be the only new offshore radio station to launch in 1984. A new frequency was used for the Caroline service on 576 kHz, as a Dutch radio partner joined them; Radio Monique was aimed, like Mi Amigo and the Dutch Caroline service before, at listeners in Belgium and Holland.

> Radio Monique was a great radio station and earned money. The deal involved supplying the ship with fuel, food and supplies in exchange for the use of the powerful 50kw transmitter. Most of the programmes were taped in Hilversum at Music Media International, they were intended for a small similarly named radio station in Belgium and also a number of Spanish radio stations but, like the Radio Mi Amigo programmes, they somehow got to be heard on Radio Monique. We had national advertisers for well-known products and we soon had listeners; in surveys we had between 1.7 and 2.2 million listeners. When we were live from the ship we'd have fun and present the shows like a 'play on the radio'. We'd make a lot of the rough seas and we'd kick a bucket around and thump the desk to make it sound rougher than it was.
>
> Ad Roberts, DJ, Radio Monique

In seas described as being 'as high as a house' by a lifeboat man, the *Ross Revenge* dragged her anchor in a January storm during 1985 but programmes continued for much of the time. Walton lifeboat stood by, but fortunately their services weren't needed.

An office in Russell Street in Covent Garden was the centre of operations for Radio Caroline in the first few years of her return. Ronan was regularly in residence, when he wasn't conducting his business in Kings Road coffee houses or from telephone boxes, always in a secretive way, convinced that his every move was being followed by the authorities. Throughout the mid-'80s, a land-based organiser was responsible for booking tenders, liaising with DJ's, buying supplies and collecting records. It was a difficult and complex job, with the shipborne crew dependent on their organisational skills.

Between 1983 and 1986 I organised more than one hundred tenders out to the ship. My daytime job was at Marks & Spencer, but I'd go to record companies around work, collecting new product, some companies were really friendly and very forthcoming, it depended on who you knew. Then I would collect money from Ronan and spend hundreds of pounds in Tesco on groceries, then meet the boat in Ramsgate where we'd load two or three tons of water. Still in my business suit and stilettos, I'd go out to the ship, once there I'd make notes about what they needed, I'd be writing these long lists in the middle of the night. Then we'd return in time for work next morning. They'd ask me what I saw on TV last night, I'd always say, 'Oh, nothing much, I was a bit busy'.

I did confide in my supervisor, he was keen and interested in what I was doing, so I asked if he'd cover for me if ever I was held up, I was marooned out there for three weeks once, when the wind blew up, luckily my boss covered for me.

In rough seas I'd sit on the bridge feeling the ship tugging on the anchor chain as the bow came up out of the water and then watching the wave coming right over the bridge as the bow went straight down, I always felt safe out there.

Stevie Lane, DJ & Co-ordinator

The arrival of a supply tender was always unpredictable and it was usually a mystery as to how many new crew members would arrive. Sometimes short-term gloom would set in amongst those on board if none of the regular replacements or new faces could be spotted from the deck of Caroline as the supply boat approached. If there was no replacement, it would invariably mean an extended stay on the *Ross Revenge* or more work for

those colleagues remaining on board. Chris Pearson was a new
recruit in March 1985:

> I was picked up from the old Blue Star garage in Dartford and
> driven to Ramsgate. Whilst en route, I was asked what name
> I'd be using on-air. I thought I'd use my own name, but it was
> pointed out that this may not be the smartest idea ever, so I
> looked around for inspiration. I was sitting next to a cardboard
> box marked 'Pearson's Apples'
>
> I remember climbing aboard in the pitch black at around
> 3 a.m. on a Saturday and being greeted by a bunch of very
> friendly people who thrust a cup of hot coffee in my hand. I
> so clearly remember standing on the deck, looking at the ship,
> what I could see of the mast and the famous name on the side
> and thinking to myself, 'My God, this is really happening ...
> I'm going to be a jock on Radio Caroline.' It was a cold March
> morning and as soon as we got inside, I was overcome by just
> how warm it was in the Mess room and also the overpowering
> smell of diesel and the noise from the generator. The Dutch
> crew disappeared off to set pans of water boiling to heat up
> peanut butter coated chicken satay in plastic sachets and we
> Brits sat drinking coffee and talking about radio folk we had in
> common and laughing lots.
>
> I eventually got to bed at about 5.45 a.m. and was told, 'Find
> your sea legs this weekend and you'll be on-air from Monday'.
> About 5 hours later I was woken by Jay Jackson to be told,
> 'Someone's ill, you're on-air in an hour Shag!' My studio 'train-
> ing' lasted all of 5 minutes and involved Nick Richards showing
> me how the rotary fader desk worked, how to use the geared
> turntables, where the mic fader was and then he headed off to
> make a brew! It was trial by fire that Saturday lunchtime, but I
> was only 19 and, at that age, you feel you can do anything!
>
> Chris Pearson DJ

Commercials for Bet Canada and the chance to play Lotto
6/49, The Canadian National Lottery, also started at this time.

Professional-sounding commercials were played hourly with the weekly winning lotto numbers broadcast regularly. Caroline listeners were invited to send £15 for six entries. What listeners didn't realise was that they were sending money to an agent, rather than the lottery itself, although the entries were legitimate and people did win.

> *Twice a week you could become a millionaire, you could win, tax free in Canada, one million dollars. The game is Lotto 6/49, choose any six numbers between 1 and 49, send them with your name, address and £15 cash, cheque or money order to Bet Canada, Box 55 55, Vancouver, Canada.*

There were numerous other commercials heard on Caroline at this time for a number of products and events: Hawaiian Tropic Sun Screen, Canada's Expo 86, Arabian Sands Holidays, Nikon Cameras and Singapore Airways. It certainly made the station sound busy, doing what Caroline set out to do in 1967 – survive on commercials for international companies booked overseas. For the first time in nearly twenty years, the English service of Caroline sounded like a proper commercial radio station.

eurosiege

Both Caroline and Laser were proving to be too popular for the land-based, licenced commercial radio stations, who complained to the DTI, the Department for Trade and Industry, through their governing body the Independent Broadcast Authority, that the 'pirates' were stealing their listeners. The DTI accused the ships of interfering with marine and emergency radio frequencies, something that was always denied. In August 1985, the DTI announced a blockade using a chartered boat, the *Dioptric Surveyor*, which was to be stationed alongside the ships in the Knock Deep, challenging and reporting every boat that visited either Caroline or Laser. The cost to the tax payer was reckoned to be £50,000 a month. The 'spy boat' was on station for around three months, before a larger replacement ship was used, although the initial plan was to charter a boat for a much shorter period:

> We now expect to have a vessel anchored in Knock Deep from Thursday 8th August, initially for a fortnight.[1]

The original plan, of surveillance over a one-month period, was extended and in those months of surveillance, the DTI staff on board certainly experienced 'the thrill' of being at sea, especially during rough sea conditions. The vessel often had to run for port when the seas blew up and became too rough for the small boat; there were also regular visits back to land for supplies to be replenished and for crew changes. An interesting situation occurred a few weeks into the observation process, when the *Communicator*, the Laser ship, steamed off to an area off the Galloper Sands, way out into the North Sea with the *Dioptric Surveyor* following, leaving the *Ross Revenge* unobserved for twenty-four hours. Full advantage was taken to receive supplies when the coast, literally, was clear.

The exercise attracted a huge amount of publicity; newspapers and TV text services announced the initial decision to place a boat in the area, and news reports gave more coverage to the radio ships than had been the case for many years. The *Daily Star* sent a team out to 'run the gauntlet', taking champagne and tee-shirts to the ships; they featured a full-page spread on the situation. BBC TV news sent reporter Garry Lloyd to the Knock Deep where he asked Caroline's Peter Philips if they were 'robbers of the airwaves' and if the radio station had 'stolen listeners', as the DTI had accused. 'I don't think listeners would agree that they've been stolen', was his reply. As autumn approached, the smaller vessel was replaced by a larger ship. Ironically this replacement vessel was a former sister ship to Laser's *Communicator*, the *Guardline Tracker*. With the exception of the transmitting masts on the Laser ship, the two vessels looked identical.

Little mention of the surveillance was made on Caroline, unlike the Laser DJs, in particular Charlie Wolf, who delighted in taunting the DTI during what became known as Euroseige. Giving listeners a regular 'Euroseige' update with commentary on events involving the *Dioptric Surveyor*.

Daily Reports ... In Depth Background Features ... Euroseige Update, Daily at 1.30 and 5.30 British Time ... Euroseige 85!

Although a number of boats were challenged and reported, the supplies still got through. Caroline claimed their supplies came from Spain and as they were broadcasting from outside territorial waters, the station and suppliers were legal. They also denied accusations of interference caused by their transmissions, which the DTI claimed was the main reason for their efforts to close the stations.

I remember the first day the *Dioptric Surveyor* came out. I was doing the breakfast show and it came past the studio window at about eight o'clock in the morning; it went shooting past and that was it. We thought, 'that was a quick visit by the Government', this was on the Wednesday. A couple of days later, on the Friday, they returned but this time they didn't go away. They anchored only a hundred yards away, maybe even closer than that to the *Ross Revenge*. I remember that distinctly because I had to get on the ship to shore radio and tell them they were endangering our vessel as they were so close. Eventually they moved away to a position between the two boats.

Charlie Wolf from Laser, he was the one who christened it Euroseige 85, used to go on the air each evening and really take the mickey out of the folks from the DTI and the IBA. One evening it was a bit on the rough side, it didn't affect us or Laser much, but the *Dioptric Surveyor*, which was quite a small boat, I think it was only around 99 tons, and remember this was 17 miles off the coast, were bouncing around a bit, so Charlie goes on the air, and obviously they're monitoring all of this and says, 'Hi, this is for all the folks on the *Dioptric Surveyor* who are tossing their cookies today'. When it was really rough we used to wind them up because we knew there weren't many good sailors aboard, I'd go on air and say things like, 'oh, what a wonderful breakfast I have in front of me this morning, bacon, eggs, and there's so much grease on my plate the eggs are swimming around, they're doing the breaststroke', you could almost see half their crew on the deck 'praying to the great green goddess of the sea!'

When one of our supply boats came out, it was a sort of 'cat and mouse game' because they would up anchor to get closer trying to see the supply boat 'handing over goods', so our supply boat would keep circling us, the 'spy boat' would keep circling us, and as soon as our supply boat was on the blind side there'd be 'bang, bang, bang', all the records would come across, all the food would come across. It was good fun really.

I think it had the opposite effect to what the Government wanted; they were trying to knock our morale by closing us down, but what actually happened, well, it was something that kept us going, and I remember all the publicity that we got from the BBC and the local IBA stations. The press was absolutely amazing, that gave us the encouragement to go on, it was like Ronan once said to me, 'it was like £20 million worth of free advertising', there we were on the front page of every national newspaper and on every news bulletin. The mail that we got suddenly increased with people saying, 'good grief, we didn't realise Caroline was still on the air', and others would say, 'we've never written to a radio station before, but good luck and keep going.

Johnny Lewis, DJ

Perhaps sensing victory, the surveillance of the ships continued into November 1985. At the start of the month, time ran out for Laser 558, the ship's captain asked for assistance from the *Guardline Tracker* after a series of generator failures and the station was forced to close.

The *Communicator*, which had previously been the *Guardline Seeker*, was escorted into Harwich by its twin, the *Guardline Tracker*, the ship chartered by the DTI. It seemed that Laser's finances had just run dry, but the DTI could claim that their operation had hastened Laser's end. The surveillance ship returned to sea to monitor Caroline, but within a few days the operation was called off.

28

INTO OVErDrIVE aND PLaYING THE HITS

Following the demise of Laser 558, Caroline wasted no time in moving from their frequency of 576kHz to the now vacant 558kHz, one of the clearest on the medium wave and also one that had been allocated to the new BBC local radio station for Essex. In a smart, swift move Caroline 576 became Caroline 558 after the entire crew had assisted with adaptations to the aerial system overnight.

> *Caroline 576 is closing for essential transmitter maintenance; join us tomorrow morning at six o'clock for the breakfast show with Nick Richards*

> *Good morning and welcome from Caroline 558 on this Thursday morning …*

This was the start of one of the most settled periods of broadcasting from Caroline since the 1960s. For the next two years, a regular, reliable radio service with two strong, clear signals was broadcast from the ship. The daytime Caroline service veered towards a Top 40 format similar to that of Laser. The Dutch service, Radio Monique, broadcast throughout the daytime hours. This was followed by Viewpoint 963, a regular programme of American religious broadcasts that not only attracted an audience and response, but also brought in money. A further service was broadcast later in the evening, after the religious output, playing more specialist music. For a while, Jammin' 963 played reggae and dub exclusively, but this was soon replaced by Caroline Overdrive. Championed by Tom Anderson, Overdrive played heavier album tracks with a format similar to Radio Seagull that had broadcast from Caroline in the 1970s.

> *Throughout the night on 963 kilohertz this is Caroline Overdrive.*
>
> *Welcome back my friends to the show that never ends ... This is Overdrive.*

Overdrive came about with my dissatisfaction with the daytime format at the time. Caroline as a station had become far more pop orientated than the album station that I originally joined back in the Seventies and, with all due regard to those that wanted to make it a success doing that, I saw little point in going through all the hardships of being on a ship at sea and all that entails, and to be there for no purpose, other than to repeat the music that everyone else was playing, so, by various means, I managed to twist Ronan's arm and ended up with him giving me the 963 frequency at night, after the Dutch and the 'Gods' had finished, hence Overdrive was born. It really was Fergie MacNeil and myself sitting down with a pile of records and a load of ideas and spending a couple of months putting it together. We were the only two initially, at which point, when we wanted to go ashore, we obviously had to recruit others, such as Mark Matthews and Nigel Roberts who came along and got involved. The idea was to be as far removed as possible from the daytime format and I expect if you speak to Peter Philips he will say he wanted it so far apart that we never shared a record.

Tom Anderson, DJ

Peter Philips had worked on land-based pirate station Radio Jackie and also on The Voice of Peace, broadcasting from a ship off the coast of Israel. He was to be responsible for changing Caroline's output and drastically increasing the audience by introducing the new Top 40 style sound of Caroline 558.

The station had lost its way musically; it was partly an album station but it was also playing club and dub reggae music and it didn't work on medium wave and I was having this discussion in a bar with Tom Anderson. I'd told him that I didn't think it was working and suddenly Ronan walked in. It was the first time I'd met him and he asked what I thought of the station. Well, having just had a similar conversation with Tom I thought I had to voice my thoughts so I told him that I thought it was rubbish, I think its lost its way, and he said, 'I completely agree. What would you do about it?' I said, 'much of the music we were playing wasn't working and we should take a more commercial approach and a more professional approach to the presentation' and he said, 'would you like to do something about it?' and that's how I became programme controller, I sort of talked myself into it really.

Peter Philips, programme controller and DJ

There were times though when the music had to stop. A major hazard of being permanently moored at sea was when an anchor chain broke and the ship cast adrift, and if there was any risk of entering British waters, the transmitters were always switched off. This happened in January 1986, lifeboats stood by the *Ross Revenge*, but the situation was controlled by starting the ship's engine, not something that can be done quickly, and sailing to safer waters where a temporary anchor held the ship roughly in position until a more permanent solution was found.

The weather had been very rough, supplies were getting low and a few of the crew wanted to go home. It was rough as hell but I coped pretty well with the sea. Mike Barrington saved us by cranking up the engine to avoid the sandbanks but things did get hairy, with the engine starting to overheat. A couple of Dutch tenders were looking for the anchor and broken chain to weld it back on, but they failed and we put the spare anchor down. It was a very scary time for us.

Jerry Wright, DJ

Disc Jockey Richard Jackson had gained a good deal of radio experience on land, having worked for Radio Jackie, a land based pirate station with a history almost as long as Caroline's, and the Irish super-pirate, Radio Nova.

> I was 'collected' and taken to Ramsgate and we joined a ferry to Zeebrugge and then spent eight hours on board the tender boat, appropriately called 'Windy', we went through an incredible storm and I felt extremely sick. I was onboard for Christmas 1986 and I remember our new supply ship, 'Bellatrix' loaded to the brim with festive stuff, trees and puddings … we had a brilliant Christmas and it showed on air.
>
> We went through a massive storm in January 1987 – we survived, but always in the back of your mind you'd think, 'is a stay holding the mast going to go ping?' You were always aware of what could go wrong and keep out of the way, off the deck. Despite the weather, Caroline would rock on. I was fortunate, whilst I was out there Caroline was in a good place, we had a great signal, we were now playing more pop music than album tracks and we had some good DJ's. Life was good. I'd get up in good weather and take a bowl of cornflakes onto the back deck, sit in a deckchair and enjoy my breakfast.
>
> Richard Jackson DJ

The Dutch language station, Radio Monique, was hugely successful with tens of thousands tuning in every day. The Monique organisation was responsible for the main supplies and a regular system was operated with the tender officially leaving Dunkirk. The French authorities knew where the boat was going and the purpose of its business and whilst perhaps not encouraging it, they were hardly hampering the exercise. Probably because France was not directly affected, there were no French language programmes, but also because large amounts of money were spent on fuel and supplies in Dunkirk.

Lots of people in the Netherlands and Belgium listened to
Radio Monique, but the station was more popular in Holland.
The signal was very strong on 963kHz, especially in coastal
areas; reception was quite good in much of the Netherlands
and Belgium. I think it was successful and it made money.
Monique had some big advertisers like Singapore Airlines and
Bose. There was money enough from Monique to pay for the
expensive tender trips with diesel, water and food and to pay
the DJs on board. The English side was responsible for the ship,
maintenance, studio-equipment, generators and transmitters.
Monique was using the big transmitter on 963 and a lot of
commercials generated the money to keep things going, and
of course there were the religious programmes bringing some
money in; the God tapes were very important. The *Bellatrix*,
used as the tender, was a former pilot-boat. It was a very comfortable ship with cabins on board. She replaced the much
smaller *Windy*, which had previously supplied the *Ross Revenge*
with diesel and water. Because the *Bellatrix* was much bigger it
could bring much more diesel and water in one go. Every two
weeks they came out from Dunkirk which was a great experience because the *Bellatrix* was as big as the *Ross Revenge*. The
trip took about six hours. Life on board the *Ross* was fine; she
was a big ship and there was plenty of room [and] it was very
stable when the sea was rough. Most of the time there were
thirteen or fourteen people on board, English and Dutch, and
a good atmosphere. It was a very special time of my life, I'm
happy I was one of them, great memories.

Jan Veldkamp, Radio Monique DJ

Without the Dutch it would have been a more rundown operation. I was surprised when I arrived that the ship was warm,
was lit and there was food – there was even beer. The Dutch
turned up regularly, every ten days or so, with another 15 tons
of diesel oil and a few tons of water, plus frozen food, tins and
fresh stuff. They were much better organised and I don't think
their tenders were anything like as closely scrutinised as the

English ones. They were coming out of Dunkirk in France and going through all the formalities of port clearance, telling pilots when they were going and coming back.

Kevin Turner, assistant programme controller and DJ

Life on the radio ship was never dull. With two radio stations broadcasting from the same vessel, several broadcast staff were needed, the number onboard was subject to availability at the time of the departing tender from land. A full ships compliment at this time was usually about twelve, sometimes six British broadcasters and three Dutch, a transmitter engineer and a marine engineer and very occasionally, a cook. Steve Conway joined the team as a newsreader in February 1987, later becoming a regular programme presenter and in latter days at sea, Programme Controller.

I loved the music, it was always on, wherever you went on the ship and it was so great to be a part of that and to be helping to provide that for the tens of thousands of people listening all over Europe … and the excitement as well, no two days were ever the same, you would wake up and something was always different – something had gone wrong, something had gone right, new people had arrived, something was always happening … and there was peace as well, it was incredibly peaceful, you had the wind, the sea, the sun, the moon, it could be a very tranquil and beautiful place to work.

Steve Conway, Newsreader

An air of contrived mystery and covert telephone conversations usually surrounded the clandestine activities of Caroline on land. Often unnecessarily complex arrangements would be made for those intending to join the crew.

I had a coded telephone message from a guy called Cosmic, to meet him in a pub car park in Chelmsford. Cosmic looked every bit as you'd image someone with that name would look; he had wild dark hair, beard and moustache and was dressed in shabby jeans and jacket. With him was 'Captain Keith' with long trailing hair and wearing an oily boiler suit. Kevin Turner made up the trio, dressed smartly and with neatly groomed hair. We made our way to Felixstowe, where we boarded a ferry for Zeebrugge, 'Try not to look conspicuous,' instructed Cosmic in lowered tones, as we drove onto the ferry with boxes of records and suitcases in the overloaded, clapped out Volvo estate car.

Mick Williams, DJ

Getting on board the *Ross Revenge* could be quite an adventure, even from the large *Bellatrix*. In calm weather the *Bellatrix* would tie up to the stern of the *Ross Revenge* and crew would simply step from one ship to the other, but in rough weather the supply ship would anchor some distance away and transfers of personnel and supplies would be shuttled by a rubber boat, often in seas rising and falling by several feet.

I went out on the back of a storm and although the seas were calming down it was still very choppy. Two of us got into the rubber boat with Willy [member of the tender crew] at the helm. We bounced over and were alongside the *Ross*, the small boat rising and falling 19ft or so in the swell. We were soaked and cold. When my turn to climb aboard the *Ross* came I grabbed the remains of a rope ladder as two waves came up to my chest. Willy was trying to pull me back onto the launch; I was hanging onto the rope. I heaved myself over the side of the ship and tumbled upside down at the feet of Ad Roberts who helped me up. It was far from a dignified arrival.

Mick Williams, DJ

Regular 'anorak' visits were also made out to Caroline at week-ends when weather conditions allowed. Since the mid-1970s, small boats, chartered by loyal Caroline supporters Albert and Georgena Hood, would take nearly three hours to travel out from various small ports with several Caroline fans on board who were able to view the ship and meet the DJs. The look of amazement and pleasure on supporters faces at seeing 'the world-famous Radio Caroline' at close quarters was often reward enough for them and the crew – gifts of magazines, drink and chocolate also helped.

I hate to think how many times we went out there, it was 1975 that I started the boat trips, taking sight-seeing trips. I'd planned to do one trip a week, but often did more. I had no boat myself, so I advertised for boat owners to take me out and two or three replied. Most of them said no when they knew where we were going, but one man stayed loyal throughout. The North Sea can be a horrible place when the weather's bad: We went out from Southend on a fishing boat, it was New Year 1984. On the way out we found some horrendous weather and when we were alongside it was really bad, this was about three minutes to midnight. The crew were saying don't hang about, please get back, they're giving a force 10 imminent, so we threw everything on board and turned for home, but then off the top of the Long Sand the engine broke down. We were able to get it going, but we couldn't believe the size of the waves.

Albert Hood, boat trip organiser and supporter of Caroline

Caroline fans could also keep abreast of developments at sea, with magazines and newsletters available from various organisations set up to champion the offshore stations: *The Caroline Movement, Anoraks UK* and *Offshore Echos*.

Communication from the ship to shore was now via CB radio with a complex method of transmitting and receiving on different pre-arranged channels.

We worked out an 'enigma' code, transmitting on one channel, but listening on another and only one person on land and those on the ship knew the channels, so even if you were listening you'd only hear one side of the message. Twice a day

we'd make contact, usually early morning and around teatime.
We'd use very short messages and make contact by whistling:

'Are you in there mate?'

'Nothing for you from here. How about you?' and the reply
might be.

'Yeah, short of such and such,' followed by a coded message
relating to the requirements. All the Lotto 649 numbers were
passed this way too: '42, 21, 33, 06, 10, 49, bye' and the next
day you'd tune in and hear the Canadian lottery results read
on air.

Bill Rollins, land liason

*The lucky numbers in the latest Lotto 649 draw are 42, 21,
33, 06, 10 and 49. Keep listening to Caroline for more Lotto
6/49 information.*

Another reliable way to send coded messages from the ship was
via dedications played at the start of the hour. Listeners were
blissfully unaware that the crew could be short of particular supplies. 'This is for so and so who will be 16 on the 19th, I hope you
have a great day, from your friends at Number 36 ...' would mean
shortages related to those coded numbers.

There were a number of regular DJs on Caroline at this time
and limited wages were paid, when money was available. But
because of Caroline's unique situation not all DJs returned for a
second spell on board, either because of their personal circum-
stances on land or because they were unable to handle a life at sea.
The turnover of DJs was high, but many would-be radio stars had
their first break on Caroline.

Peter Philips was programme controller and had been running
the station for the previous two weeks with a shortage of disc
jockeys; this meant all on board had been working extra-long
hours. His relief at seeing a full complement of presenters,
including two new recruits, was evident but his pleasure was
short lived when he asked what radio experience we had.

'None,' I replied. 'F***ing marvellous,' he said as he stomped off. We've been good friends ever since.

Mick Williams, DJ

During the Eighties many songs and albums were championed by Caroline. Some were 'paid for, plug songs', but a number were favoured by the radio station on merit and whilst Caroline no longer had the ability to put a song high into the charts just by playing it, as had been the case in the Sixties, many of these songs were certainly helped by Caroline plays. Notable examples include 'Radio Africa' by Latin Quarter, 'Living in a Box' by the group of the same name; 'Relax' by Frankie Goes To Hollywood, 'Money's Too Tight to Mention' by Simply Red and the Dire Straits album *Brothers in Arms*, which DJ Jay Jackson claimed Caroline had the world exclusive on as he featured selected tracks on his Sunday morning show. Other than the recognisable, commercially popular songs, there were still plenty of obscure album tracks that appeared on the station in the first two years after her return, but by 1987 the sound of Caroline 558 had changed considerably from the album format. Radio Caroline now featured many of the big chart hits of the day, albeit with a 'rocky' edge, plus classic hits from the 1960s and '70s.

Playing the best of the old and the best of the new. This is Caroline 558.

We'd start the hour with a Sixties or Seventies track, follow that with a current from the Top 10, then Eighties, more or less mixing old and new on an alternating basis, but all done by clocks, with an odd and even hour. You just picked from a card index in the record library, that gave you your oldies and the current stuff was all in the boxes in the studio. We were getting fairly reliable supplies of singles and albums out there; what we didn't have on vinyl we acquired on Sunday evening by recording it from the chart show on Radio 1. It was a badly kept secret amongst the record companies, that if they were to deliver an extra copy or two to Radio HMV or

Radio Top Shop in London's West End, these records would find their way out to a ship on the North Sea. We also had 'plug' songs, usually one an hour. We were told they were worth about £500 a week to the radio station and there were usually about six in rotation at any one time, coming around about every three hours. We had some quality stuff that was 'on plug' from some big artists, but there were always some dodgy tracks too.

Kevin Turner, assistant programme controller and DJ

Working as part of the Caroline team wasn't just a case of playing the music.

Once on board the radio ship, you were resigned to being there for some time – often weeks, usually months – the tender boats certainly didn't run to a regular timetable, and there was no guarantee that you would get off within a certain period of time. All new recruits were quickly expected to adapt to life within this isolated community, floating eighteen miles off shore.

It was like living on a remote tropical island – except it wasn't an island, and it certainly wasn't tropical. It was a very small community of people who were entirely inter-dependent, they all had roles within that community; yet still not self-sufficient, they were entirely reliant upon supplies arriving from outside. However annoying people can sometimes be, you were always pleased to see people, 'cos people meant friendly faces, somebody different to talk to and stuff: fuel, water, food and the necessities of life.

Peter Philips DJ

Everyone was called upon to 'muck in' and assist when needed; there was a washing up rota (using salt water, but you could get lather if you used enough detergent) and those with a talent for cooking shared that task. Some very imaginative meals were served up, with most of the crew eating together every evening.

The best meal I ever had was provided by a fisherman called
Tony who came alongside one day with two lobsters that he'd
caught, but nobody on board knew how to prepare lobster, so
he came and cooked them for us. We even had fresh salad at
the time; it really was a memorable meal.

Kevin Turner, assistant programme controller and DJ

Those with an engineering talent were always welcome and their
abilities, other than playing records, were put to good use. Peter
Philips, besides programming the music, reading the news and
presenting programmes also had a good head for heights.

We often had situations when work needed to be done on the
mast and, perhaps surprisingly, there weren't many people who
were keen on climbing it. It was around 300ft high and being
on a ship at sea was never 100 per cent stationary. The main
things that needed to be replaced were the stays. The tower
was an absolute masterpiece, held together with these stays,
steel cables that led down from various points on the tower to
various points on the deck, but being metal they all had to be
insulated, so at various points there were porcelain insulators
to prevent electric current coming down from the tower and
electrocuting people on the deck. When sea salt built up on
the porcelain or they came into contact with sea spray you'd
get a flashover with sparks which would either burn the cable,
crack the porcelain or both, so after a few rough days there'd
usually be various parts that needed replacing.

Now if just one needed attention you could ignore it for a
while, but if you had half a dozen or so at critical points in the
tower that were broken or needed attention then someone had
to go up and replace them. If you were lucky, depending on
where they were, you might only have to go up about a 100ft,
but if you were unlucky they might be nearer the top of the
mast at 300ft.

The tower on the *Ross Revenge* had no ladder and as it was a lattice tower you climbed up the lattice, as it got narrower towards the top it got easier, at the base the gap between the lattice was probably about 5ft and that took quite an effort to get going, by the time you got to the top it really was like climbing a ladder as the lattice was much tighter.

The first 50ft were the worst, the first time I went up there I got to that point and sat there for about ten minutes thinking I'm never going to complete this climb alive, but after that it gets easier, not least because you think, if you fall from any higher it's no more dangerous than falling from 50ft; the end result would be much the same. So once you'd got over that initial fear it became easier. In fact, once you got towards the top it was really rather nice up there, people down below didn't know what they were missing; you got a terrific view from up that tower, you could see what seemed like half of Britain from up there. There was a certain amount of movement when you were up there, but you expected that. The thing that worried me was because the thing was so large it was considered by the RAF to be an excellent thing to fly around by what I imagine were trainee pilots, who would suddenly come out of nowhere at something in excess of the speed of sound and go past the tower just 3ft away from it, just to show off or maybe test their piloting skills. You'd see the whites of their eyes sometimes, you'd be up there and this thing would go roaring past, you'd just have to cling on to the tower and collect yourself for a while after that happened. There were never any incidents, we were convinced that one day they'd hit the tower or the rigging, but they never did, so I suppose they must have been quite good pilots really.

Peter Philips, programme controller and DJ

The new *Mi Amigo* studio. (Carl Thomson)

All's well, thumbs up from a smiling Ronan O'Rahilly as Caroline South is back in business from *Mi Amigo*. (David Kindred)

```
KEE RAMSEYMAN

HARCOURT HARWICH 22/8/66

RECEIVED FROM JERRY LEIGHTON NEW YORK .

GEORGE ON PLANE    YOU KNOW JERRRY IT'S FUNNY ON A TOUR
LIKE THIS WITH A GROUP OF PEOPLE TRAVELLING WITH YOU, THE
ONES YOU THINK ARE GOING TO BE DRAGS TURN OUT TO BE QUITE
THE OPPOSITE, AND THE ONES YOU THINK WILL BE GREAT ARE JUST
NOTHING.

JOHN- I DONT GO BACK TO LIVERPOOL MUCH EXCEPT TO VISIT MY
RELATIVES. THERE IS NOT MUCH POINT REALLY, AFTER ALL ITS
NOT MY HOME ANY MORE .

PAUL -   RE HOUSE.   I BUY QUITE A LOT OF OLD STUFF FOR THE HOUSE,
USUALLY AT AUCTIONS.  ITS NOT BECAUSE ITS CHEAP, ALTHOUGH
THATS GOOD REALLY, BUT I REALLY LIKE VICTORIANA -  I THINK
ITS GOT CHARACTER.

JOHN -  RE RADIO.  (I THINK THAT AMERICAN RADIO ISN'T HALF
AS GOOD AS ENGLISH BECAUSE THEY TALK TOO MUCH.)  WH

WHY DON'
               5 697 @9 9,

(WHY DON'T YOU GO ON TO THE SOUTH SHIP JERRY - I'D BE ABLE
TO HEAR YOU IN LONDON THEN.  MIND YOU, I THINK THE NORTH
SHIP IS THE BETTER OF THE TWO -   GARRY STEVENS NO. 1  D J
IN NEW YORK JOINED US IN ST. K  LOUIS AND FLEW BACK TO
NEW YORK WITH US .)

HARCOURT HARWICH

KEE RAMSEYMANO
```

WOW! *

Telex report from Caroline's Jerry Leighton on the Beatles US tour. (Gord Cruise)

Radio City is off the air as Shivering Sands Fort is boarded. (Getty Images)

Gord Cruise, on air with Caroline North. (Gord Cruise)

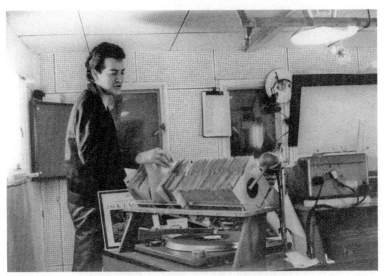

Caroline North on air with Mick Luvzit. (Carl Thomson)

A pirate marriage that made world headlines. (Gord Cruise)

The biggest hit on Major Minor that never was. (Author's collection)

Robbie Dale, Johnnie Walker and Caroline prepare to
take on the Government. (Getty Images)

MANS FIGHT FOR FREEDOM

by Johnnie Walker

This is the story of man's fight for freedom.
The beginning is in the past, the middle is now, the end is
in the future.
It is a story of sadness and triumph.
August 14th. as Disc-Jockies Robbie Dale, Johnnie Walker and
Russ Brown leave Liverpool Street Station spurred on towards
the sea by the hundreds of cheering people.
See them now as they stand on the tender. There are tears in
their eyes as their families, their homes and their loved
ones are left behind.
Three O'clock on this Monday afternoon and on 266 Big L is
heard for the last time.
Caroline is alone.
These three men prepare for midnight, for in a few hours
time they are to challenge the might and power of the British
Government. They will become criminals.
Midnight approaches and it is August 15th.
Johnnie Walker announces that Caroline belongs to YOU, that
she loves you and she will continue. The Beatles sing "All
You Need Is Love". These men sound happy, but underneath
they are sad, for they now know that they have passed the
point of no return.
They are not sad for long. They are joined by other men who
also gave up so much to fight for Freedom. The seas are rough
and cruel, life is hard but as each day passes the moment
of triumph draws nearer.
The British people rally round. They send food, they send
comfort and they send their love. All you need is Love -
and Love overcomes.
The British Government relents.
Caroline raises her anchor and heads for England.
See her now, majestically and proudly sailing up the river
towards the Capital that has welcomed so many victors in
British history.
But none as victorious as these men.
They stand on the deck waving to the millions of people who
line the Thames. This time the tears flooding from their
eyes are tears of happiness. The insurmountable odds have
been surmounted.
They re-unite with their families, with their friends, with
their loved ones.
We are near the end of our story. London's sky-line has a
new landmark pointed towards the Heavens -Caroline's aerial-
at last beaming out it's love and music to a free and peaceful nation.
We have over-come. The battle is over. Free Radio becomes
a way of life, but never taken for granted.
For no man will ever forget Monday, August 14th, nineteen
hundred and sixty seven.

Johnnie Walker

Johnnie Walker's 'Man's Fight For Freedom'. (Offshore Echos)

Caroline North is towed into Amsterdam. (Hans Knot collection)

Both Caroline ships tied up and abandoned in Amsterdam. (Rob Olthof)

The *Mebo 2*. Home to RNI and for a few days in June 1970, Caroline International. (David Kindred)

Prepared for take-off, Ronan promotes Caroline TV. (Offshore Echos)

The ship that nearly became Radio Caroline, *Oceaan* 7, Radio 270.
(Authors collection)

The end for the former *Fredericia*. (Karel Gerbers)

Mi Amigo is rescued from the breakers and is to become a pirate radio museum.
(Rob Olthof)

Mi Amigo with a new, short-lived mast 1973. (Hans van Dijk)

The *Mi Amigo* comes home to the Essex coast. (David Kindred)

Mi Amigo in rough seas. (Theo Denker/Hans Knot)

Caroline DJ's in disguise as men from the Ministry pass by. (Felixstowe and Offshore Radio Facebook page)

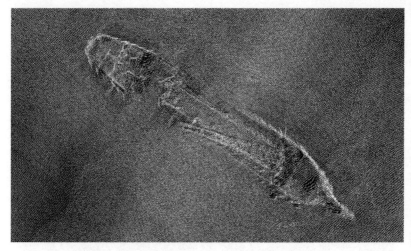

Mi Amigo – still there as seen in this sonar scan of the sunken ship with collapsed mast still attached. (Port of London Authority)

The new Radio Caroline ship takes shape in Santander. (Carol Maszka)

Ross Revenge in dry dock. (Carol Maszka)

The original studio complex, in a portable cabin welded to the deck. (Carol Maszka)

Ross Revenge heads for England. (Carol Maszka)

Caroline returns, *Ross Revenge* at anchor. (David Kindred)

Communicator, home to Laser 558. (Author's collection)

Dioptric Surveyor keeps an eye on Caroline and Laser. (Charlie Wolf/Offshore Echos)

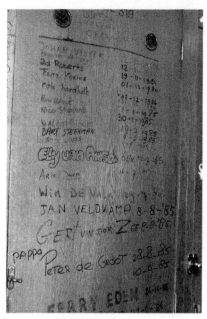

The writing's on the wall: The Radio Monique DJs leave their mark in the Dutch cabin onboard *Ross Revenge*. (Author's collection)

DATE	DAY	S	L		DATE	DAY	S	L
1		26	38		17		31	2
2		16	29		18		11	
3		10	2		19		38	2
4		30	7		20		17	
5		28	3		21		25	10
6		37	16		22		2	34
7		1	36		23		28	6
8		15	23		24		3	13
9		32	4		25		29	35
10		16	1		26		7	31
11		33	27		27		13	28
12		8	39		28		5	37
13		23	4		29		39	4
14		34	22		30		22	16
15		40	5		31		35	27
16		3	11					

1) Main anch.gon
2) Spare down
3) Spare dragging
4) Unit under pw
5) Inside limits
6) Raid
7) Police off
8) DTI off
9) Suspect off
10) Attempted boar
11) Serious illnes
12) Serious injury
13) Taking water
14) Guy wires
15) Rigger reqd ur
16) Coastguard/L.B
17) Posn:Long/Lat.
18) Tug for st.by
19) Tug for tow re
20) Tender busted

21) Exp.tender nig
22) Exp.tend.today
23) Tender reqd
24) Unable to deli
25) In contact wit
26) Generator
27) Diplexer
28) Big rig
29) Small rig
30) Ant.damage
31) Mod trans.
32) PA fault
33) Exciter fault
34) Stanton carts
35) Stanton styli
36) Swivel
37) Keep 24hr watc
38) Monique
39) 4ft fluro tube
40) 60w lamps

The 'enigma' code book. (Bill Rollins)

Emergency repairs to the aerial. (Author's collection)

The last photograph of the mast, intact, taken just days before the collapse, from the bridge of the *Olau* ferry. (Author's collection)

It's amazing what you can do with an upturned water butt –
the new, improvised aerial feeder! (Author's collection)

Before: The well-equipped Caroline studio before the raid. (Author's collection)

After: The Caroline studio is re-equipped after the raid. (Author's collection)

High and dry on the Goodwin Sands. (Mike Nichols)

The Goodwin Sands seldom give up their prey (Mike Nichols)

Ross Revenge in Dover harbour after salvage. (Authors collection)

The author, Ray Clark, known as Mick Williams aboard *Ross Revenge* in 1987.
(Francois L'hote/Offshore Echos)

29

Hurricane Force 12

Since 1974, all Caroline broadcasts had been from the sheltered Knock Deep channel off the English coast, with few passing vessels, other than dredgers and fishing boats, but changes were to be forced on Caroline once again; the British territorial limit was extended and the Knock Deep anchorage was now within UK waters. In June 1987, with the help of a crane vessel to lift the anchor, the *Ross Revenge* moved to a new position, well into international waters, close to the South Falls, midway between England and France. The main shipping lanes were nearby, but the ship was now in a more exposed position. However, there were some advantages.

> After the move to the South Falls, the Olau ferry would come past twice a day. We'd always speak to them on the ship's radio as they passed and as they went by on one occasion we just happened to mention that we'd run short of onions and potatoes. The next we knew was this huge ferry stopping very close indeed and they're throwing vegetables onto our deck and we were out there scrabbling around, picking them up in buckets.
>
> Kevin Turner, assistant programme controller and DJ

But now the *Ross Revenge* was no longer protected from the worst of the seas. Sometimes the waters in the Knock Deep were so flat calm that the ship's reflection could be seen, but this was seldom the case at the South Falls. Life on board would never be as comfortable again.

Conditions were certainly uncomfortable on 16 October 1987, as hurricane-force winds hit the south of England … and the *Ross Revenge*!

On the day of the hurricane I was doing the breakfast show, normally I would have expected to get up around 4 a.m., but this morning the engineer, Mike Watts, banged on my door sometime earlier and said, 'Oh, you'd better get up, there's a hurricane going on outside'. Well, it didn't seem like it, the ship just wasn't moving that much. The reason was, our mast was acting like a sail and the wind was blowing against it and holding the ship still, so I told him to go away, or words to that effect, but he insisted there really was a hurricane blowing. I got up and made my way upstairs to the mess room, and although it was still dark and only 3.30 a.m., you could see sheets of white outside the portholes, it was sea spray, even after day break you just couldn't see through it, it was just a solid wall of sea spray.

We turned on the radio to check what was happening on land and there was nothing on, no BBC stations, and no local commercial stations. We managed to hear one far off transmitter that was giving stories of no trains, motorways closed and no power and I didn't know whether to believe this or not. Then we listened to the ship to shore, channel 16 coastguard and we heard stories of ships washed up on beaches and ferries not running, so by now we started to think that maybe there was a hurricane going on out there and we were on a ship, 18 miles off the coast in the middle of it.

We'd turned on our transmitter and that was doing what it should, so we thought well if everything else is off the air this is a bit of an opportunity, we'll pick up some new listeners this morning; it'll be a bit of a hoot. So we just started doing a Caroline breakfast show, it was just a normal morning; the ship wasn't moving because the winds were so strong and apart from a restricted view out of the windows because of this spray all was fine. The only glitch we had was when a stay on the mast broke loose and started banging against the aerial feed wires during the programme. These feed wires carried the signal to the top of the mast and as the loose stay came into contact with them it resulted in lots of sparks and blue flashes as thousands of watts shorted between the cables. For listeners they heard an annoying 'clicking' as the wires shorted out. By this time I was getting a bit 'gritty' and thought we're not going to have this, so I told the listeners that we had a minor problem and had to switch off for about ten minutes. With the power from the transmitter turned off and wearing waterproof clothes, we tied a rope around my waist and the other end onto a deck rail and I went out into the full force of the wind and I'd never known anything like it. The wind was so strong, it was impossible to walk, the only way to make any progress was to pull yourself along using the deck rail, my legs weren't really doing very much. I managed to climb to the roof of the bridge and could see this stay flapping around, but couldn't reach it, so still holding on I 'flew' a piece of rope, rather like a kite until the rope captured this wire stay as they wrapped around each other. It was the wind that did the job rather than me, and I was able to pull this stay in and roped it off as best I could and climbed down, back into the ship. Mike, the engineer fired up the transmitter again and, as you'd expect being Caroline, we just carried on with the show.

Peter Philips, programme controller and DJ

A song from Katrina and the Waves there on Caroline 558 … don't talk to me about waves, outside it's just a seething cauldron of saline hostility.

The 300ft high radio tower and its supports had certainly been strained, almost to the limits. Temporary repairs were made by the crew on the ship, but riggers would be needed to restore the structure to the standard necessary to survive. The rigging had been stretched and the many porcelain insulators had been damaged and urgently needed replacement and repair. Sadly the riggers didn't get to the ship in time to prevent a disaster; in the early hours of 25 November 1987 the tallest mast ever built on a ship came crashing down. Radio Caroline was off the air.

Fortunately for those on board, Chief Engineer Ernie Stevenson took charge; he had seen most things during his long nautical career.

I was in bed and I heard this crash, sort of thundering noise, and I thought, 'what the hells happened now?' I got out my bed and I'm a bit deaf, so I was going to tear a strip of the DJs for waking me up, but I was informed, 'the mast's fallen down chief', by now we had really bad seas whacking the ship.

It would appear that where the mast broke off, the top had pinned into the sea bed and it was holding the ship, but luckily enough with the tide change, we swung around it. Around 4.30 a.m., there was this horrible banging and crashing on the ships side and we wondered what it was. I tried to get the light to see and I saw it was the remainder of the ship's mast crashing into the ship's side.

Well the seas were that bad that I got them all together with their life jackets on, that's when one of them piped up, 'Chiefy, chiefy, 'scuse me, you've got no trousers on.'

'Trousers? I'm trying to save yer bloody life, stop worrying about trousers' so they were all mustered and settled down and then the weather was easing off, although we still had great seas crashing about, but we were all safe. So then we looked at what was hammering at the vessel. It was the mast still attached to us by the guy wires, so with Peter Chicago holding me and ropes around us, we went cutting wires with great seas crashing over the top of us as we were there with the oxyacetylene torch.

We managed to cut most of them away, but left a few in case we could recover the mast, but eventually the ship decided herself that she didn't want that mast, so about twenty-four hours after it had come down there was this awful 'whipping' sound as it parted, quite violently. All the DJs were thinking she was going to sink because now the ship was behaving as she should, she no longer had the mast up and she was shying about and bouncing about something absolutely wicked which was hardly surprising because she had no top weight, but over 200 tons of concrete ballast down below, this for the mast she no longer had. It was so rough, cups wouldn't stay in one place, we had to get the cupboards opened up and the 'fiddles' on the table so that all the plates would stay there, watching them it was comical.

Ernie Stevenson, chief ship's engineer

Ernie Stevenson had retired from a lifetime at sea on deep-sea trawlers – he had been the chief engineer for the Ross fisheries fleet. Ernie had seen seas in all conditions on many ships, including the *Ross* in her fishing days and, now in his 70s, had been persuaded to work for Caroline. As with all problems that beset Caroline, the first thought was always to get back on air as soon as possible.

We needed a replacement mast and it was Ernie Stevenson who pointed out an old pipe running the length of the ship that could be used to get an aerial up, he didn't initially tell us that it had been used in the ship's trawler days for carrying liquefied fish livers from the back deck where they were processed to a tank at the front of the ship where they were stored and it had probably been about twenty-five years since this pipe had last been used, but they were all still there, so when we cut this pipe out with a welding torch the ship smelt from top to bottom of fried cods' livers. The smell was everywhere, it got into the walls, the carpets, the furniture, everything , but we persevered and washed it out with a high pressure hose over the side and probably fed these remaining livers to something in the sea, possibly giving them salmonella or something. We strengthened this pipe with bits of angle iron so that it didn't wobble around too much and welded a cross bar to it, and connected our aerial array to it, then using the ship's crane we dangled it over the side and hoisted it into place, it was

quite a moment as we'd been working on this thing for about
two weeks.

> Peter Philips, programme controller and DJ

Using the cod liver oil pipe as an aerial mast was certainly a stroke
of genius, but the unique and hugely expensive ceramic aerial
feed had also been smashed when the tower came down, but in a
true example of Caroline's innovative solutions to technical difficulties, it was replaced by an upturned plastic water butt ... and
it worked!

> It was time to connect all the wires onto the top of the mast,
> there was only one bloke who was good at climbing and that
> was Peter Philips, he trusted my knots so we hoisted him
> up, tied onto a rope that was connected to the winch and I
> wound him up and he connected the aerial up and we were
> back in business with the best signal we'd had since the mast
> came down.
>
> Ernie Stevenson, chief ship's engineer

Keeping the ship supplied and the transmitters on air had now
become even more of a task than it had before. The momentum
of an adaptable and reasonably well structured organisation had
been lost and without the limited, but regular income that had
kept the radio stations operating in the past, the future looked
uncertain. Worse still, there was no Dutch service, and the Dutch
had provided fuel, oil and food. With no income these were now
in short supply. But efforts to rebuild Caroline continued.

By now the disc jockey line-up was changing frequently as
regular presenters left the ship, many in search of work ashore at
independent local radio stations. Consequently there was now a
rapid turnover of mainly inexperienced staff joining Caroline. Nick
Jackson had wanted to join the radio station since leaving school.

> It was early January 1989 when I arrived alongside *Ross Revenge*
> for the first time on a cold, overcast morning. The North Sea

hadn't been kind to us but our tender *Fairwind* and legendary skipper Dave 'The Fish' Turner, delivered us alongside safely. The next challenge was to transfer to the *Ross Revenge*, easier said than done on a cold January morning when you are frozen stiff and the small fishing boat you are standing on is pitching and rolling around on an angry sea, trying to free itself from the mooring ropes securing it to the radio ship. Supplies and personnel transferred, we gathered in the messroom. I remember the ship being lovely and warm, which was wonderful having endured such a miserable journey out into the North Sea lasting several hours.

Engineer Mike Watts gave me a full tour of the ship after my first show and I was blown away by the sheer size of *Ross Revenge*. It was the engine room that left a lasting impression. The mighty 10-cylinder Werkspoor engine was still in working order at the time and was to be fired up within days of my arrival. The fully equipped workshop with its various machinery and hardware left over from the ships trawling days impressed me just as much as the warm transmitter room on the other side of the bulkhead. With two AM services and the Short-Wave religious service all operating, the TX room was an amazing place to be, not to mention deadly if you weren't careful and Mike took time to point out the various 'danger areas' around the ship.

I settled into life on board very quickly and loved being there. As well as a daily show on Caroline 558, I also kept an eye on the Short-Wave religious service, 'World Mission Radio'. A few of the crew would take it in turns to do 'The Gods', making sure the right pre-recorded programmes were played out at the correct time following a schedule provided by the owner. We were also paid for our efforts!

The first major event came about a week after my arrival when a massive tug arrived one morning. They brought out a number of crew members for the Dutch language service, Radio 819. Transfer complete, they then used their giant onboard crane to raise our anchor for inspection, moving us slightly closer to the Falls Head buoy at the same time. Re-anchored, they flushed clean just about every freshwater tank on *Ross Revenge* and filled each one to the brim. Finally, several months-worth of diesel was pumped aboard. With the job complete, *Ross Revenge* sat incredibly low in the water.

Nick Jackson DJ

30

WHO are THE real PIraTes Here?

Further attempts were made to improve the aerial system, including the use of new technology in the form of a flexible mast made
from fibre glass with a toughened outer shell. With yards of copper
wire inside, it was reckoned to be capable of taking a high-power
feed from the transmitter. Fixed to the deck at the base, the mast
swayed wildly as the wind blew and the ship moved. When it was
tested at low power it failed spectacularly, caught fire and went
into self-destruct. During this time the Dutch service had been
off the air and they were eager to return, this time as Radio 558,
taking over the English Caroline frequency. Ultimately two new,
substantial masts were built to a height of about 80ft by those on
board using assorted mast sections that were transported out to
the ship until, over a two-year period, the technical adaptations
eventually enabled three separate radio services to broadcast from
the *Ross Revenge*.

> I found myself in the back of a rusty old Transit van going to
> Herne Bay on a cold Sunday evening in January 1988. Here I
> encountered 'Dave the Fish' for the first time and we boarded
> his boat, *Fairwind*, for what seemed an eternally long and rough
> trip out to the Falls Head. I joined just a couple of months after
> the mast had been lost, we weren't even on air at the time and
> I remember much excitement over a shortwave test transmis-
> sion. By the end of the month, Peter Chicago had rigged up
> an antenna that allowed us to broadcast on very low power on
> 558, but it was so low that only the closest coastal areas were
> able to pick us up. Later, we went to collect several sections of

galvanized steel tower that were then loaded, at considerable danger, onto the *Fairwind* and then winched aboard the *Ross* in the dead of night. The new tower allowed us to increase power on 558, I climbed it on several occasions to attach stays, and with it we were able to get the Dutch back on board with Radio 819. In January 1989, we were given the go ahead to start Caroline 819 –the overnight alternative, which ran from 10 p.m. until 6 a.m.

Rob Harrison, DJ

Caroline returned, the Dutch service continued and a new short-wave service broadcast religious programmes and was known as World Mission Radio. Against all odds, Caroline was once again back in business.

But behind the scenes the Dutch authorities had decided to act against those responsible for the broadcasts from the ship and the British Government was happy to go along with their plans. The authorities believed that the ship was now stateless and there were police raids and arrests in Belgium and Holland. Those involved behind the scenes were questioned and on Friday 18 August 1989 a launch, chartered by the British Government, moored close to the *Ross Revenge*, giving the Caroline crew an ultimatum – throw in the towel or face the consequences. The crew on the radio ship contacted those ashore in England and made them aware of the situation; Peter Chicago needed to be on board.

The first I heard about any impending trouble, was an announcement on the Radio Caroline news and there was a call 'for the attention of the office' added onto the end of the bulletin which indicated a problem. We had a telephone out on the ship at this time, it was quite a recent addition, I was able to telephone the *Ross Revenge* and find out exactly what was going on and apparently a British boat chartered by the DTI had gone out to the ship and invited the crew to stop broadcasting and leave the ship, under pain of some unspecified threat. Needless to say, nobody was prepared to just walk away from the boat, but they had been given to understand that if they weren't prepared to stop broadcasting, something more serious was going to happen the following day; it all appeared rather vague and odd. I realised the best thing I could do was to get out to the ship. Well at this time I had a small 10ft inflatable rubber boat and an outboard engine and the weather was quite good, so that night, I went out for a quiet drink in the pub and then loaded the boat into the car, drove down to Broadstairs, inflated the boat on the quay, put this boat over the side and went out to the ship. It was quite exciting; I'd never attempted to get out to the ship just on my own in a small boat before, but it was a clear, moonlit night and the sea was reasonably calm.

I got to the ship in the middle of the night and got a bit more detail to the story. We'd been told that the Department of Trade were going to return at eleven o'clock in the morning to receive an answer – were people prepared to close the radio station down and leave the ship or not? So we waited and at eleven o'clock the boat, *The Landward*, came into sight. It was a fairly misty day so we didn't see them until they were quite close. They hinted that the people involved in the station were involved in serious crime, 'we realise that you're only out here broadcasting in all innocence, but we have to tell you that there are much more serious matters involved and your offices in Holland and England have all been raided.' Well, I knew that this was rubbish because I knew all of the people involved intimately. There'd been suggestions that the boat was used for drug running or laundering money, but all simply because people couldn't believe the truth, which was, we all enjoyed doing what we were doing and that we weren't making much money at it, but we did enjoy the broadcasting and the freedom of being out there.

Well, when they saw that these implied threats, 'you don't know what you've got mixed up in, but be good boys and leave the boat and nothing more will happen to you' when that angle didn't work, they said, 'we have to tell you that phase two is due to come into operation soon, and if you're not prepared to leave the boat now, you'll have to take your chances'.

Well, about half an hour later, a much bigger boat came into view, it was a Dutch boat, the *Volans*. They were coming straight towards us and it was quite obvious that they were intending to come alongside. I called them on the radio to try and find out what the intentions were and they ignored the calls. I called North Foreland Radio to say that we were under threat and again, North Foreland Radio ignored the calls and before I had a chance to do anything else the boat had actually come alongside.

                                        Peter Chicago, broadcast engineer

Anybody hearing this broadcast perhaps can help us by telephoning the coastguard to register a complaint, possibly by contacting anybody in authority that you think could help us. This is the radio ship Ross Revenge *broadcasting from the international waters of the North Sea.*

There were uniformed Dutch police officers on board the *Volans* and one of them started to come over the side and I pushed him back and he made another attempt to come over and I pushed him back again and at that point he started to draw a pistol and I didn't back off and he changed his mind. The next thing I knew, I'd been hit pretty hard on the chin, hard enough that I blacked out for a few seconds. By the time I came to, there were several uniformed officials on board. The ship had been boarded. A spokesperson who worked for the equivalent of the DTI in Holland, explained that they were taking action under Dutch law which in his own words 'entitled them to come out and seize any transmitting equipment that had been used to make broadcasts towards Holland' and that their instructions were to take the equipment intact. He sent some technicians down below and within a couple of minutes they'd come back up again and said this was completely impossible; it would take them about two weeks to dismantle the equipment. There was more discussion in Dutch and finally they made communication with their superiors back in Holland and they decided they were going to take the major components out of the transmitters and, as we discovered later, just about everything else that they could get their hands on.

As the day progressed, more and more damage was being done and the components they did take out of the transmitters, a lot of them were smashed or cut out, there was an awful lot of broken porcelain, wires hacked through and even transformers which had been too large to remove were damaged by chipping hammers. In other words the ship was being completely gutted of all viable broadcasting equipment. They even turned their attention to the ship's generators and they had put one of the generators out of action by smashing the pump housing, but before that had got too far advanced, I pointed out to them, that these were the generators that supplied power to the whole boat and that they were putting the boat itself and those on it in danger by disabling the power plant and they did at that point stop, but not before it was too late for one of the generators.

The whole thing was just an extremely unpleasant and soul-destroying experience; I'd been instrumental in putting the whole transmitting installation together, even the studios. I'd put a lot of the woodwork together, planned the layout of the studios and to see it all destroyed … it was really a horrible day, the only, slightly good thing that did happen was that over the course of the day I tried my best to argue the Dutch technicians out of what they were doing and I think was able to appeal to their better nature to the extent that at five o'clock they announced that they were going to take a break back on their own ship, and this to me was a pretty clear signal from them saying, 'well, if you've got any sense go back down below and take as much as you can and put it away and at least have something to get back on the air with, at least I think it was quite deliberate … a nudge and a wink sort of thing. Well of course we did just that, taking enough equipment to get one of the radio transmitters back on the air again, and that's the only reason that we were able to go back on air again so quickly.

Peter Chicago, broadcast engineer

Supporters of the radio station were outraged and there was talk of legal action being taken on behalf of Caroline, but in the end the Caroline strategy of getting back on the air as soon as possible, proved the best way ahead. Within days, various bits of replacement radio equipment had made their way out to the ship, much of it provided by friends of Caroline and former employees, who were now working for land-based commercial stations. A demonstration was held in London and many gifts were donated by those present. A lot gave records, something Caroline was without as the vast record library had been taken during the Dutch raid. Yet another return to air was seen as the only way ahead for the station and this time the fans were encouraged to contribute towards the future of Caroline.

Caroline limped back on air in early October 1989. Shortly afterwards, I returned to the ship as there were only three presenters who were each doing two shifts a day. This time, *Fairwind* was weighed down with all of the donations from the London rally. The fish hold was full of gifts for the crew, tins of food and boxes and boxes of records. Some supporters had donated their entire record collections. Arriving alongside the *Ross Revenge*, Peter Chicago spotted the mountain of supplies and shouted, 'I suppose you've brought a kitchen sink as well?' at which point, Dave 'The Fish' reached into his hold and produced a fine example!

It was a very sorry looking ship that I re-joined that October, but we battled on. I stayed for a few weeks before heading ashore and, following in the footsteps of a number of colleagues, I sent out some demo tapes.

Nick Jackson DJ

31

COULD THIS FINALLY BE THE END?

Using the parts that found their way to the ship, and the equipment stashed away during the raid, Peter Chicago was once again able to get Caroline back on air, but any quality of content and signal had all but gone. No longer did the large tender, *Bellatrix*, service the ship. Likeable, but fanatical, Caroline fan, Dave the Fish, used his small fishing boat to deliver whatever parts could be acquired, despite almost constant surveillance on movements around the *Ross Revenge*. Now the radio station was financed purely by donations and the income from a premium-rate telephone line, and much of the magic had disappeared from the broadcasts. Many long-standing Caroline supporters thought the time had come to retire gracefully.

Just two years earlier, the *Ross Revenge* had been clean and comfortable; the ship had been run in an orderly fashion and was treated like home by the small community of radio personal. On approach you were aware of major activity on board, with bright lights blazing and powerful generators screaming – it was a hub of power and professionalism. Now the ship was often without fuel and it was getting harder to find people prepared to endure living in such basic conditions.

> I lodged an interest to help fill-in, on a strictly short-term basis, and about ten days later I was asked to go out with a Dave the Fish tender. His small boat was laden down with tools, electrical materials, some crates of tinned food and beer and me, plus a very large PA system with big speakers, an amplifier and a radio receiver that blasted out the live broadcast of Caroline at a volume that hurt.

I found the ship was in quite a mess generally, parts of her looked as if she'd been turned completely upside down and upright again. Disappointingly, tins of non-perishable food were still on deck from the previous tender, well over a week ago and had not been stowed. There was a definite air of lethargy amongst the small number of people remaining out there. The engine room was not bad, albeit a bit oily, considering the main ship's engine didn't work at the time. I was told to take my pick from two of the better (least damp) vacant cabins downstairs. There was little to choose between them, a well-used quilt would help keep me warm with my clothes on. The galley was in a better state than I imagined, although it was still pretty grim by anyone's standards. There was no sign or smell of any imminent cooked food, so I unloaded my tins of meatballs and spaghetti and commenced heating a very basic snack.

Chris Watford, DJ

Once, we had almost run out of drinking water and were reduced to showering in salt water and drinking a mixture of putrid white wine mixed with lemonade to make it more palatable. Another time, we ran out of diesel and only had enough to light the navigation lights. The transmitter had to be turned off and there was no lighting inside the ship. The worst incident was The Great Tobacco Famine of 1989, when we were reduced to pulling up the decking on the bridge to find old fag ends to roll up.

Rob Harrison, DJ

Broadcasts were erratic throughout the winter, but in spring 1990, it appeared that the final confrontation had been engineered by the DTI as a new radio station for London, Spectrum, was allocated 558kHz, the frequency that Caroline had been using for five years. Interference made both stations difficult to listen to and those supplying the ship at this time were subject to intensified surveillance. After thirty-six years of fighting to survive, it seemed the luck and spirit of Caroline was gone. Peter

Moore, who had assumed control in the absence of anyone else coming forward, maintained efforts to continue, but as fuel and finance finally ran dry, Caroline made her last broadcast from sea on 5 November 1990. The ship remained at anchor at the Falls Head, but she was now silent. What had been an impressive unit capable of broadcasting clear, professional and reliable high-powered radio programmes, listened to by millions across Europe just a few years before, was now a near-derelict wreck.

Manned by volunteers who appeared to have little interest or ability in keeping the vessel in a safe condition, she was without power for even the most basic needs such as lighting, heating or cooking. The crew even resorted to the ridiculous situation of putting candles in portholes, in an attempt to light the ship, which was moored close to the busiest shipping lanes in the world. As conditions became unbearable she was abandoned; the crew could take no more and called for help, they were airlifted off.

The chance was here for the authorities to make their grab on the abandoned radio ship, but once again they failed to act. Risking his life to retake the ship, Peter Chicago was able to get back on board, but any hope of broadcasting from the ship again was thwarted by the introduction of a new Broadcast Act. From January 1991, armed forces would be given the right to board any ship suspected of broadcasting in international waters and use whatever force was deemed necessary to curtail the transmissions. Whilst over the years, Caroline had managed to defend herself against nature and Government bureaucracy, there would be no chance of defence against armed forces boarding the ship. A draconian end to a service that had been provided free of charge and given untold enjoyment to millions over the years, to a service that had started an industry and promoted British music which had influenced the world. There appeared to be no future for Radio Caroline, but was it the end?

With the ship still at sea, there was hope that some foreign power would grant Caroline a licence to broadcast legally from her position off the English coast. Contact was made with authorities in Cuba via a European embassy, and one of Caroline's religious programme providers had links with Equatorial Guinea. The plan was that tourism to these countries could be promoted in return for the use of their flag and a licence to broadcast, but no agreement was reached.

The *Ross Revenge* Support Group, made up of Caroline fans prepared to donate money in the vain hope of a future at sea for the radio station, provided limited food and fuel supplies. An uneasy truce was made with the DTI who allowed goods to be taken out to the ship, providing no attempt was made to broadcast, but every move to the ship was watched.

The once proud radio ship remained at sea throughout the summer, but during November 1991, the *Ross Revenge* again lost her anchor in huge seas. The caretaker crew, living in near squalor, were unaware that the ship was adrift until a violent lurch was felt as they ran aground on the Goodwin Sands, a notorious sandbank that had been the final resting place for most ships that have ever beached there. The crew were once again airlifted to safety in a hazardous operation by an RAF rescue helicopter.

We'd been in a ferocious storm, a North Easterly force eleven and when we ran aground, the ship was bucking and tearing around underneath us and we ended up at this thirty to forty-five degree angle, and each wave that was hitting us was pushing us further onto the sandbank and we were tilting over farther.

The helicopter was coming out to try and rescue us, the lifeboat, the wonderful, brave people from Ramsgate RNLI had run aground themselves, and there was a time, for about five minutes, when we were absolutely convinced that before the helicopter could reach us the ship was going to roll over, we were going to be in the water, and we were all going to be drowned.

We were clinging to various pieces of equipment in the bridge, 'cos the ship was at such an angle, so we got together into a little group and we shook hands and we said goodbye because we were absolutely convinced that we were going to die and then just when it seemed that things couldn't get any worse the helicopter arrived and we made our way outside and we were rescued … it's a day that I will never ever forget.

Steve Conway

We all crossed the wet and sloping deck and hung onto the rear transmitting mast. As the waves crashed over us the RAF man was lowered to the back of the stern deck. I slipped on the wet deck and slid down to the starboard rails. Fortunately I hit a spare section of mast and from here I managed to crawl to the back of the deck. The RAF man was able to drop the rescue harness over me and then attached himself. I felt my feet leave the deck, but then they got stuck under the safety rail. With the helicopter pulling and my safety boots refusing to bend something had to give way. I started to fall out of the loop; the rescue man grabbed my lifejacket and stopped me falling. The helicopter moved away from our stricken ship and finally we were winched up.

Stuart Dobson, crew member

Reports that the abandoned *Ross Revenge* was on her side gave little hope of the ship's survival, but as tides receded, the 1,000-ton ship was high and dry, and upright on top of the sands. Salvage tugs made their way to the Goodwins. For a while it was doubtful that the ship could be saved, but eventually she was heaved clear of the sands and into deeper water, although it took two powerful tugs to haul her clear, reputedly on their last attempt. The *Ross Revenge* was then dragged into Dover docks. Dover Harbour Board had salvaged the ship, but who owned her and were the owners' prepared, or able, to pay the salvage costs?

Peter Moore, initially just a fan of the station, had become more embroiled in the organisation, until now he *was* the organisation. As Caroline's caretaker, he was recognised by the salvagers and negotiated a drastically reduced salvage fee of £20,000 to reclaim the ship. But even this amount was unavailable, supporters were able to come up with some of the cash, but unless they wanted a wreck permanently taking space in the Western Docks, Dover Harbour Board had to accept Moore's plea for time to pay.

The salvage money was now being paid, albeit in instalments, but even if the bill had been settled outright, *Ross Revenge,* because of her condition, was still trapped in the harbour. The ship was effectively a wreck, completely unseaworthy with a huge list of necessary repairs to be completed before she could move beyond the confines of Dover's Western dock.

Inspectors from the Marine Safety Agency arrived, spending two days examining the *Ross Revenge* concluding, not surprisingly, that she was the worst, most unseaworthy ruin of a ship they had ever seen. A mighty list of faults was assembled. Major items such as, the steering gear was destroyed, through to facts that the crew had no marine qualifications at all and that there was no safety equipment not even an anchor. It was noted that there was little lighting; no running water, no heating, insufficient furnishing, and the list was endless. I was handed a thick book of defects. The contempt of the inspectors was evidenced by their parting comment that anyone who went to sea on such a ship deserved to drown.

Peter Moore

Again fans, friends and supporters with various abilities came to the rescue, and a call was put out for the one man capable of over-seeing the work to make the *Ross Revenge* seaworthy once again. Ernie Stevenson had left Caroline while she was still on air. He wasn't a young man and his health was suffering, but he was tracked down and journeyed south to rejoin his former ship.

My wife was reading the evening paper here in Hull and she said, 'oi, look at this, radio call for Ernie', she read it out, then all my cousins were calling up telling me that I was wanted. Well I knew the telephone number, so I called up Peter Moore, he told me that she'd been aground; she was in trouble and needed help. He was asking questions about different parts of the ship, so I managed to mend the central heating from up here, and then they said, 'when are you coming back down?'

I went down and I looked her all over and it was a disaster area, but if you start with a disaster and keep repairing small corners, you eventually get to the middle and complete the picture, and that was my intention.

Ernie Stevenson, chief ship's engineer

Ernie immediately took control of the situation, helped by those that had relevant expertise. Others, who he saw as surplus to requirements, were encouraged to leave the ship, but the challenge ahead was huge.

32

WHat DO WE DO NOW?

It became obvious that if Radio Caroline had a future it would no longer be from a ship anchored outside British territorial waters. As work on the ship continued, history was made, Radio Caroline applied for a licence to broadcast, and a restricted radio licence was granted for one month while the ship was in Dover. It was the first of many similar licences to be granted over the years to come. Disc Jockey Tony Kirk had served three spells onboard *Ross Revenge* when she was still at sea and became involved with the start of this new era for Caroline.

I was in the Caroline office and remember talking to Peter Moore, he was saying 'What do we do? We have little money, the ship is impounded in Dover.' It was a real tale of woe, but he mentioned the twenty-eight-day Restricted Service broadcast Licences (RSL) that the Radio Authority issued and suggested I call them to ask if we could apply for one and broadcast from the ship in Dover harbour. The initial response was no, as we were considered a pirate, I explained that nobody had been prosecuted, so the lady I was speaking to went away and five minutes later I was then told that our application could go ahead.

We then needed a site high enough to base our transmitter and contacted Dover Castle, they were happy to accommodate us, but had to check with English Heritage head office. They'd recently appointed a new Chief Executive, an original Caroline backer from the 1960s, Jocelyn Stevens, I can only speculate whether this had any bearing on English Heritage's helpfulness, but I was awarded the licence and we went on air on 7 April 1992.

Tony Kirk DJ & Licence Applicant

With a low-powered FM signal, the Dover broadcast certainly gained publicity through press and local TV and radio interest. The programmes were presented from the ship by some who had served in offshore times and a selection of new volunteers. This was Caroline's first ever licensed broadcast, but compared to even the weakest signal from her days at sea, the range was miniscule. However, limited advertising and the sale of merchandise provided funds towards the salvage bill and escalating harbour costs.

Caroline's broadcasts were no longer seen as a threat to European Governments and now official bodies, if not helping, certainly were not hindering Caroline's continuance unduly. Agreement was reached with the Dutch authorities who had raided the *Ross Revenge* just a few years earlier and the broadcast equipment that had been ransacked from the ship was returned, collected from a security compound in Holland, and refitted.

A further RSL was arranged for Chatham Dockyard, the hope had been to have the ship moved to the Medway but, as work progressed, she was still impounded in Dover, so an expensive relay of signals was set up enabling the broadcast to go ahead from Dover. Although the broadcast served to keep the name of Caroline alive, it ultimately cost money and confirmed the urgency to leave Dover and reduce expense.

All effort was put into clearing the debt owed to Dover Harbour Board, and finding an alternative mooring, but for a one thousand ton ship with a 17-foot draught, this was no easy task.

With very few other possibilities, a suitable mooring was found in the River Blackwater in Essex. In the years following the war, the river had been used as a safe, deep water anchorage for many 'resting … and rusting' ships, but the practice of mooring ships whilst they waited for work had stopped – nowadays a ship without work was scrapped, rather than incur mounting costs. The mooring had been found, but meeting the conditions to her moving there, were daunting.

Had it not been for Ernie's motivation I doubt she would have made it out of the dock, except maybe to the breakers. Sam Parker from the Marine Coastguard Agency was very encouraging. We all sat around the table in the mess room and he said, 'Well gentlemen, you have a huge task ahead of you, but from what I've seen so far you have definitely made big inroads into addressing the list of what's to do and Mr Stevenson has the knowledge of what is required to make the vessel suitable for a dead tow. I cannot believe that she has lasted this long and the fact that she came off the Goodwins is a miracle in itself.'

Howard Beer, Boatman

The DTI were satisfied that, providing I was around, they'd let the ship go out. They left me five jobs, I got them done, but I extended them in all directions so I had about thirty jobs in total. All they had to do was get it registered and get in dry dock and I could do the rest of it, or at least tell the lads what to do.

Ernie Stevenson

Preparations were made to leave Dover. The tug, *Sea Challenge*, arrived alongside the *Ross Revenge* and commenced the tow. The Department of Trade detectives had mixed feelings about the departure, but they would soon have discovered that nobody wanted to return to the awful final days at sea. There was no intention to dismiss the tug mid voyage and lower the new anchors. Officials surmised that maybe the intention was to sink the ship and claim the insurance. Had they checked they would have discovered that the ship had no insurance.

Peter Moore

It was a grey, wet morning with a fresh north easterly wind. The *Sea Challenge* connected us up with assistance from a harbour board workboat and we were swung in the dock to enter the lock, which had to be done at high water because of the size of her.

Howard Beer

The new anchorage was far more scenic than that at Dover. The ship was anchored mid river, about half a mile from shore with access available from boats based at nearby Bradwell Marina. Publicity once again came with the arrival of the ship, an eight-hour broadcast by the local Essex radio station, Breeze, was made from the vessel marking the radio station's thirtieth birthday. More than forty interviews were recorded with former disc jockeys and staff from the station's history, together with live links by Caroline DJ's Peter Philips and the author and appropriate music from Caroline's days at sea. One of those live interviews was with the station's founder, Ronan O'Rahilly. It was very unusual to see him onboard, and it was an extremely rare occurrence for him to be heard on his own radio station. The broadcast attracted hundreds of visitors to Bradwell, many of whom boarded sight-seeing boats to the ship. Television coverage of the event also boosted public awareness that Caroline still existed. The interviews from that broadcast form the basis of this book!

Plans were made for a further RSL broadcast to coincide with the East Coast Boat Show, being held at nearby Burnham-on-Crouch. Once again a number of former 'offshore' presenters from the latter days at sea were on board for the broadcast, including Barry Lewis, Steve Masters and Chris Kennedy. This broadcast also saw the 'return' of veteran Caroline DJ Johnnie Walker to the station after nearly thirty years, bringing with him further publicity, even if a national newspaper article was far from complimentary about a group of middle aged men attempting to relive the glory years of Radio Caroline, 'Still seasick after all these years' was the title of the piece.

Mechanical repairs to the ship continued throughout this period with much work completed and a good morale amongst all onboard. A team of engineers from 'up north' caught up with maintenance on much of the equipment that had been ignored since becoming an offshore radio ship.

> We were called 'The Northern group' [and] there were about twenty-four of us at one time: Tommy the welder, Terry the train … some have stuck, some have gone and come back. I think over the years I must have touched or repaired everywhere on the ship, there's about 3 miles of piping and the welding goes on forever. We had some good guys out there, Barry Lewis and I had a plan. We'd place a newspaper and milk bottles out on the deck and then told a new recruit to go and fetch them, they thought we were getting a regular delivery in the middle of the river – until they noticed the date on the newspaper.
>
> Peter Clayton, Ship's Engineer

After eighteen months in the relative safety of the River Blackwater, the opportunity arose to broadcast to the seaside town of Clacton-on-Sea, further around the Essex coast. Even by 'tweaking' the allowed transmitter power, a listenable signal from the ship would not be possible, so a further move was needed, but rules and regulations relating to the ships condition were still in place.

> It had been made clear that the Dover to Bradwell voyage was the only one possible. However, Sam Parker, the marine inspector who initially had been so appalled by the ship, watched us doing our best for four years and had warmed to us. He suggested that the *Ross Revenge* might now be classified as an unpowered barge and offered to examine the ship, release it from detention and detain it again off the coast at Clacton.
>
> Once again the ship was offshore and broadcasting with its own transmitter and generators. For residents of Clacton with long memories, the glory days of pirate radio had briefly returned, added to by the return of yet another name from the 60s, this time it was one of the Caroline disc jockeys from

the very early days returning to sea, Tom Lodge. As the final days of the event approached, knowing that radio inspectors had no means of arriving on board, the crew stood down the tiny transmitter and turned on one that had been used at sea. Ofcom engineers listening at their base in Baldock, 75 miles away, knew what was happening, but just sent a message that they were enjoying the music.

Peter Moore

Further RSL broadcasts followed, with the ship moving under tow to a number of anchorages around the Thames Estuary. Following Clacton, the next port of call was Southend-on-Sea, this time mooring at the end of the longest pleasure pier in the world. In keeping with the Caroline story, each chapter had an adventure associated with it, this time during a summer storm the entire electrical system on the pier was blacked out by a lightning strike. *Ross Revenge* with her huge onboard generators, little used since the offshore days, saved the day and powered the entire pier until the necessary repairs were made. Once again Caroline was in the news, and this time for all the right reasons.

The next move was into London's Docklands. A pressure group aimed at involving youngsters in politics, was prepared to finance a further 28-day broadcast to London, presumably the thinking was that Radio Caroline, a former pirate station, appealed to young people. Sadly, the youngsters that remembered the heyday of Caroline were now middle aged. However, this latest adventure once again gave ample opportunity for the public in general to be reminded that Caroline still existed.

In the defiant days of 1967, disc jockey Johnnie Walker had recorded a stirring speech about the day when 'Caroline would raise her anchor and sail, triumphantly, into London, witnessed by cheering crowds lining the banks of the Thames.' Well, this was the day! Although Walker boarded the ship on her voyage upstream to West India Dock, there was a distinct absence of cheering crowds.

The broadcast, and the ships accessible position, once moored within the Docklands complex, provided the opportunity for several Caroline 'old boys' from the 1960s to pay homage to the latest Caroline ship and their former leader, Ronan. Those present had all had successful radio careers launched on Caroline, and included Tony Blackburn, Mike Ahern, Johnnie Walker and Tom Lodge, the photographs again made the daily press.

Yet again adventure and mishap were just hours away. Shortly after the ship departed Docklands, the IRA detonated a huge truck bomb in South Quay. It killed two people and caused huge damage to buildings adjacent to the position where the *Ross Revenge* had been tied up for the previous month, another close call for the ship.

Luckily, *Ross Revenge* was now in dry dock in Chatham, the first time the aged ship had been out of the water in nearly fifteen years since her conversion from a deep sea trawler to a radio ship in Santander in the early eighties and only because the shipping inspector had demanded action if she was to continue being hiked around the Thames estuary.

There was insufficient budget for all that could have been done, just enough to ultra sound the hull thickness, overhaul the sea valves and paint the hull from the keel to the bulwarks. The previous hull damage was noted and one option was to detain the ship in dry dock for repair. But as the metal thickness was good and since such action would bankrupt the supporters, the ship was permitted to moor back on the River Medway. Now that it was at least proven that the ship was fit to float, the Marine Safety Agency offered another concession. The process of releasing the ship and detaining it the next day was becoming farcical and costing Radio Caroline £500 each time. It was agreed that, thereafter, *Ross Revenge* could go anywhere at will within the smooth water limits of the Thames Estuary. Time passed, staff retired and officialdom forgot that the ship existed.

Peter Moore

Further RSL broadcasts followed. For a while the ship was moored in full view of passing traffic in Chatham, then, after a return to Southend pier, her visit was dramatically cut short when, with approaching bad weather, it was deemed likely that the ship was stronger than the pier and could destroy the seaward landing stage.

Another move took *Ross Revenge* to a remote, exposed anchorage off Queenborough, Isle of Sheppey. For much of the time she was locked and unattended, however, on Christmas Eve 1999, with a caretaker crew aboard, she broke adrift and again the services of a tug were needed to pull the ship to safety and a quieter mooring.

As the new century approached, new communication technology was evolving. Former Caroline DJ, Chris Cary had become a maverick businessman, successfully operating the hugely popular Irish land-based station Radio Nova during the '80s. When Nova was closed by the Irish Government, Cary invested money into various technical innovations that increased his wealth. He'd experimented with satellite-delivered radio, but the return was not adequate for him, he closed the station and offered Caroline use of the remaining booked satellite time. Satellite distribution of radio broadcasts was believed to be the way ahead at this time and was seen to be the future for any chance of getting Radio Caroline to a wider audience. The internet, still subject to telephone dial-up connections, was not considered viable.

With Carey's satellite-delivered station now off the air, the need to get Caroline heard was challenging. EKR, European Klassic Rock, was operating on the Astra satellite from the Maidstone television studios and a few hours of satellite time was offered to the small Caroline team. David Foster had been a member of the offshore team in 1987 and together with Caroline stalwarts, Nigel Harris (known in the '70s when he first joined the station as Stuart Russell) and Johnny Lewis (also known as Stephen Bishop) were responsible for those early programmes.

A friend of mine from the hospital radio station where I was presenting programmes, suggested I visit, 'You'll like the studio down there' then while I was there, in walked Nigel Harris, 'You did Caroline didn't you?' he said, 'well we're starting up Caroline on Sunday, do you fancy doing some programmes?'

David Foster DJ

Nigel Harris asked if I'd like to do some stuff for Caroline on EKR, it was only going to be for one weekend as far as I'm aware, I closed the programme down and said we'll be back next weekend. Peter Moore was pulling his hair out saying 'How are we going to do that?' but we did and we continued with EKR until they ran out of money – just Sundays from 9 a.m. till 6 p.m. Then we thought how can we keep Caroline on air? We had meetings to see if there was any possibility of us hiring time, we couldn't afford all week, but we thought we might be able to do Saturdays and Sundays. Nigel, myself and Andrew Austin went to this meeting. Ronan had once said to me 'If you go along to a meeting, and you look like you have money, then it's as good as having money', so we all had brief cases, but they only had our lunch inside. It worked; we secured a weekend deal, and then gradually increased our hours. Then we went onto Sky, on 0199, just like the early days of Caroline, and we went 24 hours.

Johnny Lewis DJ

Meanwhile the search for a suitable permanent mooring for the ship continued, new ideas for exciting new ventures involving the ship were mooted by councils, developers, film makers and other radio stations, but ultimately none came to fruition. The ship was looking scruffy, the once bright red painted hull, now faded to a washed-out pink, and debris and assorted junk was piled up inside her. An approach was made to take her to Tilbury dock, and surprisingly she was invited to tie up against a public jetty, before being moved further into the dock and away from public view. Although Caroline was again broadcasting regular programmes from the land-based studio in Kent, the future looked bleak for the rusting radio ship. She was seen by some as a liability, but the point was made that Radio Caroline without a ship could never be Radio Caroline.

The makers of the film, *The Boat That Rocked* made an approach and appeared interested in using the ship, but with limitations as to where she was allowed to move, another ship was used for the film, though Caroline's authentic studio equipment did appear.

The local BBC radio station for Essex, made a number of successful broadcasts from an old lightship off Harwich, marking various offshore radio anniversaries. Many former pirate DJ's from the '60s were involved and although the surrounding publicity raised awareness of Caroline's continuance, it was, ironically, the BBC taking the glory, whilst reliving the magical broadcasts of 'pirate radio'.

Throughout the period of virtual imprisonment of the ship in Tilbury, developments on air continued. Satellite costs were becoming too expensive but a slow increase in interest in internet radio meant that more people were listening to the station. A full-time radio studio was built in Strood, Kent, and programmes that had once consisted of computer generated non-stop music now had a presenter as the number of volunteers increased. Some had earned the reward of a programme after chipping rust and endless painting of the ship; others were former presenters returning to Caroline. More low-powered RSL broadcasts were made, this time from the ship in Tilbury, and although not making money directly, they were able to promote merchandise. With the shabby ship showing little outward signs of her former radio career, a benefactor arranged for a new radio tower to be supplied and fitted to the deck of *Ross Revenge*. Although considerably shorter than the massive original tower, and of no practical use now that the huge onboard transmitters were no longer needed, it at least made the ship 'look the part'.

Licenced commercial radio stations had broadcast to the UK since 1973, but Radio Caroline had never wished to become part of the establishment. Her broadcasts, ethos and operational structure were never compatible with the boardrooms, suits and the world of takeovers and consolidation of the powerful groups now controlling an ever-increasing number of radio stations. However, times were very different now and listening trends and new developments meant there was less demand for, what was seen as old technology, medium wave. Many stations, both commercial and BBC, were giving up their AM frequencies, but the point was made to anyone who would listen, that Caroline had more experience of using AM than any other station in the country and would be happy to have a go at making it work – legally this time.

Bob Lawrence had started his radio career on the *Mi Amigo* in the late '70s and began lobbying those he thought might help to give Caroline the full time licence that many believed she justly deserved.

I guess the first contact with officialdom came in 2010, when I approached Ofcom asking if Radio Caroline could have a medium wave licence. As expected, they came back and said that whilst they'd love to help there was no structure in place to offer Caroline a licence. Dealing with any large corporate authority is so difficult nowadays when what you're asking for doesn't exist, it's so difficult for them to understand when you say, 'I know it doesn't fit into any of the boxes on your computer screen, so could you create a new box?' They just don't know how to deal with it, other than saying NO!

Teresa Pearce, Labour MP for Erith and Thamesmead, gave me the courage to grit my teeth and challenge the rules. She replied within minutes of my asking for support. She explained that listening to Caroline fighting the 1967 Marine Offences Act had fired her up and inspired her to fight for what is right – Caroline inspired her to go into politics. Then Tracey Crouch, Conservative MP for Chatham and Aylesford, took our side. Tracey put forward an Early Day Motion in the House of Commons, signed by seventy-two MPs. It was a fantastic display of support and took the whole idea straight to the heart of the policy makers.

I think there was genuinely a desire to get Caroline a frequency, the problem was the people in positions of authority
just didn't know how to achieve it. The vast majority of MPs,
from all parties, gave me the impression that they wanted to
acknowledge the debt owed to Caroline. We didn't fit into any
of the boxes. It was a long process because the politicians can
only think in terms of 'the rule book says'. It took the help
of a 'tame' politician' but ultimately, once again, it was Radio
Caroline that took on the might and power of the system and
came out triumphant.

Bob Lawrence, DJ

Pressure to leave Tilbury Dock was increasing. *Ross Revenge* had
long outstayed her welcome and despite further attempts to find
a safe, accessible mooring for the ship, ultimately none seemed to
be available. The inevitable eviction from Tilbury was held at bay
for as long as possible, each new repair project aboard the ship was
shown as being 'in preparation of the move', but in truth it was
buying time until Tilbury Dock threatened to seize the ship and
have her scrapped. Despite attempts to use any number of disused
docks, wharves and jetties along the Thames and surrounding
rivers, the only possible place of refuge was to return to the River
Blackwater, where the ship had been moored twenty years earlier,
and the amicability of The Tollesbury Oyster Company.

After years of evading insurance, for fear of being presented
with an insurmountable list of requirements, a company was
found that was prepared to take on unusual marine risks, very
few though were quite as unusual as the *Ross Revenge*. Even with
insurance in place for the voyage to Bradwell, other improvements had to be made. The ship had to undergo stability tests
and extra pumps and fire safety equipment also had to be fitted,
together with an anchor and chain for her eventual security.

A few items were left to luck, so departure was planned for
mid-day on a Friday when officialdom was at lunch. There
was a heart stopping delay in the lock when it was feared that

objections would be raised and that the whole house of cards would crash down, but as tensions were escalating, permission was granted and the convoy of two tugs and the radio ship headed out on to the river. The speed of the tow was specified at four knots, but the tug, *Avenger*, had a lot of horse power and there was a great desire to get out of the area controlled by the Port of London Authority, so the speed was built up to eleven knots and by the evening the smaller of the two tugs, *Horton*, had been dismissed while *Ross Revenge* and *Avenger* waited off Harwich until the tide enabled them to enter the River Blackwater. By dawn the two ships were off Bradwell, the location that *Ross Revenge* had left behind two decades ago.

Peter Moore

Old acquaintances were renewed with local boatmen, who were needed to provide access to *Ross Revenge*, now anchored nearly half a mile offshore. After further improvements were made, insurance was granted to allow members of the public to board and visit the ship, providing a rich source of income.

During recent years, internet accessibility had improved hugely. It had become quite normal to 'listen to the radio' via a computer and with the introduction of WiFi radios, access to any radio station anywhere in the world had never been easier. Some Caroline listeners remarked on the format of the radio station. Many were quite happy with the 'album music format' that paid homage to the programmes of Caroline from the '70s, but others remembered the music played in the '60s with a passion and yet more were fans of the '80s output from the days of Caroline 558. As the audience increased, Caroline was becoming a victim of her past success. With multiple internet accessibility, provision of another 'strand' was quite possible and talk of a 'gold' service was suggested.

There was an idea to create another online stream; the original idea was for it to be called Caroline Extra. I'd been working on this idea for a while, scheduling music and building up the data base of songs, then someone said 'let's call it Flashback', and by this time much of the work had been done. We trialled it internally for quite a while before going live, so really it just evolved, and continues to evolve. At present it's a mixture of non-stop music and pre-recorded programmes, so it's really self-contained, I run it from home.

I'm an IT man, it's my business and I've followed the progress of internet radio with interest from its infancy, but I never thought it would replace conventional radio.

Mike Brill, Engineer

Caroline Flashback has started to see a noticeable increase in audience in recent months, with many 'returnees' rediscovering Radio Caroline, with advances in technology allowing for a worldwide audience.

The 'hoped-for' chance of obtaining an AM licence still showed no sign of happening, but Ofcom did start a project to allow small-scale DAB services on an experimental basis. Some of these operators approached Caroline offering space on their multiplex, they considered having a well-known name as one of their contributing stations added credibility. Launching first in the Aldershot/ Woking area, Caroline then expanded to Norwich, Brighton, Portsmouth, Birmingham and Glasgow. A DAB service for London was added. It is not known if these trial services attract a large audience, but to the loyal supporters of the station it indicated regular expansion and also, as in the case of internet radio, it's extremely useful to have a presence, just in case this is 'the next big thing'.

Now, fifty years after Radio Caroline first came on air, a quirky twist of fate renewed an old friendship. Back in July 1964, Radio Caroline and Atlanta formed an alliance, building a network of Caroline North and South. The original ship, anchoring off the coast of the Isle of Man and opening broadcasts just weeks after the island's own official radio station, Manx Radio, came on air. Despite the local community station being a minnow when compared to the powerful transmitters of Caroline, the residents of the island and their politicians formed an affinity with the pirate station, fighting Westminster in 1967 when the bill outlawing the original offshore stations was extended to include the island.

An approach to Manx Radio was made by Caroline presenter Barry Marsh with a view to both radio stations coming together to celebrate fifty years of broadcasting. A series of shows produced over a long weekend by Caroline was agreed upon, featuring interviews and recounting the history of Caroline North.

The listener response was overwhelming and led to the invitation of a regular link up between the two stations, with Caroline using the Manx Radio AM frequency of 1368 kHz for monthly, weekend-long broadcasts. Better still, with continually advancing technological developments, broadcasts now come directly from the *Ross Revenge*. Even more remarkable, is that rather than use high powered transmitters and a huge aerial mast to enable programmes to leave the ship, all that is needed is a small 6-inch square 'dongle' attached above the ship's funnel. These highly popular broadcasts are presented by disc jockeys 'in residence' onboard the ship over the broadcast period. Most of them have returned to Caroline having previously been a part of the successful Caroline 558 period in the mid-80s and since had successful careers in British broadcasting.

We'd already done a test broadcast from the ship one Friday in August 2015 to see if the 4G link was reliable enough to make regular programmes possible. With that successful, the next thing was to organise the first of the Caroline North weekends which Manx Radio said they wanted to come from the ship. I wasn't originally supposed to do that, but this being Caroline, someone or other dropped out and I was asked to put the weekend together at the last moment.

Originally Manx wanted a '60s station so that's what we did, but after a few months, I think we all felt we'd done that to death. So I put the idea to them that we could tell the Caroline story through the years over successive broadcasts, as, to a lot of listeners on the Isle of Man, Caroline had disappeared in March 1968, never to be heard of again. So we covered the return from the *Mebo 2*, then the return to sea of the *Mi Amigo*, the sinking, and the arrival of the *Ross Revenge*, including in all the broadcasts some short interviews with the staff that were there at the time and extending the music accordingly.

Kevin Turner, DJ

The radio regulator Ofcom appeared to have little sense of urgency. Decisions concerning Medium Wave radio were delayed on a number of occasions. However, there were many Caroline enthusiasts within Ofcom and the radio industry as a whole, who looked to see how they might help Caroline's plight.

In recent years, several hundred low-powered community radio stations had been granted licences. The idea was to use local, often inexperienced and normally volunteer staff, covering local matters, using a permitted power that limited the signal to ten miles at best. In 2016, the latest wave of applications were invited from several locations, including an area serving North Essex and South Suffolk, to be broadcast on the medium wave, AM. Radio Caroline applied, asking Ofcom to interpret the term, not as a geographical 'community', but as a community of people who liked listening to Radio Caroline. Taking the view that 'if you don't ask, you don't get' a request for 1,000 watts (1 kilowatt) of power was made, rather than the normal 20–70 watts. The application was successful and with the announcement in May 2017, came the offer of the requested, more powerful output. Once again Caroline was in the news as all national newspapers carried the story that, eventually, those pirates were going to knuckle down and 'go legal'. When ITV National News at Ten reported from the ship the reporter asked, 'Will you miss being pirates?'. 'Even Jack Sparrow adapted,' was the reply.

14 August has been an important date for all long-term Caroline supporters since the introduction of the Marine Offences Act in 1967, outlawing the original pirate stations. A huge event to mark the occasion was held at Clacton Town Hall, attended by several hundred listeners. Programmes from the ship were relayed via Manx Radio as an extended weekend of

Caroline North was broadcast. The weather, unlike 14 August in
1967, was beautiful; the date had fallen as it did fifty years earlier
on a Monday. BBC Breakfast news, broadcast an extended report
about 'the pirates' and Caroline in particular. A reporter, complete with drone-operating cameraman, had made a visit to *Ross
Revenge* days earlier and ITV and Sky also gave extensive coverage to the subject. Once again BBC Essex recreated their version
of a pirate radio station, based on the LV18 Lightship, alongside the Ha'penny pier in the historic naval town of Harwich, a
few miles up the coast from the Caroline ship. Former Caroline
DJ's Roger Day, Norman St John, Tom Edwards and Johnnie
Walker broadcast until their closedown at 3 p.m. in tribute to
the Radio London closedown fifty years earlier.

This time though, things were certainly different, after a
few seconds of respectful 'dead air', the recognisable sound of
seawash and seagulls could be heard on the BBC's frequency,
as for the first and almost certainly last time the BBC carried
Caroline's special one hour commemorative programme live
from the ship, linking the output of BBC Essex, Manx Radio and
Radio Caroline.

The planning for Caroline AM continued as Ofcom issued
Caroline the best possible medium wave frequency, 648 AM.

The BBC World Service had used Orford Ness on the Suffolk
coast to send programmes on AM directed across Europe, and
had done so for decades. These activities were funded by the
Foreign Office. But after the financial crash of 2008, funding
was withdrawn. The powerful World Service signal on 648AM
was shut down in March of 2011. The premises were vacated
and locked but left intact. Orford Ness was then sold to two
adventurers who described their purchase as 'a folly of enormous proportions' and who found that they now owned all
of the BBC hardware including aerial systems designed and
built at great expense and tuned for 648. By chance, or maybe
not by chance, Caroline was offered this frequency and after

negotiating a tenancy agreement, now had a regional station for East Anglia.

Peter Moore

A suitable transmitter was sourced for the new project and, as you'd expect with Caroline, even this acquisition had a story behind it.

The transmitter came to us via quite an interesting route. Of Canadian manufacture, it spent its working life in Switzerland, this service was switched off in 2006 and the transmitter was destined for the skip. However, it was intercepted and was put into storage in case 'it might be useful one day'. However, in 2015 the guy who stored it for eight years needed to clear out his garage and it was destined for the skip once more. An Ofcom engineer heard about this, and knowing Caroline and my background in AM mentioned it to me.

Eventually, at the end of October 2017, Peter Chicago, George our electrician, myself and a couple of helping hands, assembled on Orford town quay just as the sun was rising at 8 a.m. on a Friday morning to catch the little tender boat that runs across the creek to the Orford Ness spit of land where the transmitter station is sited – there being no conventional road access to the site. As Peter commented, it had been a few years since he had been on a quayside at sunrise, waiting for a boat to take him out to a transmitter! The installation took most of the day, and by 6 p.m. we had to leave the site with the installation not quite completed. It was a couple of weeks before we were all able to get back together, but on Saturday 11 November 2017 at just after 10 a.m., we powered up the transmitter into its test (dummy) load and David, the Ofcom engineer, started his acceptance tests. At 10.40 a.m., we had the antenna connections and transmitter tests completed, and pressed the 'go' button with the obligatory 'test tone'.

Although a few people had been tipped off and were asked
to listen for tests, it took just 40 seconds for the first report to
appear on a public website, after which the floodgates were
well and truly open. As the date was 11 November we removed
the test tone and observed two minutes silence at 11 a.m.,
then came back with some non-stop unannounced music.
I don't think anyone listening doubted that it was Caroline,
but it was interesting to read all the forum speculation about
where the transmissions were coming from. I finally left site
at around 5 p.m., and drove home down the A12 listening to
Caroline all the way. Absolutely amazing, we had pulled off, an
incredible coup.

                                          Alan Beech, Engineer

As with the very first tests from Caroline, back in 1964, Ray
Charles' records were played as part of the initial tests. The original position of Caroline in March 1964, just off Felixstowe, was
visible from the Orford Ness site. Broadcasts officially started on
20 December 2017, with a day of live programmes broadcast
from the ship.

33

Past, Present … Future?

Radio Caroline is now in a far better place than it has been for many years. Financed by generous supporters and advertisers and helped in no small measure by the many friends that the station has made over the years, Radio Caroline operates two twenty-four-hour daily services worldwide. Broadcasts are also available in East Anglia on 648 AM. DAB output is available in Central London, Brighton, Portsmouth, Woking and Aldershot, Birmingham, Glasgow and Norwich. It can be heard on smart phones, smart speaker and online at www.radiocaroline.co.uk

The ship, *Ross Revenge*, now has a legal owner and is recorded on the Register of Historic Ships. There is an urgent need for many thousands of pounds to be spent preserving this iconic ship for generations to come, not just as Britain's only authentic off-shore radio ship, but as the largest ever trawler in the deep sea fishing fleet. When it comes to reliving British social history, *Ross Revenge*, ticks every box, providing the food we ate and our radio entertainment for many years. Plans are being made for restoration to take place as soon as possible.

The Caroline audience is growing rapidly, although discussions continue on a regular basis as to what Caroline's musical format should be. It's unlikely that total agreement will ever occur but, as always, the radio station continues to offer a unique sound, unlike any other radio station. There can be no denying that Caroline is different.

There is some debate that the present radio station isn't 'the real Radio Caroline'. No amount of reasoning will persuade otherwise, but with several presenters still involved with the output for more than forty years, the heritage and the ship, these broadcasts are as close are anyone is going to get. Others speculate that the complete true story of Radio Caroline can never be told. I would agree with them, it would be an impossible task to chronicle every crazy event that has happened throughout the radio station's history – so far. But the aim of this updated second edition of the book is to repeat the stories told to me by many people involved with this most unique radio station, and I have no reason to doubt them.

At the time of writing, in June 2019, a new national breakfast show is about to be broadcast across what were once more than fifty truly independent radio stations, each with their own sound and staff. Many of those people previously employed in the industry are now searching for work, but with very few opportunities of finding it.

Ironically, when Radio Caroline first came on air the BBC had a broadcasting monopoly, fifty-five years later there appears to be little more choice than a duopoly, yet all Radio Caroline wanted was a licence to broadcast. All these years later it has one – what was all that unnecessary fuss really about?

Radio Caroline developed a reputation for surviving regardless of difficulties encountered. But some major setbacks, not of our making, and maybe a couple of own goals, sent the station in to a downward spiral in the late '80s, culminating in a disastrous shipwreck.

No other radio station would have survived so many setbacks, but the fact that we have is due to the famous name, that still opens many doors, and to the amazing loyalty of our supporters. For our part we have always tried to deliver on our promises even if that delivery was a long time coming. Also we remain independent.

By early 1992, Caroline had all but ceased to exist with the choices being to walk away or start all over. We chose the latter path.

The revival was agonisingly slow. There were few means by which broadcasts could be made and any opportunities that did exist were minor and not prestigious. The *Ross Revenge* was, and is, a costly mascot, but Radio Caroline has to have a ship.

Satellite radio and the internet provided opportunities for international and then global range and we were delighted to achieve 20,000 hours of listening a month. Now 23,000 hours a day is the norm and rising. For credibility in the old style, we now have AM transmissions across our traditional stamping ground of East Anglia with DAB outlets in various towns and cities.

There is something magical about the station and if that magic does not fade there will always be Radio Caroline. Maybe the best comment came from Johnnie Walker more than thirty years ago, when he said that while he sometimes was unable to listen, it made him happy just to know that Caroline was out there 'somewhere' doing what it always had done.

The future should be one of continued expansion, with a team of presenters who started their careers on Caroline and who are now returning to their roots.

Peter Moore, Station Manager

Ronan O'Rahilly

The man who started Radio Caroline, Ronan O'Rahilly is unwell and being cared for in his native Ireland. In his younger days, he was a hugely charismatic man, with far reaching foresight and a brilliant mind, although some people see brilliance as eccentricity. Many still idolise the man who, with his radio station, revolutionised what was heard on the radio in Britain. Others, perhaps with good reason had a different take on his ideals, beliefs and business style.

In 2004 I asked Ronan if all the events that had occurred during Caroline's days at sea had been worthwhile:

> Absolutely worth it, well it was to me, was it absolutely worth it to all the listeners? I think the answer would be yes, to a lot of them anyway. It definitely changed the whole radio thing in Britain, and that was a healthy thing. It was all about feelings, about expression, about lots of young people being able to 'kick out the jams' and that turned on all kind of things. The '60s were fantastic and they did a lot, not just for Britain, they did a lot for all around the world and a lot of people were involved in that, everything came together at the right time, it was an extraordinary moment in musical history for Britain.
>
> I did it as a way of getting exposure for unknown bands, and that's what it was about.
>
> Ronan O'Rahilly

Caroline continues ...

NOTES

All interviews by Ray Clark, except where marked.

1 Before Caroline

1   Jack Kotshack, *The Radio Nord Story* (Impulse Books, 1970)
2   National Archive HO_255_601. Quote from newspaper article:
    John Thompson, *Sunday Telegraph*, 4 March 1962
3   National Archive HO _255_601.
4   National Archive HO _255_600.
5   National Archive HO _255_601.

2 Project Atlanta

1   The Pilkington Committee on broadcasting was set up in 1960 and
    its findings were published on 27 June 1962. It concluded there
    was no need or desire for commercial radio in Britain.
2   Interview Colin Nicol.
3   Interview Colin Nicol.
4   Interview Colin Nicol.
5   Interview Colin Nicol.
6   Interview Colin Nicol.
7   Interview Colin Nicol.
8   Interview Colin Nicol.
9   Interview Ingemar Lindqvist.
10 National Archive HO_255_602. Government Document;
    23/1062.
11 Interview Colin Nicol.
12 Interview Colin Nicol.
13 houstonradiohistory.blogspot.co.uk/search?q=radio+nord.

3 The 'Why Not' Business

1 Ray Anderson, EAP Studio & Radiofab.com. 'The Radio
   Caroline Story'
2 Interview Colin Nicol.
3 Interview Colin Nicol.
4 Interview, Ingemar Lindqvist.
5 Interview Colin Nicol.
6 Correspondence Colin Nicol.
7 Guardian News & Media Ltd 2004.

4 Chug-a-lug, Chug-a-lug, Chug-a-lug

1 *Galveston News*, November 1963.
2 Interview Colin Nicol.
3 Ralph C. Humphries, *Radio Caroline: The Pirate Years* (Oakwood
   Press, 2003).
4 Interview Colin Nicol.
5 Interview Colin Nicol.
6 Interview Colin Nicol.
7 Interview Colin Nicol.
8 Interview Colin Nicol.
9 Interview Colin Nicol.
10 Interview Colin Nicol.
11 Interview Colin Nicol.
12 Interview Colin Nicol.
13 Interview Colin Nicol.

5 Genius

1 Ray Anderson, EAP Studios & Radiofab.com. 'The Radio
   Caroline Story'.
2 National Archive. HO_255_1001.
3 Interview Colin Nicol.
4 Interview Colin Nicol.
5 Interview Colin Nicol.
6 *Hansard*, 5 February 1964: Postmaster General Reginald Bevins.
7 National Archive HO_255_1003.
8 Ray Anderson, EAP Studios & Radiofab.com. 'The Radio
   Caroline Story'.

6 Your All-Day Music Station

1   Ray Anderson, EAP Studios & Radiofab.com. 'The Radio
    Caroline Story'
2   National Archive. HO_255_1001.
3   National Archive. HO_255_1002.
4   National Archive. HO_255_1001.
5   'Second pirate Radio Ready in Two Months', *Sunday Telegraph*,
    April 1964.
6   National Archive HO_255_1001.
7   Mark Frankland, *Radio Man: The Remarkable Rise and Fall of
    C.O.Stanley*. Institute of Electrical Engineers, 2002.
8   BBC Written Archive Document, 1 April 1964.
9   *Hansard*, 7 April 1964@ Postmaster General Reginald Bevins.
10 '"Pirate Radio" draws advertisers', The Times, 26 May 1964.
11 *Hansard*, 12 November 1964 Lord Airedale.
12 *Hansard*, 12 November 1964 Lord Hobson.
13 Interview, Paul Braithewaite, BBC Radio Cumbria.
14 *Hansard*, 12 May 1964: Written Reply by Chancellor of the
    Exchequer to Roy Mason question, 6 May 1964.

7 The Ship That Rocks The Ocean

1   Interview Colin Nicol.
2   Interview Colin Nicol.
3   Interview Colin Nicol.
4   Interview Colin Nicol.
5   Jon Myer, Offshoreradio.co.uk.
6   Interview Colin Nicol.
7   Interview Ingemar Lindvist.
8   'Radio Atlanta fails to come on air', *Essex County Standard*, 1 May
    1964.
9   Interview Colin Nicol.
10 Production, Advertising, Merchandising Services: PAMS of Dallas
    supplied identification jingles to radio stations around the world,
    but not, at this time, to the UK, a situation that would change by
    the end of the year.
11 Jon Myer, Offshoreradio.co.uk.

8 The Caroline Network

1   Interview Colin Nicol.
2   Interview Colin Nicol.
3   Jerry Leighton, Caroline Broadcast.
4   Captain Hangeveldt, Caroline Broadcast.
5   Isle of Man commercial, Caroline Broadcast.
6   Interview Colin Nicol.
7   Interview Colin Nicol.
8   Interview Colin Nicol.
9   Internal memo from David Block, Spectre Promotions (Caroline Club) Colin Nicol collection.
10 Denny Cordell went on to produce countless chart hits, including 'Go Now by The Moody Blues and 'A Whiter Shade of Pale' by Procol Harem.
11 Interview Colin Nicol.

9 You're Hearing Things …

1   Chris Edwards, Francois L'Hote, Offshore Echos: Correspondence.
2   Interview Colin Nicol.
3   Interview Colin Nicol.
4   BBC Written Archive Centre R31/138/2.
5   Research by Brian Long: The London Sound.
6   BBC Written Archive Centre R78/2254.

10 Bringing News to the Nation, Fast and Factual

1   Hansard, 12 November 1965. Prime Minister, Harold Wilson.

11 The Tower of Power

1   Interview Colin Nicol.
2   Interview Colin Nicol.
3   Interview Colin Nicol.

12 A Sudden Swing in High Command

1   Internal memo.
2   Chris Edwards, Francois L'hote, Offshore Echoes.
3   Interview, Paul Braithewaite, BBC Radio Cumbria.
4   Interview, Colin Nichol.

13 Mayday, Mayday

1   Colin Nicol.

15 The Sound of the Nation

1   Interview, Paul Braithewaite, BBC Radio Cumbria.

16 Oh, Mr Benn, You're a Young Man

1   Interview, Colin Nichol.
2   Radio Caroline Newsbeat, 22 June 1966.
3   *Hansard* 22 June 1966, Hugh Jenkin, MP.

17 Let me Marry You …

1   National Archive RG48_2958.

19 The Fight for Free Radio

1   100 gns Health Trips to Sea Fort' *The Times*, 29 June 1967.
2   Essex Police Document; Essex Police Museum.
3   Ronan O'Rahilly, BBC Interview.
4   Ronan O'Rahilly, Newspaper Interview, Unidentified.

20 Caroline Continues

1   Excerpt from *A***holes and Anoraks*, Andy Archer.
2   National Archive DPP2_443_10168.
3   National Archive DPP2_443_10168.

4   National Archive DPP2_443_10168.
5   National Archive DPP2_443_10168.

21 Cutting the Chain

1   Excerpt from *A***holes and Anoraks*, Andy Archer.
2   Excerpt from *A***holes and Anoraks*, Andy Archer.

22 Television, Who Do You Think You Are Kidding …?

1   National Archive HO_255_1210.
2   National Archive HO_255_1211.
3   Interview Bill Rollins.
4   'Caroline TV fails first test', *The Times*, 2 July 1970.

23 Unseaworthy and Barely Habitable

1   Interview, Bill Rollins.
2   Interview, Bill Rollins.
3   Interview, Bill Rollins.
4   Excerpt from *A***holes and Anoraks*, Andy Archer.

24 Caroline Comes Home

1   Essex Police/DPP Document; Essex Police Museum.
2   Essex Police Document; Essex Police Museum.
3   Extract from Nigel Harris, Ships in Troubled Waters (My Way Publishing, 2009).
4   Interview, Bill Rollins.
5   Essex Police Document; Essex Police Museum.
6   National Archive HO_255_1221.

25 Ship in Distress

1   Extract *Monitor Magazine*.
2   Ship to Shore Messages: *Mi Amigo* to Thames Coastguard.

27 Eurosiege

1   Essex Police Document; Essex Police Museum.

INDEX